J. M. BARRIE

The Man Behind the Image

J. M. BARRIE
The Man Behind the Image

JANET DUNBAR

COLLINS
St James's Place, London
1970

TO

GRAHAM WATSON

SBN 00 211384 8

© 1970 by Janet Dunbar

Printed in Great Britain
Collins Clear-Type Press
London and Glasgow

Contents

Illustrations

Acknowledgments

I WISH to express my gratitude to Mr Nicholas Llewelyn Davies, Mr Simon Asquith, Mr Walter J. Beinecke, Jr, and Miss Marjorie Wynne of the Beinecke Rare Book and Manuscript Library at Yale University, for their kindness and assistance all through the research for this book. My debt to them is great.

My thanks are also due to the following, for permission to quote and for much helpful information:

Mr W. A. Darlington, the Hon. Mrs W. Fraser (Pamela Maude), Mrs Richard Gandy (Veronica Irvine), Lady Malise Graham, Madame Karsavina, Mr Denis Mackail, Sir Compton Mackenzie, Dame Daphne du Maurier, Mrs Scott (Audrey Lucas), Miss Mary Scott of Kirriemuir, Mr Peter Scott, Mr Roger Senhouse, Mr W. G. R. Smith, Town Clerk of Kirriemuir, Professor G. P. Wells. I am also grateful for assistance from Miss Marian Harman of the University of Illinois Library, Mr Douglas Matthews of the London Library, Mr Gilbert Turner and the staff of Richmond upon Thames Public Library, and Mr Paul Meyers of the Library of the Performing Arts at Lincoln Center, New York.

I must especially thank my daughter, Lysbeth Merrifield, for her skill and patience in assisting me to decipher hundreds of letters in Barrie's microscopic, often illegible handwriting; and for the index.

Preface

MANY books have been written about James Barrie and his works. His plays, novels and short pieces have been annotated and analysed, and made the subject of innumerable articles and theses. He became something of a man of mystery in his lifetime, and since his death he has often been a debating point with those who try to interpret his complexities in terms of modern psychological theory.

It is probable that during the next fifty years there will be more books written about the flawed genius who was J.M.B., and there will be fresh interpretations of his works, especially of *Peter Pan*, which Peter Llewelyn Davies called 'that terrible masterpiece'. Barrie's autobiographical writings, shorn of their ambiguities and embellishments, will be studied in the light of further psychological knowledge.

The basic difficulty of arriving at the truth, however—whatever the 'truth' may be—will remain. Where, in all Barrie's writings about himself, does fact end and fantasy begin? Where the two are so interwoven, how does one disentangle them? How far is one entitled to guess at what a man wishes to keep private about himself?

W. A. Darlington, a perceptive critic and notable man of the theatre, writes of Barrie:

That a man so famous and so solitary should become a figure of legend even in his lifetime was inevitable. In these days, any man of mark who is detected in the act of trying to keep himself to himself is considered to be acting in a manner prejudicial to good order and the public interest. If no intimate details of his life are known, Rumour will embroider them. Only by sacrificing his privacy can such a man hope to be known for what he is; generally he prefers to acquiesce in the legend concerning himself. He outdid Rumour at her own game. In his youth he kept silence about himself, or at least entered the confessional only in disguise, as the Little

Minister, or the schoolmaster of Glen Quharity, but in his later years, when he added public speaking to the arts in which he excelled, he became communicative, and sometimes added to the legend characteristic touches much more picturesque than any that Rumour had been able to invent, but even less reliable. Anybody who proposes to write, or for that matter to read, a biography of Barrie must have it always in mind . . .

He has given us a wealth of biographical detail, always set forth with supreme craftsmanship and bearing the stamp of truth. But its truth is the truth of the artist, not of the historian. Barrie wrote about himself as he wrote about a character in a play or book, selecting, rejecting and inventing what material he needed to make his creation lively and life-like.

*   *   *

In an individual of such complexity, it is useful to study facets in depth, if possible. This book is an attempt to understand James Matthew Barrie in the light of his relationships with four women who influenced his life to a powerful degree: Margaret Ogilvy, Mary Ansell, Sylvia Llewelyn Davies and Cynthia Asquith. The first, the over-possessive mother, unwittingly sowed seeds which were to lead to much misery in her son's life. With the other three he was able, in some degree, to be himself; through his letters to two of them one catches glimpses of his inner life. He had moments of self-revelation, and these give clues to the man behind the image which he showed to the world.

The study has been made possible by the present writer being given access to three valuable sources of material. One, the archive of Barrie material collected by Walter J. Beinecke, Jr, over the last twenty years, consists of hundreds of Barrie's letters, his working notebooks and many of his manuscripts, and photographs, cuttings and other material. The second source, in private hands, consists of Lady Cynthia Asquith's diaries, written in great detail during the nineteen years she was Barrie's secretary and close friend.

The third source, also in private hands, is the Peter Davies collection of personal papers. Peter Llewelyn Davies, one of the five brothers unofficially adopted by Barrie, put together a mass of family letters and added explanatory notes. They were, in every sense, private letters; he wanted his own children, and his brothers and their children, to have a true record of the tragedy which befell the five sons of Arthur and Sylvia Llewelyn Davies, bereft of their parents and an exceptionally happy home life, at an age when they were too young to fend for themselves. The impact of the domineering, possessive, extraordinary 'little Scotchman' on their lives, and of his infatuation with their mother, is brought home in these papers with terrifying clarity. Some of the letters also shed fresh light on the failure of Barrie's marriage.

This record was not intended for publication, but Nicholas Davies, the only surviving brother of the five, inheriting the papers, takes the view that they are important to an assessment of Barrie's complex personality, and has generously made them available to the present writer without conditions. They have, therefore, been quoted wherever they are directly concerned with Barrie or are otherwise relevant, together with Peter Davies's comments, also when relevant.

Chapter 1

EARLY DAYS I

There is no acceptance of honest poverty in Scotland as a station to which the Lord has called us. The ways of God may command respect, but the humblest Scot believes that he can improve the divine dispensation, so far as it touches him personally, by exerting himself to the betterment of his position.

J. A. HAMMERTON wrote those words in 1928, but in spirit they have been taken for granted by generations of Scotsmen. They were the invisible text which pervaded many a poor household during the nineteenth century, and especially was this text the driving force in the house at Lilybank in the Tenements, Brechin Road, Kirriemuir, where James Matthew Barrie was born in the year 1860.

Kirriemuir, then a small weaving town, is in the county of Angus (formerly Forfarshire), about five miles north-west of Forfar, the county town. The countryside around has a gentle beauty, rising to the heights of the Grampian Hills in the distance. It was an undistinguished little town, once described by Robert Louis Stevenson as a haphazard group of houses 'squeezed round that square like chickens clustering round a hen'. The square was the centre of the place, its main feature the Town House, which had once been a prison and courthouse.

In the mid-nineteenth century, when horse and cart provided the usual form of transport and trains were an expensive luxury, a town like Kirriemuir was a self-contained, stay-at-home community, where everybody knew everyone else—and what kirk they attended, and how regularly. What was not actually and absolutely known about neighbours' private affairs was inevitably the subject of speculation and deduction. There was little privacy in Kirriemuir.

The clackety-clack of the flying shuttles could be heard in every street in this town of linen-weavers, for there were hand-looms in most of the houses. The women no longer spun the yarn made from the flax growing at the edges of farmland, as their mothers had done; this was now grown commercially, brought into the town by cart from the spinning mills, and distributed to the weavers. Alexander Whyte, a noted son of Kirriemuir, who began life in a poverty-stricken cottage and became Principal of New College, Edinburgh, spoke in his inaugural address of his early days in the little town:

There were rows and rows of weavers' shops in the Newtown [the Southmuir] where I was brought up; generally comprised of a 'but and ben'—the 'but' being the kitchen with maybe a little room as a bedroom or sitting-room. Then at the other end there were four weaving looms. The father would have one, and perhaps two daughters would have one each, and the son would have one; if he had not, then some other person would have it. It has always amazed me how these people managed to live. The father might make twelve or fourteen shillings a week, and with a little extra work he would perhaps make sixteen shillings, while the others would have perhaps only five or six or seven shillings. It is amazing to think of the way they turned out, and always had a little to give to a good cause, and sometimes—who would believe it?—were able to send their sons to college. But it was done!

The Barrie home was more than a 'but and ben'; there were two small rooms downstairs, one a living-room and the other the bread-winner's 'web room', taken up by his loom, which filled most of the space. There was only one loom; David Barrie had no intention of putting any of his children to the weaving—he and his wife had other plans for them. Steep, narrow stairs led up to another pair of rooms, one a kitchen that contained the usual boxed-in bed, the other a bedroom. Cramped as it was, the house was larger than most of the other weavers' dwellings, which had only the two rooms Alexander Whyte describes—the 'but and ben' of later comedians' songs, but grimly cabined and confined to live in.

David Barrie, one of the most respected men in the community, was known for his probity and a passion for self-education, as well as for his ceaseless industry; his mind was as active as his fingers. He was described by Alexander Whyte, who became the close friend of his eldest son, as 'a typical Forfarshire figure of a man; a fine, open, intelligent countenance, the mouth mobile and humoursome, the brows broad and full, and a fringe of whisker framing the face, of which both lip and chin were shaven.'

In 1841, at the age of twenty-seven, David Barrie married Margaret Ogilvy, the twenty-one-year-old daughter of a local stonemason who was one of the most fanatical upholders of that fiercely puritanical brand of Protestantism known as the Auld Lichts. Following the Scottish custom of the time, Margaret Ogilvy kept her maiden name after her marriage, but, also by custom, she dutifully changed to her husband's kirk. This was the Free Church, a sect which had hived off from the Established Church of Scotland in 1843 on the issue of the Established Church's relationship with the State. The Free Church lacked patronage, and its funds came only from its independent-minded adherents, but there were many in Scotland who valued religious freedom, and they somehow raised enough money over the years to build churches and found a few theological halls.

Religion, especially the puritanical brands of Protestantism, had a strong grip on Scottish family life. The Presbyterian Church of Scotland was splintered into sects, and the Auld Lichts were the most uncompromising of them all. They had seceded originally from the Establishment in 1733 on the question of the right of a congregation to nominate its own minister, instead of leaving that right in the power of the Elders. There was soon trouble among themselves over the text of the National Covenants, which gave the State authority to interfere in church affairs. The dissident party was divided into New Lights, who strongly objected to this power, and the Old Lights, who were prepared to accept it, provided it did not interfere with their beliefs.

These beliefs were fundamental: their model was the primitive church of Apostolic days. 'If any man have not the spirit of the Lord, he is none of His,' was their most fervently held tenet, and they declared, just as obstinately, that their worship 'must at all costs be held free from the carnal work of man.' This prohibition applied to instrumental music of any kind, to hymns, written sermons and written prayers. They clung tenaciously to the creed that the spirit of the Lord was opposed to any manifestation of graciousness of living, that existence on this earth was earnest and could never be anything else.

The Free Church had more liberal elements, but though Margaret Ogilvy went over to her husband's sect, in her heart and mind she never left the narrow self-righteousness of the Auld Lichts.

*   *   *

David Barrie and Margaret Ogilvy had ten children in all, seven daughters and three sons. The fourth and fifth children, Elizabeth and Agnes Matthew, died in infancy. Alexander Ogilvy, the eldest of the family, was born in 1841, Mary Edward, the eldest daughter, in 1845, Jane Ann Adamson in 1847, David Ogilvy in 1853, Sara Mitchell in 1854, and Isabella Ogilvy in 1857.

On May 9th, 1860, James Matthew Barrie was born, and baptized the following Sunday, according to custom, at the foot of the pulpit in the South Free Church. With a growing family, David Barrie had rented an adjoining house as a 'loom-shop', where he had installed extra looms and employed a few weavers on his own account. Average wages were miserably low—there is a record of a weaver who wove a 90-yard web and received eight shillings for it—but David Barrie was able to earn more money than his neighbours by his own tireless industry and his willingness to take on more responsibility by employing a few others and overseeing their work. What money there was to spare went into savings; and as David Barrie now had his own loom next door, Margaret Ogilvy was able to bring her kitchen down to the ground floor, thus making more space for beds upstairs. There was also space in the living-room for a set of six horsehair-seated chairs, which Margaret Ogilvy had long hankered after, and which came up unexpectedly at a 'roup'—a sale.

David Barrie took the birth of his ninth child with his accustomed calm; he was not a demonstrative husband or father, and the fact that he worked for many hours a day to support his large family meant that he had little time for each one personally. That was Margaret Ogilvy's province: she kept them clean and decent, they never missed service at the South Free Church on a Sunday, they knew their Bible, and were, in turn, diligent pupils at the school attached to the church.

The standard of education in such a small town was surprisingly high. A contemporary record, *Dr Easton's Statistical Account of the Parish of Kirriemuir*, listed sixteen schools in the town and neighbourhood in the 1830's, and added: 'The number of persons upwards of fifteen years of age who cannot read or write is not one to a thousand.'

David Barrie had had little schooling himself, having been put to the weaving as a young lad, but he had learned to read at an early age, and his bookshelf was full of works on philosophy and theology, together with books borrowed from the minister or one of the

dominies, and regularly changed for others. It was with great pride
that he saw his eldest son growing into what he had always wanted
to be himself, a scholar.

Alexander, at eighteen, was a tall, broad young man, very much
his father's build. He was steady, ambitious, and a born student—a
son after his father's heart. He had gone on from the South Free
Church school to a bigger school at Forfar, where his close attention
to his books won him a bursary to Aberdeen University.

The eldest daughter, Mary, also liked studying. There was, of
course, no question of a girl trying for a bursary and going to the
university; but Mary, at the age of fifteen, became a pupil teacher at
a local school and brought a modest salary home to augment the
family income. Her sisters, except Jane Ann, in due time followed
her example.

Margaret Ogilvy had taken her first-born very much for granted;
she had never had any doubts from the day of his birth that he
would grow up and bring credit on his mother, and the fact that he
was set on a straight course for an M.A. was a natural source of
satisfaction. She concentrated her ambition on her second son,
David. He had gone to school, as the others had done, at the age of
five, and quickly rose from class to higher class, showing signs that
he would one day follow his elder brother in an academic career.
His mother was sure that he would outdistance Alec, and that after
his M.A. he would set his sights for a D.D. The highest reward on
earth any mother could hope for was to see her son a Doctor of
Divinity.

*   *   *

The third son, James—Jamie—gave no signs during the first six
years of his life of being other than an ordinary small Kirriemarian,
playing at the local games, getting into trouble for misdemeanours
with his mother or with her right hand in the household, Jane Ann.
He, too, was good at reading, but what Jamie really liked, besides
games, was the world of entertainment. One of his school-friends, a
boy called Mills, the son of the local bookseller, had a toy theatre at
home, and Jamie was fascinated by the gaily painted peepshow. He
and young Mills pushed the tiny figures on and off the stage, and
enjoyed themselves greatly. Soon they were carrying on larger
activities in the wash-house opposite the Barries' house in the
Tenements, acting stories—often taken from the Old Testament—

which they dramatized on the spot, and charging other small fry
'peeries' (tops) or 'bools' (balls) for admission.

Jamie was now at school, but not the one which his brothers and
sisters had attended. The Misses Adam, two daughters of a retired
minister, had opened a small school in Bank Street, and Margaret
Ogilvy, wishing to help them in their venture, sent Jamie there.
This was the original of the 'Hanky School' in *Sentimental Tommy*,
where the pupils were required to bring clean handkerchiefs every
day, not for their noses, but to place on the floor when they knelt
for prayers. The sisters were kind and refined, but Jamie did not
learn much beyond his letters, and he was presently taken away and
sent to the school attached to the South Free Church at Southmuir.

Alexander did well at Aberdeen University. In April 1862 he
graduated M.A. with first-class honours in Classics, and soon afterwards opened a private school at Bothwell, in Lanarkshire, where
there was a good opening for an establishment conducted by a
principal with such excellent qualifications. Mary left home and went
to Bothwell to assist her brother both with the teaching and the
housekeeping.

Having settled in his school, Alexander's thoughts turned to his
brothers. Jamie was too young to leave home, but David, now rising
fourteen, was ready for more education than Kirriemuir was able to
provide. His mother had not wished to part with the boy when
Alexander had suggested earlier that David should go on to the
school at Forfar, as he himself had done, and at which he had gained
his bursary to the University.

Margaret Ogilvy had never been able to disguise the fact that
David was the favourite of all her children. He was quiet, studious,
and would undoubtedly have a brilliant and glorious future. She had
become intensely ambitious for this boy. Her eldest-born was a
teacher, and therefore respectably placed in life—but David, she
determined, was to be the minister that all mothers of sons hoped for.

Small, sparely made, with a gentle voice, David Barrie's wife was
outwardly the perfect complement to her burly, industrious husband
at his loom: a thrifty housewife, a good mother, a regular attender at
the kirk. That every decision, important or otherwise, was decided
by this unassuming little woman was so much taken for granted that
no one in the household had ever questioned it. Jane Ann had long
taken over the actual work of the house, and Sara and Isabella were
still at school. Another daughter, Margaret, had been born in 1863,

bringing the number of living Barrie children up to eight. As usual, no great fuss had been made over the new arrival, though Jamie played a great deal with his little sister, for he was good at childish games.

Alexander, doing very well with his private school, now wrote home suggesting that young David should come to Bothwell and continue his education there. He was sure that the boy would get a bursary to either Glasgow or Aberdeen University, if necessary with extra coaching, and there would be Mary to look after him; they had comfortable lodgings adjoining the school and there was plenty of room.

Margaret Ogilvy was torn between parental common sense and her own obsessive love for her second son. The father had no doubts whatever; it was obvious that the lad must take this chance of higher education. He was certain that David would do well under Alec. The mother was certain that he would do more than well, and again came the constant day-dream—he would one day attain the highest honours and be a minister whose name everyone in S cotland would know. So she agreed to David's going, though what it cost her to part with this dearest of her children can only be guessed.

Young David accordingly made the train journey to Bothwell, and settled down happily in his brother's school. Theology was one of his strongest subjects; there was no question but that he was destined for the ministry. He was not, however, a solemn youth; he was as cheerful and as full of high spirits as the next, in spite of his formidable capacity for learning.

Regular reports were sent home on David's work; and Alexander was able, at the end of 1866, to give the family some good news of his own. He had applied for, and been appointed to, the position of Classical Master at Glasgow Academy, and would be selling his school in order to take up this important post in the following September. Mary would still be his housekeeper, and David, of course, would go with them. It was a wonderful opportunity for the boy; Glasgow Academy was a school with a high academic standard.

Margaret Ogilvy, who had never ceased to miss her favourite son, could only rejoice at the news, and it was a proud and happy family that stopped on the way home from the kirk on a Sunday, giving news of the two scholars to anyone who cared to ask.

January came in with an extra cold bite in 1867, and there was a

frost at Bothwell hard enough for skating. Alexander had given his
brother a pair of skates, which he shared with a school-friend. On the
eve of David's fourteenth birthday, the two boys went skating.
After a few turns on the ice, David took off the skates and gave them
to his friend, who strapped them on and went spinning away at
great speed. In doing so he cannoned into David, causing him to fall
heavily, head first, on to the ice.

There is little hope with a badly fractured skull. David survived
for a few hours, remaining unconscious. While there was still some
glimmer of hope, Alexander sent a telegram to his parents, telling
them to come as soon as possible, but presently he had the grim task
of sending a second telegram, saying David was dead.

In Kirriemuir, the news made an impression on the small James
Matthew Barrie which he was never to forget to the end of his life.
In *Margaret Ogilvy*, the book he wrote about his mother, he says:

She had a son who was far away at school. I remember very little about
him, only that he was a merry-faced boy who ran like a squirrel up a tree
and shook the cherries into my lap. When he was thirteen and I was half
his age the terrible news came, and I have been told the face of my mother
was awful in its calmness as she set off to get between Death and her boy.
We trooped with her down the brae to the wooden station, and I think
I was envying her the journey in the mysterious waggons; I know we
played around her, proud of our right to be there, but I do not recall it,
I only speak from hearsay. Her ticket was taken, she had bidden us
goodbye with that fighting face which I cannot see, and then my father
came out of the telegraph office and said huskily, 'He's gone!' Then we
turned very quietly and went home again up the little brae . . .

Chapter 2

EARLY DAYS 2

MARGARET OGILVY was 'always delicate from that hour'. She was only in her late forties, but she was completely overwhelmed by her grief, and she seems to have made no effort to achieve that searing but necessary discipline which is essential when a child dies and there are brothers and sisters who cannot understand the calamity which has suddenly thrust them out of a mother's heart— or so it seems to them. They feel bereft, and the trauma of rejection may persist, buried under the later accumulated emotional experience of years, but still there until the end of their days.

Barrie's book about his mother, written when he was thirty-six, is our only real record of how his relationship with his mother changed after David's death. One day he was the youngest brother, noisy and carefree, not yet ready to be dreamed over but still his mother's own and separate child. The next day he was a substitute for one who could never be replaced, and so, he knew with a deep instinct, it would always be.

Margaret Ogilvy lay in bed holding the christening robe in which all the children had been baptized. 'I peeped in many times at the door, and then went to the stair and sat on it and sobbed.'

Jane Ann found him, a solitary figure, at the head of the stairs, not knowing what to do. Jane Ann was twenty, and the entire management of the household had devolved on her since her mother's illness; she was housekeeper, nurse, the prop and stay of her father and the rest of the family.

This sister . . . came to me with a very anxious face and wringing her hands, and she told me to go ben to my mother and say to her that she still had another boy. I went ben excitedly but the room was dark, and when I heard the door shut and no sound came from the bed I was afraid, and I stood still. I suppose I was breathing hard, or perhaps I was crying, for after a time I heard a listless voice that had never been listless before say, 'Is that you?' I think the tone hurt me, for I made no answer, and then the voice said more anxiously, 'Is that you?' again. I thought it was the dead boy she was speaking to, and I said in a little lonely voice, 'No, it's no' him, it's just me.' Then I heard a cry, and my mother turned in bed, and though it was dark I knew that she was holding out her arms.

From that day on the small boy determined to take the place of his brother. 'I sat a great deal on her bed trying to make her forget him, which was my crafty way of playing physician.'

If he saw anyone doing something which brought a laugh, he hastened to his mother's side to imitate the joker. He would stand on his head in the bed with his feet against the wall and call out: 'Are you laughing, Mother?' Sometimes he succeeded, and then Jamie rushed to tell Jane Ann, but by the time she got to the bedroom Margaret Ogilvy's face was again wet with tears. Jane Ann told him to try to get their mother to talk about the dead boy, and presently Margaret Ogilvy began to recall fond memories. At first Jamie was jealous, crying out: 'Do you mind nothing about me?' but that did not last. He was obsessed by the intense desire to become so like David that his mother would not see the difference. He learnt his brother's special whistle from the dead boy's friends, put on a suit of David's clothes, went into his mother's room, cried 'Listen!' and began to whistle. It was not until many years later that he realized how deeply he must have hurt her.

The days and weeks passed. Life had to be lived, in spite of grief, and when he was away from the sick-room, Jamie Barrie was a perfectly normal small boy of nearly seven. He still played with young Mills's toy theatre, and though the wicked theatre of the adult world was not even mentioned in the Barrie household, the playwright James Barrie could remember days in his early youth when he managed to be at the back of the tent audience when travelling shows of jugglers, tumblers and other mummers passed through Kirriemuir on their sinful way to the larger towns.

With his friend James Robb, a fellow-pupil at the South Free school, he went fishing the trout streams which abound in the district; but best of all he liked to play cricket. This is surprising, as Scotland is not a cricketing country, but it was very popular in the town, played on the level turf on the crest of the Hill of Kirriemuir. The boys played with a home-made bat, the wicket was a flat boulder set on end, and rolled-up jackets marked the fielders' positions.

But at home—there was always the sick-room. A different world. Denis Mackail writes in his book, *The Story of J.M.B.*:

It is the story of how a mark was set on a child's soul, as well as of the beginning of twenty-eight years of incessant and unalterable devotion. Here, already at six-and-a-half, is the presage of what he won't afterwards escape or try to escape. Already his mother has let him be a little different from other boys, as she still thinks only of a boy who has gone. Yet even if she had guessed for a moment that she was fanning a spark, would this mean that for such extremity of sorrow she is to have nothing but praise, and no syllable of blame? . . .

Day follows day for the living, and *they* don't know, in the midst of it all, what they are really doing to their own and each other's lives. Many will still be unconscious long after they have done it. The inmates of that little house in the Tenements, simple as they may seem to us, weren't nearly as simple as characters in a play. They were far more complex and fluid. Even the mother wouldn't always weep, nor her son be free of infectious high spirits. Time would always be moving a little faster, and producing subtler developments, than could ever be followed by the human eye.

A perceptive analysis, and one that is inevitably in the mind many times as one studies the years to come. A dichotomy was slowly forming in this little boy; there was the world outside, the world of reality, and the shadowed home where fantasy was being woven. For Margaret Ogilvy was at last finding some relief from her desolation by talking to this eager son who was proving to be a splendid listener. She began telling him about her own childhood, which had not lasted long, for at the age of eight she had lost her mother and she had had to be both housekeeper to her father and substitute mother for her five-year-old brother, David, now minister at Motherwell.

Her father, Alexander Ogilvy the stonemason, had always been the hero of her childhood. As she talked of him, and of that distant past, she carried the listening Jamie along with her, firing his lively imagination in such a way that he re-lived that childhood with her— escaping, with the stricken woman, into a world where sorrow had not yet entered. The old stonemason had died nine years before Jamie was born, but so persuasively did Margaret Ogilvy tell her story that Jamie felt as if he had known his grandfather intimately, known the weather-beaten face, hard as the stone on which he chiselled, his face dyed red by its rust.

Margaret Ogilvy related how she would carry her father's dinner to the distant places where he was at work, how she mothered her younger brother, and scrubbed and mended and baked and sewed, carried water from the pump, had her washing days and her ironings, gossiped like a matron with the other women. There were times when childhood would have its way, and she would run out and play with the other children of her own age. Jamie identified himself completely with those memories, too:

I see her frocks lengthening . . . and the games given reluctantly up. The horror of my boyhood was that I knew a time would come when I also must give up the games, and how it was to be done I saw not . . . I felt that I must continue playing in secret, and I took this shadow to her, when she told me her experience, which convinced us both that we were very like each other inside.

She made him see herself as she had been, with a magenta pinafore tied over her frock, or, later, in a pale blue costume and a blue bonnet with white ribbons beneath the chin. He was steeped in her past: the present had no reality for him when he was with Margaret Ogilvy. Thirty years later he wrote:

The reason my books deal with the past instead of with the life I myself have known is simply this, that I soon grow tired of writing tales unless I can see a little girl, of whom my mother has told me, wandering confidently through the pages. Such a grip has her memory of her girlhood had upon me since I was a boy of six.

*   *   *

In September 1867, Alexander took up his appointment at Glasgow Academy, living in a terrace off the Great Western Road in the Hillhead district of the city, about half a mile from the school. Alexander's thoughts soon turned to the question of Jamie's education: it was time the boy moved on. He wrote home, suggesting that it would not be difficult for Jamie to get an entrance to the Academy; the fees were only a few pounds a year, and Alec himself would be glad to provide board and lodging.

Fifteen or sixteen months ago it had been young David who had been destined for this step-up, and Margaret Ogilvy must have read her eldest son's letter with a pang. She was still an invalid, though her illness had never been diagnosed. Jane Ann looked after her with loving patience, and Margaret Ogilvy was content to leave everything in her devoted daughter's hands.

Jamie, on being told that he was going to Glasgow, was loth to leave his mother, but a parental decision had been made, and it would not have entered his head to make the slightest demur. He travelled to Glasgow—an excitement in itself to the boy, going by train—and on August 19th, 1868, James Matthew Barrie, aged eight, was entered as a pupil at Glasgow Academy.

He seems to have been neither happy nor particularly unhappy at this school, though he disliked Glasgow. Here were gaunt streets with cliff-like rows of houses, instead of the village wynds and passages with Kirriemuir's farm-fields and the Commonty beyond, which he had always known. He was away from his friends at the South Free, there would be no Jimmie Robb to go fishing with him, and already a new sensitivity and shyness were taking hold of him at the prospect of getting to know a new lot of boys. It was a relief to have Mary at their lodgings when he went back for midday dinner, and in the evening. He had never seen much of his schoolmaster brother in his younger days, but Alec was unfailingly kind, taking him for walks on Saturdays in the country beyond Hillhead along with his own constant companion, Alexander Whyte from Kirriemuir, who had been at Aberdeen University with him and who was now a minister at Free St John's in George Street.

One day Alec put Jamie on the train for Motherwell, to visit their mother's brother, the Reverend David Ogilvy. This was an excursion which gave Jamie his first glimpse into High Life, for the minister employed a servant! 'As I was to be his guest she must be my servant also for the time being . . . My relative met me at the station, but I wasted no time in hoping I found him well . . . at once I made for the kitchen, where, I knew, they reside, and there she was.'

In Kirriemuir, forthcoming changes were beginning to cast shadows over the weaving community. Power-looms were coming to the town. There had been factories in Dundee and other towns for several years, Laird's Linen Works at Forfar would probably be expanding, and now a factory was being built by Wilkie's in Kirriemuir itself. When it was finished, a large number of the mill-hands would be girls, as in the other towns. Everyone knew that the age-old cottage economy of hand-loom weaving was coming to an end.

David Barrie, always a far-seeing and shrewd man, had no intention of waiting for the inevitable. If power it was to be, he would begin to learn as much about the machines as he could. He was fifty-six years of age, but he did not think he was too old to acquire new knowledge. He went to Forfar one day to seek an interview with the manager of Laird's Linen Works. His character and reputation as a hard worker were known, and he was taken on, but not in the weaving shops. He knew the trade through and through, he wrote a good hand, and he would be of more use in the offices of the works, so he was given the position of clerk.

Margaret Ogilvy was hesitant at the idea of leaving her home when her husband got back to Kirriemuir and told her that they were moving. But it was obvious that he could not travel five miles each way every day between Forfar and Kirriemuir, and she was bound to agree. David Barrie had no hesitation in uprooting himself; the wages at Laird's were more than he had ever earned. He found a house in Forfar that still had only four rooms but which was larger and more convenient than the one in the Tenements, and the Barrie family prepared to leave Kirriemuir.

Jamie was still in Glasgow with his brother, but now Alexander had news of a further step up the educational ladder. His sights had for a long time been set on the schools Inspectorate, and when the Education Act of 1872 was passed, Alexander resigned from Glasgow Academy, having good reason to think that he would be appointed to the Inspectorate when the Act reached Scotland the following year. He put in the intervening time doing some inspection of Free Church schools, and was presently appointed, as he had hoped, as H.M. Inspector under the new Act, being given the district of Dumfries.

As this new post would necessitate his travelling round a large area, he would no longer be able to look after his young brother. After the summer holiday that year, Jamie returned to Glasgow Academy for a further session, but when Alexander departed for Dumfries the boy returned to the family, to the house in Forfar.

The new home stood in a lane called the Limepots (now Canmore Street) and had a garden. On rising ground behind the lane was the turret of the castle said to have belonged to the historical Malcolm Canmore, the reputed slayer of Macbeth. Jamie liked the house because it was so spacious—almost like the Manse at Motherwell, the grand place where his uncle the minister kept a servant. And, best of all, his mother seemed better, and openly admired her fine kitchen. Margaret Ogilvy was still delicate—she would always be that—but she had begun to bake her bannocks again, and Jane Ann would consult her about household matters.

Jane Ann was now twenty-three, and looked older than her years. If she ever thought of marriage and a home of her own, no one knew it. Kind, loving, faithful, she waited on her mother from morning till night; a quiet young woman who was always at hand when she was needed, but seemed to have no existence of her own.

There was now the matter of Jamie going to school again. He was entered at Forfar Academy, and soon settled down there. Jamie had become an avid devourer of books, and he and Margaret Ogilvy read them together, taking turn and turn about to read aloud, though Jamie liked the lion's share of that satisfying exercise. *The Pilgrim's Progress* was an old favourite, and *Men Who Were Earnest*, which she gave him on his tenth birthday, was conscientiously worked through. Jamie's favourite was *Robinson Crusoe*, which had been borrowed from the library for a penny for three days, and then bought. At school he discovered Sir Walter Scott, and his mother made haste to borrow as many of that author's historical romances as Mr Mills's bookshop-library had in stock. She and Jamie read them aloud, as usual, and Jamie's flights of fancy began to soar. Before long he was improving on Sir Walter. A contemporary of his at Forfar Academy, David Elder Anderson, has left a recollection of his friendship with young James Barrie at this time:

I well remember happy afternoons spent around about Forfar, chiefly because of the stories Barrie related, many of which must, even then, have evolved from his own vivid imagination. There were others, however, that were based on what he had read. Once he told me the gist of Ivanhoe in such a vivid and picturesque manner as to arouse in me a love for the works of Sir Water Scott which I have retained ever since.

Charles Laing, another schoolfellow of Barrie's at Forfar Academy, relates an even more characteristic episode. They were walking home from school together and Jamie began telling him a story. When they reached the Limepots, Jamie invited young Laing in.

The cottage and garden were surrounded with stone walls, and when the garden door was closed there was a strange silence as of a cloister. No one was about, so we sat on the grass in front of the house while Jim continued his story. It was a 'strange, eventful history' told with sparkling eye, full of the minutest detail and entrancing to the listener. The story is long since lost to my memory, but I recollect that on my way home -

pondered over the incident and thought to myself 'He's a queer chap, Jim. Where can he have got the story? It's not like any a boy ever told.' And I have no doubt I concluded that he had heard it from the lips of some old body in Kirriemuir.

The Barries were well liked in Forfar. They attended the East Free Church, were regular subscribers to the Sustentation Fund, and were set for a long stay in the town when David Barrie saw a chance to better his prospects yet again, and took it. The company which had built the first factory in Kirriemuir had now built a second, and David Barrie was offered the responsible position of confidential clerk, at what was for him a good salary, more than he was getting in Forfar. After only a two years' stay, therefore, the family moved back to Kirriemuir in 1872, and Jamie left the Academy with two book prizes of which one, *The Young Man-of-War*, was much to his taste.

David Barrie could now afford a better house than the one in the Tenements, and he rented the upper portion of a villa called Strath-view, the lower part being already tenanted. Here the family lived in modest comfort. Margaret Ogilvy had a good kitchen, there was a parlour, and the bedrooms were large. Sara had gone to Motherwell to be housekeeper to her uncle, the minister, and there were three daughters at home; Isabella was a teacher locally, Maggie, the youngest, was at school, while the self-effacing Jane Ann was ever in the background, ready to help anyone who needed comfort.

And Jamie? He was turned twelve, and so far had shown no particular bent for scholarship. True, he had won prizes at Forfar Academy, but they had been for excellence at English lessons, the one subject in which he was really interested and at which he worked. He was too advanced for the local schools now, and when there was a suggestion that he should return to Forfar and lodge during the week with friends, as Alec had done years before, Margaret Ogilvy fought against it. It would do the boy no harm to bide at home for a bit, and get on with his reading. She gently reminded her husband that he had educated himself by reading, and Jamie had had a better start; she was sure he would not waste his time.

Nothing pleased Jamie better than to have long days in which to read books—and to write them. Neither of them was afterwards quite sure how it all began. They took in a monthly penny magazine called *Sunshine* which was full of pretty tales, and also contained a serial about a dear girl who sold watercress—a romantic notion in itself for Jamie, who had never seen that component of a salad. One day the magazine did not arrive. They had exhausted Mr Mills's present stock of books and there was no other source of reading matter. Margaret Ogilvy—or was it Jamie?—had the idea that he might write a story himself. No sooner said than begun: Jamie raced up to the attic with pencil and paper, sat down at an old table which was there, and set to work. There was no difficulty in starting—ideas flowed through his head: the difficulty was selecting one and sticking to it. Jamie found that he had a ready pen. He began a book. The chapters were short and many, and when he finished one he ran down and read it to his mother. She thought it very good and got out her 'work'—she was making a rug out of scraps of stuff, and she prodded the pieces through the canvas as she listened.

Thus was a pattern established. James Matthew Barrie probably decided, during those days, that 'literature is my game'. Writing stories excited and exhilarated him, and there was the flattery of his mother's serious attention. Story after story flew out of the pencil. They were mostly tales of adventure, with imagined characters—he did not describe places or people that he knew. The scenes were desert islands and enchanted gardens, with knights on leaping chargers—and, of course, a girl in a blue dress and bonnet with white ribbons, selling watercress.

Chatterbox replaced *Sunshine* as a regular magazine to be collected at Mr Mills's shop, where Jamie took many a surreptitious look at the blood-and-thunder penny pulps which would never have been allowed inside the Barries' house, but which exerted a great fascination with their garish covers and manly oaths issuing in balloons from sneering faces with menacing eyes. When Mr Mills got a fresh lot of more seemly adventure books in by the weekly carrier from Edinburgh, Margaret Ogilvy was ready with her pennies to begin another delightful orgy of reading which they could enjoy together.

They told each other stories—Margaret Ogilvy, of course, always slipping back to the small girl in the magenta pinafore, and Jamie inventing and expanding and embroidering wild fantasies, his mother an unfailingly sympathetic audience, with Jane Ann sometimes coming in and marvelling.

He paid visits to the manse at Motherwell. Reluctant as she was to see Jamie go, even for a week, Margaret Ogilvy encouraged these visits. She had not given up hopes of him entering the Church, even though he did not seem to have the least interest in theological subjects. Perhaps her brother might have some influence over Jamie's choice of a vocation.

The Motherwell manse to Jamie meant his sister Sara, good meals, the SERVANT, and fishing. His uncle David Ogilvy was earnest and serious, but he did not talk religion, and he knew which of the local burns were good for trout. Jamie went to Motherwell whenever he was invited, and if the minister sometimes asked what was being done about his further schooling, Jamie had no definite answer: he did not know.

His brother had not, in fact, forgotten that Jamie was coming up to thirteen and it was high time he was back at school. Alexander had taken a house in the town of Dumfries, so he now had a base from which to travel round the country on his inspectorship duties. Mary was again with him, teaching part time and housekeeping for him. Why should Jamie not live with them, as he had done in Glasgow, and go to the Dumfries Academy? This had the status of a grammar school, and was in very good standing in the educational world. Jamie would be taught up to university level and have a good chance of gaining a bursary.

Jamie was delighted at the idea of Dumfries Academy. Cricket, as well as football, was played there, he had heard. Cricket! It meant a proper bat and real stumps. This was the best thing that had ever happened to him. Dumfries was a long way away, much farther than Glasgow, and he would not be able to come home except in the long holidays, but that did not spoil the sense of adventure which now possessed him. He felt guilty when he saw Margaret Ogilvy's woeful face, and there were moments when he would have liked to be told the whole thing was off, for it meant losing the table with pencil and paper in the attic, and his mother's ever-ready attention when he ran down the stairs pell-mell to read out his latest story.

Dumfries it was to be, however. David Barrie wrote to his eldest son making the arrangements. He could now afford to pay the fees himself, and he did not neglect to thank Alec for always having a mind to those at home. In 1873 Jamie left Kirriemuir yet again, was met by his brother and sister at Dumfries station, and began a period which he later said were the happiest years of his life.

Chapter 3

GROWING UP

JAMES BARRIE made a friend on his very first day at Dumfries Academy. This was Stuart Gordon, son of the Sheriff Clerk of the town. Stuart asked his name, and when Jamie told him, he did not like it. 'I am going to call you Sixteen-String Jack,' he said. He himself preferred to be called Dare Devil Dick—a character well known to Jamie, being the hero of one of the highly coloured penny numbers he managed to read on the quiet from time to time. A little further fencing brought out that they were both devotees of Fenimore Cooper, and a sound relationship was established.

Stuart and his brother Hal, who was also at the Academy, lived in a house called Moat Brae, which had gardens and grounds sloping down to the River Nith. The brothers had formed a pirate band with some of their schoolfellows, which met on most nights at the bottom of the garden near the river, where there were hollows in the bank suitable for pirate lairs, and great trees to climb so that passing ships could be sighted and attacked. James Barrie was invited to join the band, and was soon joining lustily in all the piratical goings-on, progressing to the office of keeping the band's log-book.

The Academy was co-educational, but Jamie was not yet of an age to take much notice of the girls there. In any case, a boy with five sisters was used to girls. He felt equal to the class-work, shining in essay-writing, but otherwise was no more than average. The important thing was the freedom the boys enjoyed to do what they liked after school, and the relaxed atmosphere at home. Mary never minded if he was late for a meal and Alec was, as always, un-demanding: he believed that a boy should go at his own pace. A solid, studious character himself, he was entirely different from his volatile young brother, yet he had an instinctive understanding of a temperament which was fuelled by an extraordinarily active imagina-tion. It is probable that he trusted to the steadying influence of the

Academy to provide a balance. If Jamie was to win a bursary to the university he would have to work hard—there were few bursaries available and many boys all over Scotland were determined to get one, as he himself had been. But there was time enough for slogging. Let the boy make the most of this year or so.

That was exactly what Jamie was doing. The taste of happiness was in his mouth and he was fully occupied in living. School in the morning, home to midday dinner, school in the afternoon until four o'clock, some homework, then hours of sheer enjoyment. Cricket! The real thing. He bowled and he batted, he kept the score. In winter, football, which he played well but which was not a patch on cricket. Fierce games of marbles which actually wore out the sole of one boot. Long walks with Alec on a Saturday; Dumfries is surrounded by lovely country, and 'Criffel, Torthorwold, Caerlaverock, Lincluden, the Solway', still sounded music in the ears of a tired old man more than sixty years later.

Holidays meant Kirriemuir, walks with his father on Saturday afternoons, fishing with Jimmie Robb. There was also the added pleasure of watching Kirriemuir play Dundee at cricket in the summer holiday, and of keeping the score on his own account. He had already formed the habit of jotting down important events in a notebook, and cricket was always important.

At Strathview, Margaret Ogilvy was still frail, and Jane Ann had grown into her mother's shadow, ever at her beck and call. This sister seemed to be ageless, neither old nor young: she was just there. She stood beside her mother, smiling and nodding, while Jamie talked enthusiastically about his ploys at school and out of it; then she would be off on her household tasks, and Margaret Ogilvy would pick up her sewing, and ask more about Jamie's doings—and somehow the talk would presently turn on the past, when she had been his age, having had to leave her dame school when she was eight. 'Well I remember the day . . .' she would begin, and softly, relentlessly, she pulled him once more into her own childhood.

Every time he went back to Dumfries after the holidays, a normal boy's life reasserted itself. He had begun to work hard at school, for Alec was now pointing out that he himself had got his university bursary at sixteen, and Jamie was already past fifteen. Jamie felt no great enthusiasm at the prospect of the university. He had privately decided what career he wanted to have, but he also knew what Alec expected of him, and did his best at school, putting in an extra hour

or two now and again. He did not need extra literature coaching—
he was nearly always top of the class with his essays—but there were
other, less interesting subjects which were needed for a bursary, and
he forced himself down to the grind.

What really mattered to the young James Barrie was his life after
school hours. He was no longer excited by the pirate band in the
garden of Moat Brae, with Dare Devil Dick's 'Advance another
step, and I will blow up the powder magazine, and send you to
eternity!' sending his temperature up. When he was sixteen, he
discovered the larger sphere of the drama, and a kindred spirit.

Wellwood Anderson, the son of a Dumfries bookseller—Jamie
seems to have gravitated to booksellers' sons—had founded a school
manuscript journal in May, 1875, called *The Clown*, to which Jamie
contributed a piece called *Reckolections of a Skoolmaster, Edited by
James Barrie, M.A., A.S.S., Ll.D*. The young editor put a note in
the Answers to Correspondents column of his next number, saying
that he would be glad to hear again from the gifted author. This was,
in fact, an editorial device to stimulate general interest; but the
journal lasted for only four numbers. The editor did not mourn, and
neither did James Barrie. He and Wellwood Anderson—Wedd to
his intimates—had become firm friends, for not only had they the
same literary tastes, but they discovered that they were both passionately addicted to the theatre.

Wedd came from a bookish home where the drama was not
anathema, as it was in so many Scottish homes of the time. He, and
soon his friend Jamie, had the run of his father's shelves, and anything in the theatrical line was pounced upon, read by them both,
argued over and enjoyed to the full. There were no inhibitions in
Jamie's mind over drama. In his parents' house the word meant
Shakespeare: anyone since the Bard was suspect. Jamie now found
that a great deal of drama had been written since Shakespeare's
time.

Dumfries had a very good theatre, which had been rebuilt on the
site of the old Theatre Royal in Shakespeare Street, the interior
being designed by a well-known stage architect, C. J. Phipps.
Because of its fine stage, it was on the provincial circuit of the top-
flight stock companies, and the Academy boys were encouraged to
attend performances, if their parents permitted. Jamie saw his first
play at this theatre, when J. T. Clynes brought his company to
Dumfries for the winter of 1876, putting on a week's run each of a

repertory which included Lytton's comedy, *Money*, Dion Boucicault's *London Assurance*, and several of Shakespeare's plays.

The two boys went whenever they could. Jamie always tried to get the end seat in the front row of the pit—there were no stalls—so that he could see what the actors were doing in the wings. No stage illusion for James Barrie! From the very beginning he was interested in the mechanics and techniques of stagecraft, as well as in the plays —in the means as well as the ends. Alec did not disapprove of theatregoing, and provided the money—after all, Shakespeare! J. T. Clynes was the first Hamlet, Othello, Richard the Third and Macbeth that Jamie saw. Occasionally, the actor-manager was able to afford a London comedian like J. L. Toole, and George Shelton (who was, years later, to create the part of Smee in *Peter Pan*) was a favourite supporting player. In general, the actors in the company had had no training, but their full-blooded hamming went down very well with the Academy boys.

One evening stood out for Jamie in that first, wonderful winter. Clynes had put on a pantomime, and there was a benefit night for the Principal Boy. Jamie, arriving late with Wedd, found the end seats in the front row occupied, and the house packed so full that there was no place in the auditorium for them. The boys were asked if they would mind coming behind the scenes and sitting in the wings, and would they keep out of people's way and make themselves as small as possible? Magical evening. Enthralling pantomime, especially when someone on the stage, asked to get a paste-pot for the Dame, answered wittily: 'I de-Clynes the task.'

*   *   *

Wellwood Anderson was the kind of boy who could suggest the most unlikely schemes and then proceed to carry them out. The season at the Theatre Royal had given him an idea. There had always been many Academy boys at the performances, so why not found a dramatic club for them? Those who were overcome by the theatric spirit could act, the rest applaud. As for plays, there were already two resident authors at the Academy, himself and James Barrie.

The Dumfries Amateur Dramatic Club thus came into being. In the first season, 1876/7 (young Anderson never let the grass grow under his feet) he put on three short plays, getting permission from the Rector, Dr Cranstoun, to perform them in the Hall of the Academy. The first, *Off the Line*, was a version of a comedy-drama of Clement Scott's which Wedd had seen, with Toole as the star, and which Wedd now re-wrote from memory. The part of Harry Coake, an engine-driver, was taken by Mr J. Barrie, attired in whiskers (at the cost of thirteen pence), a blue reefer jacket, and an ancient driver's hat (half-a-crown).

The second play was written by Mr J. Barrie himself, and was based on incidents from a Fenimore Cooper tale. It was entitled *Bandelero the Bandit*. Jamie had originally intended to play Bandelero himself, but he gave it up to one of the other boys because he thought another part was better, one in which he had to assume six different disguises. This part consisted of all his favourite characters in fiction rolled into one. In the event, it turned out to be a disappointing kind of part because he had to be constantly changing his clothes, with the result that he was scarcely ever on the stage.

In the third play, *Paul Pry*, a version of a comedy by Toole, again adapted by Wellwood Anderson, Jamie played Phoebe, daughter of a major-general, a modest girl with her hair attached to her hat. No one had considered inviting one of the actual girls at the Academy to come into the play.

The innocent amusement of amateur theatricals was suddenly attacked by a local clergyman at a meeting of the School Board, of which he was a member. He made a violent onslaught on both the dramatic club and the plays, calling the latter 'grossly immoral'. The *Dumfries Herald* of January 24th, 1877, gave a full report of what he had said at the meeting, and added a few pungent comments of its own:

It is due to the reader perhaps to explain what was the cause of this terrible outburst and unwarranted attack. In 'Off the Line,' Harry Coake, an engine driver, accepts, on a bitterly cold day, some refreshment from a young barmaid at the buffet of a rural railway station, what he terms 'Only a bit of sandwich and a drop of brandy.' Out of gratitude he offers surreptitiously to take her to the pantomime on New Year's Day. She writes him a letter accepting the invitation, and the incriminating document is found by his wife in one of his coat pockets. Trouble ensues. In the end, however, Harry explains the situation satisfactorily to his wife and all ends happily. Two awful villains, Gamp and Benshaw, were characters in Barrie's play 'Bandelero the Bandit.' They were no worse, and no better, than the average stage villain of the 'penny plain and tuppence coloured' variety and were probably based on Deadwood Dick, Spring-Heeled Jack, a Fenimore Cooper pirate, or the cruel robbers of the Babes in the Wood. Presumably these were the 'grossly immoral plays' referred to by the accusing person. Personally, he said, he knew nothing about these, but if he was correctly informed, etc. etc. One is apt to reply 'Trust not Dame Rumour, Sir, she is a lying jade!'

The affair created indignation in the town, and was taken up and commented upon in the London and provincial papers. Dr Cranstoun was very angry at what he considered to be a malicious attack on his pupils. He immediately began to collect influential names as patrons of the Dramatic Club, and was able to get no less a notability than the Duke of Buccleuch, adding the member of Parliament for the Dumfries district of Burgh, and influential doctors and lawyers, to an impressive list. The amateur actors themselves decided to widen the interest aroused, and Jamie, now secretary of the club, and Wedd, wrote to personages in the professional theatre, appealing to them to become patrons.

Henry Irving, William Terriss and other leading players replied in encouraging terms.

Then came an unexpected champion. Professor John Stuart Blackie of Edinburgh University, ever ready to champion both the drama and the enterprising young, chose the occasion at the end of a lecture which he was giving at the Mechanics' Institute in Dumfries on 'The Highlands and Islands of Scotland' to remark that he had heard of the subject which was causing such a flutter in local circles, and that if the reverend gentleman who had begun it all would step up on that platform and meet him manfully, face to face, he would undertake, so far as argument was concerned, to pound him into jelly.

Wedd followed up this mark of encouragement directly the professor got back to Edinburgh by writing to ask him to grant the Club the privilege of his patronage. He received a gratifying reply:

Dear Sir,
If my name can be of the slightest service to you, in presenting a fair front against the windy puffets of a certain class of pulpit bigots, you are free to use it.

Yours,
J. Blackie.

*   *   *

Alexander Barrie got married that year to a Miss Cowan, the daughter of an Edinburgh jeweller, and Mary returned home for a spell, before taking up a position as a teacher. She had become engaged to John Galloway, Alec's assistant in the Inspectorate, and they intended to get married in the following year.

Jamie continued to live with his brother at Victoria Terrace, where Alec had his house, and got on very well with his new sister-in-law, a pleasant though talkative woman. Alec himself was worried about Jamie. The boy was not a natural scholar, and it was clear that he would not get a bursary. But he should go to the university, all the same. Alexander Barrie had enough experience to know that a young man would get nowhere without a degree, whatever profession he took up. He would pay Jamie's fees at the university, if the boy could get a place.

Something other than university entrance was beginning to worry Jamie at this time. He had begun to notice the bigger girls at the school, had observed that though they were, in turn, noticing boys, he was not included in their sidelong surveys. And he realized that he was now looking up, in a literal sense, to Wedd and his other friends of the same age. They were becoming taller and taller. He remained the same height—he had ceased to grow. He was seventeen, and just topped five feet, while the other seventeen-year-olds were inches taller. He couldn't understand it, and though he told himself that his mother was short and he was supposed to take after her, he didn't like it: it made him feel at a disadvantage.

There was something else. His friends now began to talk about girls. About *women*. Jamie Barrie, long conditioned by his mother to guard against impure thoughts, was filled with distaste and fear when any of his schoolfellows indulged in a coarse joke. He knew it was coarse even when he did not understand the import. It came as a shock when they talked of women's underclothes hanging on a washing-line, and sniggered. At home, his sisters had been rigidly trained never to appear except when they were fully covered; washed undergarments were hung out to dry well away from the eyes of the male, or were looped in anonymous folds over the high pulley below the kitchen ceiling.

Jamie avoided lewd talk and plunged into all the activities he could cram into the day—school-work, games, oratory and argument at the debating society, walks with Wedd and a few companions at the weekend. When they went into the country to the north-east of the town they sometimes saw a man in a cloak and a shovel hat, carrying a stick—a solitary, if ever there was one, even to the eye of a schoolboy. Mr Carlyle. He would be on his way to visit his brother-in-law, Dr Aitken, no doubt—Barrie guessed at this because Miss Mary Carlyle Aitken was a friend of Alec's.

The name of Thomas Carlyle was a hallowed one in the Kirriemuir household, and Jamie always took off his cap respectfully when he met the famous man. Carlyle never acknowledged the salute. Sometimes one of the boys would grow bold and ask Carlyle the way to Lochmaben, whither they were bound, but there was no response, only the stick lifted to point the way, and Carlyle would walk on.

The second season of the Dumfries Amateur Dramatic Club opened on March 15th, 1878, this time in the upper hall of the Assembly Rooms in George Street. There were crowded audiences. The local cleric who had fulminated against them the previous season had given them excellent publicity, and everybody wanted to support the schoolboy actors. A triple bill was again presented. The first play was called *Awkwardly Alike, or Which is Brown?* adapted by Wellwood Anderson from a sketch which he had once seen and re-written to suit his cast. The second was *The Weavers*, really an old farce called *The Spitalfield Weavers* and made popular by Toole. Jamie Barrie again had a feminine rôle, a young wife called Adele, whose husband, played by Wedd, would call her Addle.

This was Jamie's last year at Dumfries Academy. He worked conscientiously but he knew Alec was disappointed, and he dreaded going home to Kirriemuir. What would they say when he told them he wanted to be a writer? For that was what he was determined to be. At the end of the session he left the Academy with an essay prize, and the distinction of having obtained the highest marks in the English literature paper. Now the good days had come to an end. It was with the greatest reluctance that he journeyed home, knowing the explanations he would have to give.

His fears were justified. David Barrie, to whom the chance of attending a university would have been very heaven in his youth, was bewildered by Jamie's declaration that he saw no point in applying for a place as he intended to be an author. An author! A writer! That was no profession, surely. Sir Walter Scott? Well, he had been a Shirra. A Sheriff was a man with important duties: his writings had no doubt been done in his spare time. Thomas Carlyle? Ah, that was different. Mr Carlyle was—well, Mr Carlyle. It was obvious that

David Barrie did not think that Jamie had yet shown any talent which warranted his being thought of as a second Carlyle.

Argument rose and fell, good-humoured enough, but with a 'snell wind blawing round the corners'. Margaret Ogilvy entered into no argument: it was not her way. She just ignored everything that opposed her point of view. Smiling and shaking her head incredulously at the very idea of Jamie making a *living* out of writing tales, she returned to the question of the university. How would he get on without a degree? She had so hoped . . .

She never put the rest into words, but Jamie knew well what was in her mind, for a special look came into her soft face. She was thinking of the son who would have got an M.A. without question, and would have gone farther than that, much farther. Jamie was always instantly aware when she thought of David, and he couldn't bear the look on her face—he would do anything to make her smile, to think of something else. Words tumbled out of his mouth: one day he would be famous, he promised her confidently. He would become a great writer, and then she would see!

The difficulty was that she couldn't see. It didn't make sense to her that with Alec ready to pay the fees and her husband willing to break into his savings for the rest, Jamie should not be eager to get his M.A.

Alexander came to Kirriemuir, and there were more discussions, this time of a positive kind. Alec did not press his own university, Aberdeen, but suggested that Jamie should go to Edinburgh, where his own old friend, Alexander Whyte, was a minister at Free St George's, and therefore Jamie would have a good friend in the city. Also—and this was the strongest argument of any—David Masson was Professor of Rhetoric and Literature at Edinburgh, and as Jamie was so keen on English, he would be sitting at the feet of one of the most famous teachers of the day. Masson, now fifty-six, was at the zenith of his powers, a man of profound scholarship who did not consider literature to be an end in itself but a means for the development of character, and a preparation for life. Although he lacked humour, David Masson was known for his clarity of exposition, and he had the humility of greatness, 'a sensitive man careful of wounding the feelings of others'. Jamie had heard much about Masson from the English master at the Academy.

He gave in, as they had known he would. He would go to the university. Edinburgh it was to be.

Chapter 4

EDINBURGH INTERLUDE

On October 30th, 1878, the name of James M. Barrie, Kirriemuir, was entered in the Matriculation Album of Edinburgh University. He had been met by Alexander Whyte, who showed him round the Old Quad and was generally welcoming. Mrs Whyte had found him lodgings in Cumberland Street, and had told him to feel free to call on them at any time.

At eighteen, young Barrie was still short and spare—'as thin as a pencil but not so long', as he was later to describe, with some bitterness, his lack of height. At Dumfries it had not mattered so much, as he had been among friends who had known him for a long time. Here, it took considerable effort not to be conscious of it. The other men seemed to tower above him as he walked among them to the lecture rooms.

Before long his innate shyness had become intense, and he made no friends during those first terms. He was not so poor as some of the students; his father gave him an allowance sufficient to pay for board and lodging, with a little over; Alec, besides being responsible for his university fees, also bought his books. Margaret Ogilvy and Jane Ann between them had seen to it that he took an adequate box of clothes to Edinburgh. Charles Laing, who remembered James Barrie from Forfar Academy days and now attended Professor Masson's classes, recalled how he recognized 'a spare, short figure in a warm-looking Highland cloak' in the Old Quad.

Barrie at first shared his lodging at the top of the house in Cumberland Street with a fellow-student called Harrison, who died a year later, and Barrie lived on there alone. It was not unusual for students to die; many of them suffered so badly from malnutrition that they had little chance of survival if attacked by serious illness. Samuel Crockett, who later became a leading novelist of the 'Kail-yard School', was finishing his course at Edinburgh when Barrie was a freshman. During his first three years there Crockett lived on nine shillings a week, his meals consisting mainly of oatmeal porridge, penny rolls and glasses of milk. He was strong enough—and determined enough—to get through those spartan years, but others were not so tough. Barrie, who had enough money for nourishing food, was observant of his less fortunate fellows:

I knew three undergraduates who lodged together in a dreary house at the top of a dreary street; two of them used to study until two in the morning, while the third slept. When they shut up their books they woke number three, who arose, dressed and studied until breakfast time. Among the many advantages of this arrangement the chief was that, as they were dreadfully poor, one bed did for the three. Two of them occupied it at the one time, and the third at another. Terrible privations? Frightful destitution? Not a bit of it. The Millennium was in those days. If life was at the top of a hundred steps, if students occasionally died of hunger and hard work combined, if the midnight oil only burned to show a ghastly face 'weary and worn', if lodgings were cheap and dirty, and dinners few and far between, life was still real and earnest; in many cases it did not turn out an empty dream.

Edinburgh was not the only Scottish university with desperately poor students, desperately trying to equip themselves for a better life than their fathers had known. Barrie, who often visited the Whytes' and heard much about his host's early life, later wrote of Aberdeen University: 'There were among Dr Whyte's class-fellows men who endured greater hardships to get an education than a traveller suffers in Central Africa.'

The hardships which Barrie endured were in the classrooms of the University. Mathematics, one of the subjects he had to take for his degree, had always been his especial bugbear. In Professor Chrystal's lecture room, a gloomy student had carved on a desk: 'All hope abandon ye who enter here', and young Barrie was often on the verge of giving up hope. In *An Edinburgh Eleven* he wrote: 'I had never a passion for knowing that when circles or triangles attempt impossibilities it is absurd; and *x* was an unknown quantity I was ever content to walk round about.' He knew that he would have to work exceedingly hard and master enough mathematics to satisfy the examiners when the time came.

Philosophy and metaphysics were tough intellectual meat, and his University notebooks give some idea of how he tried to wrestle with these subjects. There are many pages on Berkeley and Descartes, though one does not know whether these were taken down verbatim as lecture notes or were his own interpretations of the ideas expounded. However, he acquired enough knowledge in metaphysics to frighten a medical student by convincing him that he had no existence strictly so-called. 'This shows what metaphysics can do.'

Then there was John Stuart Blackie, the Highland Professor of Greek, who had championed the Dumfries Amateur Dramatic Club and remembered young Barrie. He was one of the most genial of men, who could talk six languages: 'This tends to make the conversation one-sided, but he does not mind that. He still writes a great deal . . . When he dips his pen into an inkpot, it at once writes a sonnet—so strong is the force of habit.'[1]

It was Professor Masson who had the strongest influence over Barrie; the young man went to his lectures with a high sense of anticipation. Masson was one of the greatest scholars of his time, deeply learned, yet with an equally deep sense of what really mattered in literature and life, and how they were related. Asked to define a man of letters he replied that it was not the poet, who was all soul, so much as the strong-brained writer whose guardian angel was a fine sanity, who was the true man of letters.

He [Masson] masters a subject by letting it master him; for though his critical reputation is built on honesty, it is his enthusiasm that makes his work warm with life. Sometimes he entered the classroom so full of what he had to say that he began before he reached his desk. If he was in the middle of a peroration when the bell rang, even the back benches forgot to empty.[2]

*　　*　　*

Holidays at Kirriemuir; and at Dumfries, staying with Alec and his wife. There was usually a visit, too, to his uncle the Reverend David Ogilvy at Motherwell. Sara Barrie, who had been her uncle's housekeeper for so long, also ran a little school in two of the spare rooms at the manse. The venture grew, and she had to take larger premises, sending for her sister Isabella to come to Motherwell to help her; between them they were very successful with the enlarged school.

At Strathview, Jamie's relations with his parents were unchanged. David Barrie, now a valued senior employee at the Linen Works, was earning good wages but he could not save much, with Jamie at

1. *An Edinburgh Eleven*   2. *Ibid.*

Edinburgh. This was never put into words, but the young man knew it. As for Margaret Ogilvy, every look at her son carried approval, for it was clear he was at last going along the right path.

The profession of writing was not seriously mentioned. Books were discussed and opinions given, and it was taken for granted that Jamie was interested in authors, but not from any practical point of view. It was Jane Ann, during rare moments alone with her brother, who tentatively asked if he ever had time to go on with his writing, and Jamie became suddenly aware of this sister, who had always been the background to his life at home.

Edinburgh again, more familiar after several terms, but it was not an easy familiarity. Barrie's shyness had become more constricting, and when he was not at lectures, he was much alone. He worked at his books most of the time, but he was also trying out ideas for articles, and sometimes his conscience nagged at him, for there were nights when he was spending more time on writing articles than on metaphysics and logic.

He had heard that the editor of the *Edinburgh Courant* was a Kirriemarian, and took some articles round to the paper. The editor did not find them good enough to print, and Barrie tried again, this time seeking an interview. A talk revealed that this slightly-built youth was a fanatic for the theatre, and Barrie found himself a free-lance dramatic critic for the *Courant*.

The first person to whom he imparted this wonderful piece of news was Wellwood Anderson, who had left Dumfries Academy and hoped to have a career in the professional theatre. They had carried on a correspondence for some time. Barrie was jubilant. To be given free tickets for the theatre, and then to be paid for writing about it! Wedd was the one person above all others who would understand what that meant. Barrie wrote about his theatre-going in detail:

I was at 'School' the other day . . . Most of the company would need to go to school before they seek to act in it. The play is rather artificial though rather amusing.

I have been at both pantomimes, but the 'Forty Thieves' is decidedly superior in scenery and words, not in acting, though Morgan as Ali Baba is very good. He looks so ridiculously funny dressed in Egyptian clothes made in regular English fashion. The donkey too could hardly be better. The taking song in both pantomimes is one 'Keep it Dark', it is encored half a dozen times every night. 'Ladies, you may dye your hair any colour you like, But I would advise you to keep it dark,' and so on.

The *Courant* sent him farther afield. In a later letter to Wedd he wrote:

I saw 'Little Emily' at the Royalty in Glasgow. Fisher as Micawber was very respectable, but the general impression was saddening. The villain Heep was a very mild villain, and Little Emily's ideas of pathos are decidedly vague. The Rosa Dartle mouthed it in a manner unworthy of an unacknowledged Garrick, and David Copperfield walked through his part in a perfectly unobjectionable manner.

By the following year, Barrie was also reviewing books for the *Courant*, and his dramatic criticism was growing even more assured, opinionated and illegible:

My dear Wedd,
Twaddle is twaddle. The company is to be almost the same as last season, with a few exceptions . . . I hear a burlesque is coming here, and I intend to deal with it. Pieces like this give the stage a bad name. Fancy, one of the chief scenes represents a bevy of girls bathing in real water, in the Sea of Innocence. Don't you think they might have hit on a better name for that piece of Ocean. I need not say it would give me pain to sit out such an immoral piece of inanity, so I need not say it, for I hear you telling me I have your sympathy . . . Congratulations to you for setting up *Cox and Box*, but why, oh why, did you not do the new 'Which is Brown?' Is it possible that the [illegible] can't raise sufficient company? Times are changed. You should take Paris on your next trip. Mr Michael Strogoff there has a ballet of young women dressed in tights *only*. They manage these things well in France.

There were few University clubs, but two debating societies flourished, the smaller of which was known as the Edinburgh University Dumfriesshire and Galloway Literary Society, the membership being restricted to students from those counties. Barrie joined this society, which was split on the question of whether the meetings should be opened with prayer, 'and the men who thought they should would not so much as look at the men who thought they should not.' The Society's syllabuses for those sessions have Barrie's name on many of them. In a debate between J. M. Barrie and J. C. Thomson, J. M. Barrie opposed the proposition 'Should Women Have Equal Rights with Men?' He read an essay in December, 1881, on 'Faith and Reason, or the World in Chains', and he supported the view at another debate 'That the Utilitarian Theory of Morals is Correct'. The D & G Society might be small, but there was plenty of spirit in it.

A fellow-student, Robert Galloway, who attended several of the same classes as Barrie, described him at this period: 'I remember him distinctly—a sallow-faced, round-shouldered, slight, somewhat delicate-looking figure, who quietly went in and out amongst us, attracting but little observation.'

Barrie was, in fact, leading a modest social life, but it was different from that of many of the other students—it did not include friendships with girls. This was not for lack of opportunities. Some of the academic families gave soirées and 'sociables'—especially where there were daughters—and on the mornings after such occasions, before the professor arrived in class, the talk would include sly hints of hands held in corners and trim waists encircled in a flying polka. One or two would boast in undertones of occasional visits to the disreputable houses in the Old Town. Barrie instinctively avoided all contact with such full-blooded companions.

He did, however, go to the students' suppers. At one of them, after a sword dance performed on the table by a nimble youth, young Barrie riveted the attention of the company by an imitation of Henry Irving's Matthias in *The Bells*, copying Irving's peculiarities of speech with the greatest fidelity, 'and adding just that touch of exaggeration which makes an imitation the more effective'. There is no record as to when or where Barrie saw the actor, to be able to imitate him so faithfully.

He found a friend in Joseph Thomson, the assistant librarian to the University, who had been a railway platelayer in his younger days and wrote poetry in his spare time. Thomson had reached his present status by the gruelling hard work of the traditional poor Scots scholar. It was through him that Barrie met another Joseph Thomson, no relation, who was famous for having taken over an expedition in Central Africa on the death of its leader. The explorer was only twenty-two and Barrie was thrilled to meet him several times in the company of his friend the poet.[1] James Matthew Barrie never lost his hero-worship for explorers and other men of courage and action.

When he was at home during the Christmas holiday of December,

1. When Barrie asked the explorer what was his most dangerous journey, he replied, 'Crossing Piccadilly Circus.'

1880, his sister Isabella got married, and Jamie distinguished himself by an extraordinary display of the shyness which gripped him—except when he was giving a 'performance' of some kind. There is an incident related by a friend of the Barrie girls, Joseph Alexander, who was six years older than Jamie:

When Isabella was married to Dr Murray we were invited over to a party in the evening . . . It was a young people's party and I don't think that either David Barrie or Margaret Ogilvy made their appearance. James was so bashful that he also could not be induced to join, except that under great pressure he consented to come in and recite the Dream of Eugene Aram. I remember being surprised at the dramatic intensity of the reciter, and at the time I thought he exaggerated the intended effect of the poet, but later understood it to be quite an orthodox rendering. After the recital he immediately left without speaking to one of the company!

*   *   *

Barrie went back to Edinburgh for his last year with the iron-willed determination to work even harder than before. The M.A. examination was ever before his eyes now, and he was thankful for a photographic memory, knowing well that Professor Chrystal's hated hieroglyphics would fade from the tablets of his mind once the examination was over. Meanwhile, he hoped that he had managed to drive enough mathematics into his head to satisfy the examiners.

He was getting bad headaches. This was probably chronic migraine: he had suffered from headaches from time to time since his schooldays, but now they were becoming more frequent. Never mind, he had to work. 'Grind, grind, grind,' he wrote in an almanack-diary which he had been given. Industry and an obstinate capacity to conquer difficulties were bred in the Barries, and grind he would, until he was capped M.A.

He went on Sunday mornings to hear Alexander Whyte at Free St George's, or Dr Walter Smith at the Free High. Dr Smith wrote poetry as well as sermons, and young Barrie found in his verses much 'homely sense and shrewd'. In the afternoon he might visit his sisters Sara and Maggie, who now lived in Edinburgh. On Isabella's marriage Sara had sold the school at Motherwell and come to Edinburgh with Maggie, their youngest sister, where they had obtained positions as governesses at Miss Oliver's School in Rutland Street.

Mostly he went for long walks or stayed in his lodgings—new and better lodgings—studying his notes or writing for the *Courant*. He knew he must not do too much of this, but the extra money was useful, and it was difficult *not* to write. Ideas teemed in his brain, ideas totally unconnected with rhetoric or logic, philosophy or metaphysics. What he wanted to have, more than anything else, was time—time to write, and write, and write. Well, that would come: James Barrie was sure of it. The M.A. first, if only to repay Alec for the long years of kindness and help, and his father for his patience, and Margaret Ogilvy for her faith. There was pain as well as love, and many feelings which he could not understand, when he thought of his mother. She would try to stop him doing what he must do. But the M.A.—that was the first hurdle.

On April 21st, 1882, the hurdle was surmounted. He received his degree. James M. Barrie, Kirriemuir, at the age of twenty-two, could put the letters M.A. after his name. He hired his graduate's gown for five shillings at Middlemass's, and walked in procession to the Synod Hall to be capped. He had his photograph taken, with 'the hair straggling under the cap as tobacco may straggle over the side of a tin when there is difficulty in squeezing down the lid'.

He travelled home to Kirriemuir, where he found a Margaret Ogilvy far more triumphant and 'set up' than himself; then went on a visit to Alec in Dumfries. There were two small children in the household now, and Jamie was proud to be an uncle. The main purpose of his visit, however, was to discuss his future with Alec.

University days were over. Barrie turned his back on them without regret. He liked Edinburgh, and would always go back there with pleasure, but the four years he had just passed had not been of his own choosing, and he was glad they were behind him. They had been an interlude.

Chapter 5

FLEDGLING WRITER

THE Barries now had to accept the fact that Jamie was not going to be a professor, or even a teacher, but a writer. David Barrie thought that perhaps there was something in it, after all, and Margaret Ogilvy, sensing Jamie's strong purpose, began to come round. After all, he had been *paid* for some writing in the Edinburgh newspaper. What did Alec think?

Alexander Barrie was, as usual, interested and not unsympathetic when his brother came for a visit during the summer. Authorship, he pointed out, was a precarious means of livelihood, but there was no reason why Jamie shouldn't try. Why not send articles to editors? Jamie was already doing that, but they came back. Nevertheless, he intended to go on. Alec suggested a compromise; Jamie might return to Edinburgh for a year or so, and do some research for a solid book. Alec would again stake him. At the same time he could continue with his writing, and see what success came his way.

Jamie took up the idea at once. It was not easy writing at Kirriemuir, even though his mother had put a room at his disposal for the purpose. In Edinburgh he would have access to the libraries, and he might be able to resume contact with the *Courant*, and even strike out into wider fields.

In the autumn of 1882, therefore, he returned to Edinburgh, taking lodgings with a Mrs Edwards, a motherly body who looked after him well (and who would one day be the model for the charlady-heroine in *The Old Lady Shows Her Medals*).

Barrie joined the Debating Society, and began research for a book which he had planned on *The Early Satirical Poetry of Great Britain*; an odd choice, for he had no ear for poetry and was not yet up to the subtleties of satire. He worked conscientiously, but his heart was not in it. He wrote article after article and sent them to the newspapers; they were returned. He went on writing; he had

developed the steely discipline of 'If at first you don't succeed . . .'
The work on early satirical poetry did not get very far, but he filled
notebook after notebook with all kinds of ideas, plots for stories,
synopses, outlines of plays.

A few articles accepted by the *Courant* helped to save face when he
went home for a holiday, but he had to admit that there was not
much money coming in. In the end he was obliged to return home,
and continued writing with a kind of desperation. Margaret Ogilvy
watched him anxiously, and Barrie knew that he had found his own
place in her heart. The dead brother was there—he would never be
forgotten—but the living one had now become the centre of her life.

They talked about his work; for at last Margaret Ogilvy accepted
that his writing was to be his work. They discussed the art of
authorship, and Jamie said he was of the opinion that a man must
know himself and at least one woman really well before he could
write a successful novel. Margaret Ogilvy was reassuring. Jamie
knew himself, didn't he? And as for a woman, well, he knew his
mother! So that problem was solved.

It wasn't so easy when they began to talk of more intimate
relationships. Margaret Ogilvy was in no doubt whatever that the
most wonderful relationship between human beings was that
between a mother and her son, and Jamie agreed without hesitation.
Husband and wife? Margaret Ogilvy was equally sure about that.
The private relationship between man and wife—that which was not
talked about—was necessary but regrettable. A wife must faithfully
submit to her husband: it was a Biblical injunction. And somehow
the conversation would take a safer turn. A good husband provided
for his family, and a wife would always respect a good husband. But
when it came to the really important relationships, it was the mother
who counted.

Always the same theme, and Jamie believed it. The twenty-two-
year-old young man had at last found something that he had missed
all through his life so far. His mother needed, loved and wanted
him. It gave Jamie a sensation which was to grow into a kind of
idolatry of this tiny, frail woman with the soft face and indestructible
will-power.

*   *   *

The book he had begun in Edinburgh was put aside before it was
half-finished, and Barrie began something else; a three-decker novel,

as he afterwards told people, but it was never published and nobody ever saw it. He sat up in the attic room day after day, writing, and if industrious application could have brought success, he would have been intensely happy to lay it at his mother's feet.

One day, Jane Ann was reading the *Scotsman*, when an advertisement took her eye. It was for a leader-writer on an English newspaper, the *Nottingham Journal*. Jane Ann showed it to Jamie, who was uninterested. A settled job meant regular hours, a strait-jacket well known to be a foe to inspiration. Still—and here a modicum of native common sense asserted itself—inspiration had not got him very far up till now, in spite of his utmost efforts to clothe her in noble thoughts and fine language.

Jane Ann tried again. Surely being *on* a newspaper was almost as good as writing for one? She felt that her brother had no future, sitting up here day after day, filling page after page, and getting his articles back.

Jamie agreed to send in an application, with Jane Ann's enthusiastic backing. The fact that he had never written a leader does not appear to have troubled either of them, but here was at least a chance of stepping into the world of print. Letters were sent off to Professor Masson and Alexander Whyte, asking if they would allow their names to be used for a testimonial; they agreed by return of post, and Jamie wrote a careful letter to the *Nottingham Journal* and settled down to wait. A reply came quite soon, asking Mr Barrie for specimens of his leaders. This was a poser. Mr Barrie sent them a copy of one of his university essays. Within a short time the *Nottingham Journal* wrote again, offering him the position of leader-writer at a salary of three pounds a week.

Amid the family jubilation and Margaret Ogilvy's obvious pride, Jamie was hard put to it not to show the confused feelings which now filled him. This meant leaving home, and probably for good. Nottingham was a long way from Kirriemuir, much farther than Edinburgh, and he knew in his bones that it would be London next. He had turned from a schoolboy into a student, and now the adult world lay ahead. For a terrifying moment he did not want to go on: he longed for time to come to a standstill. He did not want to leave his mother, or Jane Ann, or his quiet father, whom he hardly saw now because of the long hours at the linen works.

The moment passed. The womenfolk were already discussing his clothes, and he went to Dumfries to say goodbye to Alec and the little family there. Alec advised him to read the leaders in the *Scotsman* and every other paper he could get hold of. When at last the day of parting came, and he was on the train south, he was already excited. Writing. This was something he could do. Perhaps he would be printed every day? It was a new and marvellous prospect.

*　　*　　*

Nottingham in January, 1883, was a town known to the rest of the country mainly for its traditional Goose Fair, tales of Robin Hood, and the Nottingham lace which draped most of the windows of the land. The *Nottingham Journal* was one of the three local dailies, and not the best of them at that; its rivals, the *Guardian* and the *Express*, were livelier.[1] The *Journal* had been established in 1710, according to the inscription on the brow of the building in Pelham Street. It was now owned by two brothers called Bradshaw, who had inherited it and who were rich enough not to have to make it a paying proposition. They did not employ an editor, and the paper was 'put together' by the foreman-compositor, who was almost solely concerned with the technical tasks of getting the newspaper printed. Reporters and sub-editors had a free hand with their copy; all that was required was enough text to fill the pages. A strait-jacket for James Barrie? He found it all ideal. Here he was receiving a regular salary, and he could write as much as he liked; it would go into the paper if room could be found for it. He was very happy.

The co-proprietors of the *Journal* got their money's worth, and more. For three pounds a week—cannily translated into twelve pounds a month—they had secured the services of an M.A., and therefore an erudite person, and also a born journalist. Besides the daily leader on current topics, Barrie turned out a dozen extra columns a week—random notes, book reviews, anything he chose to write about. He became Hippomenes on Mondays, and signed the same pseudonym under a bright column headed 'A Modern Peripatetic' on Thursdays. These were all reprinted in the Saturday supplement of the paper, together with any extra articles he cared to put in. And he kept up this spate for eighteen months.

The one subject which he never treated very successfully was women, or, as he called them, Young Ladies. He could, in any article, moralize about mothers-in-law and be humorous about them, too, but directly he got on to flesh-and-blood women,

1. The *Express* absorbed the *Journal* in 1887.

Margaret Ogilvy took charge. They came out of his pen as romantic, self-possessed, sexless beings, set apart from common humanity, completely unreal. He was already developing a defensive attitude towards them which was to grow, and which came out in a heart-rending passage in an article he wrote later about a visit to Tagg's Island, on the Thames:

As for knowing a pretty girl when he saw one, nobody conceived it of the object in the corner [himself]. It was equally inconceivable to the ladies of the island . . . If they would dislike him or fear him it would be something, but it is crushing to be just harmless.

Was it his height, or lack of it? Barrie was sure that this had a great deal to do with it: he was five feet two inches and would never be any taller. Young ladies, he was convinced, never looked at short men.

He lived in lodgings Sbehind herwood Street, near enough for him to walk back after he left the *Journal* office in the small hours. On Sunday he attended St Andrew's Presbyterian Church, where an elderly Scotswoman was in the habit of getting up and walking out whenever 'Lead, Kindly Light' was given out as the next hymn, in protest at the congregation singing the words of an abominable Papist.

Saturday was his free day. He would sometimes be invited to a meal at the home of H. G. Hibbert, a sub-editor on the *Journal*, who shared his passion for the theatre and for walking in the country. They would spend hours discussing plays. Hibbert describes Barrie as being 'the most shy, the most painfully sensitive creature, with an exquisite delicacy in regard to women . . . Walking was a joy to him. I suppose we must have covered hundreds of miles of Nottingham-shire and Derbyshire together.'

Barrie also met someone through Hibbert who was later to become a close friend. This was Thomas Lennox Gilmour, a former sub-editor of the *Journal* who had decided to enter himself as a student at Edinburgh University. Besides working for a degree, Gilmour wrote for the *Scotsman* to help support himself. Barrie was in Hibbert's room on one of Gilmour's visits to Nottingham, when he had dropped into the *Journal* office. He and Barrie took to each other; they were compatriots, and though in most ways dis-similar in temperament, they each recognized in the other a kindred spirit.

Barrie had begun to send articles to London, to the *Pall Mall Gazette* and the *St James's Gazette*, and he was having some success. Thus encouraged, he spent more of his free time in writing, and though not every effort was accepted, he sold enough to awaken old ambitions. London was his ultimate goal. He knew he must not attempt to uproot himself unless he could see a fair chance of earning a livelihood in Fleet Street, but his mind was ever oriented towards the south. He was twenty-four years old, time to be thinking of a move. Not yet, however.

Forces outside his control or knowledge were combining to bring that day-dream closer, whether he was ready for it or not. The Bradshaws, faced with steadily increasing losses, decided to economize by doing without their leader-writer. Compositors, reporters and sub-editors they had to have, but they could buy syndicated articles of a general nature at a cut-price rate, and twelve pounds a month was twelve pounds a month. At the end of October, 1884, James M. Barrie, M.A., who had added, if not lustre, a considerable amount of liveliness to the pages of the *Nottingham Journal*, travelled north to Kirriemuir, a journalist without a job.

*   *   *

At Strathview he was made welcome by his parents and Jane Ann, but he imagined he saw anxiety in their faces as he settled down once more in the room at the top of the house with pads of paper in front of him, sharpened pencils, his brain flowing with ideas. At least, they flowed at first. There came a day when his mind went blank for hours at a time, and when anxiety caught him, too, by the throat.

What was going to happen to him? He had learned from Hibbert that free-lance writing from an obscure little town far away from the hub of things was not the easiest way of making a living, and though Barrie was not asked to pay anything towards his keep, he revolted at the idea of depending on his parents.

It was not all despair. Quite often he would catch an idea on the wing which interested him for its own sake, and then he wrote without stopping, fleshing the bones. Several articles were accepted by other papers as well as by Greenwood of the *St James's Gazette*. The *Pall Mall Gazette* had actually commissioned some work, which would bring in a few guineas.

A few guineas, however, were not the same as a regular salary of twelve pounds a month. Barrie went to Dumfries in December to visit Alec, and, as usual, the wise elder brother proffered good advice. Jamie had acquired good experience on a paper: why not look for a post on another? After the perusal of advertisements in several journals, a letter went off to A. G. Jeans, the manager of the *Liverpool Post and Echo*:

> Greenbank,
> Dumfries,
> N.B.
> 21 *December*, '84.

Sir,

In answer to your advertisement for an experienced sub-editor for a daily paper, I beg to submit my name for your consideration.

For the past two years I have been on the staff of the *Nottingham Daily Journal* where I acted as assistant editor. The work expected of me there included leader-writing daily as well as much dramatic and literary criticism, and I had a share nightly in the practical sub-editing of the paper. My experience of sub-editing in all its branches is sound and thorough.

I left the *Journal* about a month ago owing to a change in its arrangements, but the proprietors were exceedingly sorry to part with me, and are ready and anxious to speak cordially in my favour.

I am in Scotland at present doing some interviews etc. for the *Pall Mall Gazette* at the editor's request. For some months I have been one of the most frequent of the *Pall Mall Gazette*'s occasional contributors, and articles of mine have also appeared in the *St James's Gazette* and other well-known London papers. I should like much to send you my scrap book with a large selection of printed specimens of my work.

I am 25 years of age and an M.A. of Edinburgh University.

For references as to 'character and general capacities for filling the vacant post' he referred the editor to Professor Masson, Alexander Whyte—now a Doctor of Divinity—and others, and ended:

In conclusion I may say that should you consider my application favourably I should be untiring in my endeavours to justify the appointment. Any enquiries will be promptly attended to.

> *I am, Sir, your obedient servant,*
> J. M. BARRIE

Barrie was not appointed to the vacancy, and, again at home, resumed article-writing. There were hours when he came downstairs and sat in the kitchen, watching Jane Ann at her household business while his mother sat with her 'wires', knitting, and they would talk. Margaret Ogilvy always returned to the same theme: her father and their neighbours when she was a child; the Auld Lichts, and the tiny enclosed world of their kirk.

Auld Lichts. Barrie listened with fresh interest. He had heard many of the stories before, but now he asked his mother to tell them to him again. She was only too ready to comply, talking on long after she was tired because Jamie was listening so intently. When he next sat down in the attic-study, his pencil flew over the paper in dozens of notes, carefully numbered. Kirriemuir in the old days: a small community, full of 'characters'. Already the people, old and young, whom Margaret Ogilvy had described, were taking shape, larger than life, in that quick brain.

He intended to make it a two-thousand-word article, and the form grew out of the ideas. He began with a narrator, a dominie with a schoolhouse in the Glen of Quharity—otherwise Glen Clova, the one he knew well—and the inhabitants of 'Thrums' would be described through the schoolmaster's eyes. Thrums are the short ends of the warp on a hand-loomed piece of cloth, cut off and hung near by, so that they can be used for tying up broken threads. More often they are long ends, with many uses—plaiting into braces, twisting into bootlaces and watch-chains, weaving into small dusters. Barrie had hit on the exact name for Kirriemuir in the article which he now proceeded to write. When he had finished it, he knew he had got something which had not been done before, but he was not sure whether the *St James's Gazette* would take it. Nevertheless he made a fair copy and sent it off, giving as its title *Auld Licht Idylls*.

Frederick Greenwood, the editor, liked it straight away. He found the article fresh and original, and printed it on November 17th, 1884, having changed the title to *An Auld Licht Community*. Barrie received a cheque for two guineas in due course—top price—and at once set to work to follow up with another article, this time on a different subject, having said all he had to say on old Kirriemuir. Greenwood sent this offering back with a scribbled note: 'I liked that Scotch thing. Any more of those?'

The author was nonplussed at first, then he became excited. His mother knew a great many more stories of the same kind. There was a consultation: Margaret Ogilvy was delighted at the turn her reminiscences had taken, and from then on Barrie had many sessions with his mother and Jane Ann—the devoted daughter watching her mother to see that she was not too fatigued. Barrie proceeded to exploit this new vein to the full.

The articles were very well written, but some of them—without Margaret Ogilvy realizing it—gave scarifying glimpses of the puritanism which had, in her youth, given the self-righteous a stranglehold on the weaker brethren of their denomination. Margaret Ogilvy was very strong on the subject of adultery; she impressed upon her son that sexual sins were the most heinous of all:

Sinful women [in church] were grimly taken to task by the minister, who, having thundered for a time against adultery in general, called upon one sinner in particular to stand forth. She had to step forward into a pew near the pulpit, where, alone and friendless, and stared at by the congregation, she cowered in tears beneath his denunciations. In that seat she had to remain during the forenoon service. She returned home alone, and had to come back to her solitary seat in the afternoon. All day no one dared speak to her. She was as much an object of contumely as the thieves and smugglers whom, in the end of the last century, it was the privilege of Feudal Baillie Wood (as he was called) to whip round the square.

This was the real stuff, and Greenwood wanted more. Besides being up to standard for the *St James's*, the author was an original, and should be encouraged. Frederick Greenwood was one of the foremost editors of the day, noted for his recognition of new talent. Now in his mid-fifties, he had been in journalism from the time he left school, beginning at the bottom as an apprentice in a newspaper office and graduating by way of sub-editing and reporting to the editorship of the *Cornhill Magazine*, the *Pall Mall Gazette*, and now the *St James's Gazette*, which he founded. It was a quality newspaper, and to be printed in it, even anonymously—as Barrie was—indicated that here was someone worthy of notice.

Barrie had already had an article in another paper, *Home Chimes*, edited by F. W. Robinson. This publication was modelled on *Household Words*, which Dickens had edited, and it numbered among its contributors names which were to become famous: Swinburne, Watts-Dunton, Coventry Patmore, Bret Harte, Jerome K. Jerome. When Greenwood wrote kindly to Kirriemuir, Barrie was elated. He sat contentedly at his table, making notes, trying out passages of prose, hurrying downstairs, as of old, to read them to his mother and sister, and returning to the attic to write again. He had no shortage of ideas. From *With the Highland Smugglers* he could turn to *Scottish*

University Life, through half a dozen widely dissociated subjects, to end up with a gruesome tale called *The Body in the Black Box*. And there were several more Auld Licht tales, for Margaret Ogilvy was remembering more.

*   *   *

In 1885 Barrie decided that the time had come for him to go to London. The thought had for long been there, but now he made up his mind. The steady acceptance of articles by Greenwood and Robinson had given him confidence. 'I'll make you proud of me!' he had promised Margaret Ogilvy, and it was a promise he intended to keep. He had a foot on the literary ladder and he was determined to climb it, but the ladder was in London. He had to be *there*. To London, therefore, he would go.

There were forebodings at home. If he had had an assured position on a newspaper to go to, as in Nottingham, it would have been understandable, but—alone in London! Without definite prospects! They had seen for themselves how insecure was the life of a free-lance writer, but here, at least, there was a home at his back. In London there would be nothing. They were afraid for him. David Barrie, as usual, took no part in the talk; he offered no opinion, for he knew nothing about London except what he had read. And in any case, this son had long been an enigma. Jamie would follow his own bent, whatever was said.

Margaret Ogilvy's face grew softer than ever, and she became tearful at the thought of parting with Jamie again. She had hoped that the story-telling, with the clever lad at home making them into tales to be printed, would go on for ever. Jane Ann said little, yet Jamie knew what was in her mind. She wanted him to strike out and face the hazards. Jamie always felt strength and purpose well up in him when she listened to his sudden outbursts of frustration and the spurts of hope that succeeded them. In any case, Jane Ann was here to look after their mother, so there would be no anxieties on that account.

Alec was naturally consulted, and agreed that if Jamie intended to seek his fortune in the literary world, London was the hub. Barrie's eyes were observant even during the short visit to Dumfries. He noticed that the rooks were building their nests once more—he always had an eye for the natural world. When he returned to Kirriemuir he wrote an article which he called *The Rooks Begin to*

Build, and sent it off to the *St James's Gazette*. He also wrote a private letter to the editor saying he wanted to come to London and what did Mr Greenwood advise?

Frederick Greenwood probably had scores of letters from eager, aspiring writers, all wanting to come to London, ready to startle Fleet Street with their genius. He sent a polite but firm reply, advising Mr Barrie to stay where he was, and to continue to supply him with good articles.

Barrie noted the contents of the letter, put it in his pocket, and continued with his plans for departure. On March 28th, 1885, he caught the night train to London. In his pocket was a silver watch, given to him by his father for his fourteenth birthday, and a wallet containing twelve pounds. His luggage consisted of a square wooden box which he had taken to the University, and which had belonged to his father and his brother before him. On the inside of the lid there still adhered labels, A. O. Barrie, M.A. and J. M. Barrie, M.A.

On reaching St Pancras Station in the small hours of the morning, he began to haul his box to the Left Luggage Office, to deposit it while he looked round for lodgings. His eye fell on what was to him the most heart-warming sight in literature. A *St James's Gazette* poster leaned against the wall, left over from the previous evening, and on it he distinctly read the words *The Rooks Begin to Build* among the advertised contents of the paper. His article. He had sent it to Greenwood not a week before. He was astounded and dazzled at the same time: he had only been in London a few minutes and already he had made two guineas! What an augury for the future. He sat on the box and looked at the poster, feeling almost as if Greenwood had met him at the station. Forty-five years later, writing of those first moments, he said that this was the romance of his life.

Barrie had studied maps of London, and decided on Bloomsbury to live in, as it was convenient for the British Museum and its Reading Room. On his way there, he passed along the Gray's Inn Road, where he stopped to have breakfast, before going on to look for lodgings. He found a room in Guilford Street, retrieved his box, and began life in his new home, ready to begin the climb up the ladder of fame at the earliest possible moment. His first purchase, therefore, was a bottle of ink. The second was 'the Hat'. He says, writing of himself in the third person as Anon:

The Hat, of course, was bought for the subjection of Greenwood. H

[Anon] understood that without a silk hat he could not advance upon a lordly editor, and from first to last it was used for this purpose every few weeks. It never fitted him . . . it was not so much worn as poised on his head.

The hat evidently made little impression on the editor, for he rejected fourteen articles before accepting the fifteenth, called *Better Dead*. It began: 'No one who has thought the matter over a little can escape the conclusion that there are a number of our fellow-creatures for whom something should be Done.' The author went on to suggest with impudent irreverence that there were people in public life who would be better dead, and just stopped short of naming them all. The idea was well worked out, and the article took Greenwood's fancy.

By this time Barrie had moved to a cheaper lodging in Grenville Street, a small street near by. His room was 'not much larger than a piano case', looking out on to a blank wall, with a dank tree in between. He got into the habit of dining 'quite agreeably on four provocative halfpenny buns', which, with jam and other delicacies sent from home, made up his diet. On gala days there might be hot baked potatoes bought from an oven on a barrow in the street.

He felt very much alone. Sometimes he would stand at the window counting the leaves on the tree. He wished that he could sell some more articles—his ambition was to earn a pound a day. And he wished, too, that he knew some other Anons.

Chapter 6

LONG HARD CLIMB

ONE need not take Barrie's recollections of buns and baked potatoes in his early days too literally; they were written forty-five years later as comments on the articles he gathered together in one volume and printed privately for his friends under the title *The Greenwood Hat*. In spite of the fourteen rejected articles, the young Barrie had enough money to support him for a time; twelve pounds went a long way in those days, and he was not extravagant in his habits.

He began to work with quite astonishing industry, taking his articles round to the *St James's Gazette* offices in Angel Court, off the Strand. Greenwood read them, as a rule, within a few days of receiving them, and accepted a fair number. The Scottish author had a pleasing, quirky sense of humour, and he had, moreover, the facility of writing on a wide range of subjects and making them sound authoritative.

Barrie took care that he did sound authoritative: he possessed to a high degree the instinct for getting in as much detail as possible and making it authentic. He found reference libraries useful for this, but there was also Denny's. This was the bookshop on the corner of Holywell Street, slightly west of the present Law Courts, a shabby, narrow alley 'smelling chiefly of old books'. Like all shops of the kind, it had second-hand books displayed outside, and Barrie made many a guinea by using these shelves for reference. He would tackle any subject, even a political one. He later declared that he would say to a friend: 'Tell me what is going on in politics and I'll stop you as soon as I think I've got my article.' One of the few books he had brought down from Scotland was Roget's *Thesaurus*, next to the silver watch his most treasured possession.

Very soon he could look forward to regular cheques coming in at the end of the month, amounting to twenty pounds and often much more. There was plenty of optimism in the letters which he sent to Kirriemuir and to Alec. He was keeping well, he told them, except for occasional headaches, which he knew he must mention or Margaret Ogilvy would worry, wondering what he was hiding. He would be up to see them as soon as his work slackened a little.

His work never slackened. As soon as he finished one article he was ready to begin another: his notebooks were packed full of ideas, and he never wasted them. But he did go up to Kirriemuir from time to time, and to Dumfries to see his brother and Alec's family. Alec showed much pleasure in his growing success. Barrie also went to Bristol to visit his sister Isabella, who enjoyed being the wife of popular Dr Murray. Barrie admired their house but did not care about being shown off to their friends as a coming author; his shyness could still return with paralysing swiftness when he met strangers with whom he had little in common. It was easy enough *inventing* strangers. They were inside his head, and Barrie had got so in the way of losing himself in the rich tangles of his imagination that sometimes the life he led in there was more real to him than reality itself.

He was always glad to get back to his writing desk. A daemon possessed him, a lust for writing. He found that he instinctively became the centre of his own story or article: he lived the part. If he was writing about an explorer he became that explorer, if about a sandwich-man he became that individual, if about a grandsire his vivid fancy turned him into the old man. But when he wrote about a woman—he had the one and only model for this character firmly woven into his heart and fibre, whatever her age was supposed to be.

*   *   *

Barrie had kept up with T. L. Gilmour, whom he had met in Hibbert's room at the *Nottingham Journal* office. Gilmour was now in London, secretary to Lord Rosebery, though his duties did not prevent his doing a good deal of journalism, and he was very glad to see James Barrie again. They met frequently, dining in small restaurants and talking about their craft. As Barrie was doing well, he could afford better lodgings and he moved to rooms next to Gilmour's in Southampton Street; later going on, also with Gilmour, to chambers in Furnival's Inn (now demolished).

With so many cheques coming in, Barrie had a problem. He did not know how a bank account functioned; his father had never possessed one, and Alec had never discussed his own. Gilmour had a bank account, and Barrie suggested a scheme. He could get uncrossed cheques cashed across the counter: it was the crossed ones which were the difficulty. He would give his friend his crossed cheques, Gilmour would pay them into his bank and give Barrie what he needed in cash. Up till now, Barrie had kept the crossed cheques in his pocket, where they remained. Gilmour—fortunately an honest man—agreed to the eccentric scheme and became Barrie's banker.

In the summer of 1885, Maggie Barrie came down on a visit to London, Sara having again gone to the manse at Motherwell to look after their uncle. Maggie was a colourless girl without any particular attractions, but she shared a common trait with Jamie, a streak of hero-worship that she now turned full blast on her brother. She confided to him that she had never cared for teaching, but would have liked to do 'some writing' herself—only, of course, she had neither the time nor the talent. But she thought *he* was wonderful, and she was so wholehearted about it that Jamie began to believe that there might be something in it. At any rate, being told so with such evident sincerity was a pleasant sensation, and the London visit was a great success.

They travelled to Bristol to see the Murrays, who took them to the theatre one evening. It was a poor play, but Barrie fell in love with one of the pretty actresses in the cast; he had already seen her in another play, and he felt that this was quite a coincidence, to be seeing her again. He had an eye for a pretty woman, and actresses could be worshipped from afar—without the danger of his becoming obliterated by a non-noticing look.

When the time came for Maggie to return to Scotland, Jamie saw her off with much regret. There was no doubt about it, she was a fine little sister, Maggie. Having someone believe in one's genius was very warming to the soul.

*   *   *

It was about this time that Barrie began smoking. The author of *My Lady Nicotine* was to say, in his whimsical way, that he had never smoked anything when that book was written, but by 1885 he was rarely seen without his pipe or a cigar. He could afford cigars: he could afford a great many luxuries. Besides regular contributions to the *St James's Gazette*, his articles were appearing in the *Spectator*, *Chambers's Journal* and many other newspapers and magazines. The number of cheques which came in at the end of the month was growing, and Gilmour had sometimes to do some complicated arithmetic to keep Barrie's finances separate from his own. Any suggestion to the author that he should have a bank account of his own was met with: 'We're getting along all right as we are, aren't we?' The management of money threatened to take up time and thought which he could more usefully employ.

The wistful desire to get to know more Anons was a thing of the past. He was making many friends. Alexander Riach, a journalist on the *Daily Telegraph*, was one, and when Riach was appointed editor of the Edinburgh *Evening Dispatch*, he gave Barrie two regular columns to fill as he wished. Barrie did not hesitate to accept; he was writing a fantastic amount, and he could write more. And always in his mind was the mother with the soft face—how pleased she would be. A newspaper in Edinburgh was somehow more real to her than the London journals he sent home. 'I'll make you proud of me, Margaret Ogilvy!' was ever somewhere in his mind. He worked on, smoking, walking up and down the room, sitting at the table again to cover page after page with his small, not very legible script.

The headaches from which he had suffered since his student days had become chronic. Often he could not write at all with that cap of pain clamped on his skull, and then he would sink into fits of fathomless depression. But the next day he would be up, up in the air, fresh and receptive. His moods would swing from one extreme to another at other times, too, but the only person who noticed was Gilmour, and he was sympathetic and understanding. Gilmour shared Maggie's opinion that James Barrie was a bit of a genius.

The sheer industry, as well as the talent, of the young Scotsman appealed to Frederick Greenwood, who cordially invited him to come into the *St James's* office whenever he felt like it. Greenwood was a busy man, but he was never too busy to take time talking and listening to this short, slightly built man with the large head and outsize personality. Barrie had a charm, a magnetism, which was quite irresistible when he chose to exercise it. He never went to see the editor unless he felt in good spirits, and then he knew the visit would be a success; Greenwood stopped what he was doing, swung his chair round, pulled out another, and they would pass an exceedingly agreeable half-hour.

Greenwood sometimes took him along to the Garrick Club, where Barrie was introduced to 'names' and smiled at benignly as one of Greenwood's discoveries. It was stimulating to be considered a rising young man. Greenwood was also responsible for his meeting one of his literary heroes. George Meredith had liked one of Barrie's articles in the *St James's Gazette*, and had asked Greenwood about the author; Barrie's articles still appeared unsigned. Greenwood sent Barrie down to Box Hill, near Dorking in Surrey, where Meredith lived in a small house, Flint Cottage. Now nearing sixty, Meredith was still handsome, with curly hair and a short beard. He had a strong personality, with a great flow of talk which could be intimidating. Meredith was a difficult man and made enemies, but he had an attractive side to his combative nature, and he showed it that day to the small, shy author who had come on a pilgrimage. Barrie's shyness soon disappeared. His admiration, and the praise which sounded all the more genuine in that deep, rumbling Scottish voice, brought out the best in Meredith. The magic had worked again. When Barrie at last rose to go, both men knew this was the beginning of a friendship they would both value.

There were few idle hours in James Barrie's life, now that he had got well started in journalism. His chief recreation was the theatre, not only for pleasure but for professional reasons; he was sending dramatic notices to Sandy Riach in Edinburgh for the *Dispatch*, and writing occasional pieces on theatre matters for Greenwood and other editors. Henry Irving and Ellen Terry at the Lyceum in a gorgeous performance of *Faust*, the Bancrofts at the Haymarket, Wilson Barrett and John Hare drawing the crowds. No cheap seats these days: Barrie got Press tickets, stalls, and Gilmour often went with him. They would sit for hours later in Gilmour's rooms, talking over the play, arguing, agreeing and disagreeing in good companionship.

It was easy enough to be friends with men who had the same interests. Easy, if unsatisfying, to worship theatrical goddesses from the stalls. What Barrie longed for was a more personal relationship with women. He cringed at remembered experiences when the creatures looked through and around him but never at him:

I was in the Scotch express on my way to London and I think it was at Carlisle that five of them boarded my compartment, all husband high. When their packages had been disposed of and they were comfortably settled in their seats they turned their eyes on me and gave their verdict in the deaf-and-dumb alphabet, which unfortunately I understood. It spelt out the words 'Quite harmless', and they then disregarded me for the rest

Margaret Ogilvy.

James Barrie, aged
about six.

James Matthew Barrie, M.A. (Edin.), 1882.

A Window in Thrums, Kirriemuir. The window referred to is the small one in the gable on the right.

of the journey. They talked openly of the most intimate things as if I were far away in the guard's van. It is a treatment I am used to, but never perhaps have I been so blotted out, I who know that with another face I could be quite harmful . . .

Let us . . . concentrate with kindly interest on the mean male figure in the corner . . . it was his habit to get into corners . . . it was all owing to a profound dejection about his want of allure. They were right, those ladies in the train; 'quite harmless' summed him up, however he may have writhed. I am not speaking about how he appealed to men, but about how he did not appeal to women. Observe him in that compartment. Though insignificant he is not ugly. To be ugly, if you are sufficiently ugly, is said to attract the wayward creatures. The rubber that blotted Anon out is called (and it deserves a big word) Individuality.

*   *   *

There was one place in London where Barrie had no fear of being snubbed or overlooked by women—at Lord's. His love of cricket was unabated, and during the season he spent many sunlit afternoons 'sitting on the sward' either alone or with Gilmour, or with a recent friend, Henry Marriott Watson, a genial giant of a young man who had come from the Antipodes to conquer the London literary world, and was, like Barrie, a cricket enthusiast. They would sit on the grass, smoking, applauding, criticizing, appraising, enjoying every moment of the glorious game and each other's company.

In 1886, Barrie was ready to try another rung of the ladder. Articles were all very fine, and financially he was in excellent fettle; but ambition was goading him again. He wanted to write a novel. About what, he did not yet know. The idea persisted. All he needed was a subject, or the hint of a subject, and he would be well away in no time. He cast his mind back to some of the articles he had written, and presently remembered the one which Greenwood had taken after a batch of rejections, when he first came to London.

Better Dead, he had called it. It had a good theme, about a Society For Doing Without Some People, a public-spirited club which carried out benevolent murders with the intention of removing public characters who were nuisances.

It might make a book, thought the author. He did not see why he should not squeeze every drop of juice out of a good theme and make it into something longer. Besides, he could think of many more characters whom he would have great pleasure in removing—in a book.

He began by calmly taking Sandy Riach's surname for his hero, Andrew Riach, and for Andrew's profession Gilmour's position as secretary to Lord Rosebery; Andrew was described as secretary to 'a member of the Cabinet'. The story opens with Andrew visiting Clarrie, a Young Lady, in the manse at Wheens—otherwise Kirriemuir—before his departure for London. Her father, the minister, desires a word with the young man, obviously to ask him his intentions. Clarrie tactfully rises to go. 'The love-light was in her eyes, but Andrew did not open the door for her, for he was a Scotch graduate. Besides, she might one day be his wife.'

Greenwood (without reading the book, one would imagine) gave Barrie introductions to publishers, but none of them would take a gamble on it. Eventually it was published, unsigned, by Swan, Sonnenschein, Lowrie & Co. of Paternoster Row, at the author's expense, and sold at 1/-. Barrie lost £25 over the transaction.

Back to articles, one after the other, on every likely and unlikely subject. Barrie was now sending regular sums to Kirriemuir. Margaret Ogilvy must not lack for anything.

There came unexpected and unwelcome news in the summer of 1888, reminding J. M. Barrie that he was a free-lance, and free-lances who did regular work for a paper depended to some extent on a personal relationship with the editor. Frederick Greenwood told him that he was leaving the *St James's Gazette*; the paper had changed hands, and Greenwood found that he could not get on with the new proprietor. Barrie wondered how this news would affect *him*, and decided that it would be wise to keep his ear to the ground for possible new markets. He derived a good part of his income from the *St James's*, and he could not afford to take risks.

It was at this point in his fortunes that he met William Ernest Henley, the man who was to achieve immortality with at least one poem. Henley was one of the most magnificently courageous of the Victorians. When he wrote such lines as 'My head is bloody but unbowed' and 'I am the captain of my soul', he meant it. He stood up to misfortune where a lesser man might have sunk down in despair. Almost forty when he got to know Barrie, he was tall, solidly built, full of boisterous good nature, and a cripple—he had had a foot amputated, and further tuberculosis always threatened him.

In a milieu where writers and journalists turned out a staggering amount of work, Henley topped them all: he wrote poetry, plays and essays, he was an art critic of standing, he had edited two papers and had now started a sixpenny weekly, the *Scots Observer*, in Edinburgh, with the backing of Constable's, the publishers. Knowing that Henley was a friend of George Meredith, Barrie sent him an article in which he drew the attention of the public to some of Meredith's neglected works, including a fine essay on Comedy and three short stories 'which had all been lying forgotten for ten years between the covers of a dead magazine.'

Henley printed the article in the first number of his new paper, and a friendship began between him and his contributor. Henley's assistant editor was Charles Whibley, a young man of twenty-eight, the same age as Barrie. An individualist with uncompromising opinions and many prejudices, Whibley was nevertheless one of the most companionable of men, and was destined to become one of Barrie's greatest friends.

These were great days for James Barrie, no longer Anon but with his own name or a pseudonym on everything he wrote. 'Henley's young men' were making a reputation for themselves, and Barrie held his own in that fellowship. His shyness dissolved in the civilized talk and witty discussion, especially as his own brand of humour was evidently appreciated.

Several of Barrie's friends were getting married, and he indicated to them that he would have liked to get married himself, but there was no Young Lady on the horizon. He had fallen in love, and out of it again, countless times, always with very pretty women. Beyond that he had never been able to go. They stimulated his romantic imagination, but not his passions. If there was ever a more powerful, primitive urge, something got between him and the desirable woman. An old, soft, watchful face. . . .

It was entirely different when he was writing articles about beautiful Young Ladies. In those he wrote about matrimony and honeymoons with all the assurance of a man of vast experience, a man of the world.

On his next visit home, Barrie stayed in Edinburgh for a few days and saw Sandy Riach, who told him he was trying to inject a modern note into the *Dispatch*. It was time the younger generation made its opinion known on important subjects like religion: the traditionalists had had it their way for too long. Barrie agreed, and gleefully wrote several articles for the *Dispatch* attacking the Free

Assembly. 'Frightfully profane,' he said in a letter to Gilmour. 'Great pains taken in family to conceal authorship.'

The Barries were indeed disconcerted by Jamie's writing sardonic articles about the Kirk, for even though these were unsigned, rumours as to their authorship were sure to get about. An editor called William Robertson Nicoll, who was at the same time an ordained minister, found them pointed and amusing.

He was on the look-out for this kind of writing, which was light in the hand without being superficial, and he had no difficulty in finding out, through Riach, the identity of the irreverent author of the articles, and approaching him.

Nicoll was a remarkable character, short in stature, a dynamo of energy. Still under forty, he might stand for the archetype of the familiar Scots poverty-to-riches-through-hard-work lad o' pairts. He came from Aberdeen, the son of a minister who had regularly spent part of his small stipend on books. Young Nicoll, a tremendous reader, beginning with the advantage of an enormous library at home, was soon through the village school, grammar school at Aberdeen, and the university there, graduating at the age of nineteen. He simultaneously studied for the ministry and wrote regularly for the *Aberdeen Journal*, and after he had accumulated the responsibilities of a church, marriage and children, he still went on writing, mostly articles on religious and theological matters.

He was also the editor of a religious weekly, the *Expositor*, published by the firm of Hodder and Stoughton. After a serious illness, Nicoll was advised by his doctor to live in a less rigorous climate, and he came south, settling near London. He had to give up the ministry, but was soon extending the scope of his literary work, not a difficult achievement, for he was in high standing with Hodder and Stoughton. Mr Stoughton, in particular, was a shrewd Christian and businessman combined, and he saw the potentialities of this dynamic clergyman. The firm was starting another paper, the *British Weekly*, and Robertson Nicoll was appointed editor.

The *British Weekly* was a success from the beginning. Nicoll knew what his particular public wanted—sound religious principles, handled without pomposity and leavened with humour, where admissible—and he gave it to them. The author of the articles in the Edinburgh *Dispatch* clearly had a fresh eye on the contemporary Christian scene. Nicoll wrote to James M. Barrie and invited him to contribute to the *British Weekly*.

Barrie never turned work down, and a new market was welcome. He decided to have a pseudonym for the *British Weekly*, and chose 'Gavin Ogilvy'. His first article was an appreciation of his and his brother's friend, Dr Alexander Whyte. His second was on an entirely different subject—a description of life on a houseboat. Robertson Nicoll, who had expected a succession of articles on the Scottish church, was disappointed, but he was anxious to keep this new contributor—who was quite as obstinate as himself—and the article went in.

Barrie and Gilmour had taken a houseboat for the season, moored off Tagg's Island at Molesey, on the Thames. They could both afford this extravagance, for Gilmour was making a steady income from journalism to add to his salary as private secretary to Rosebery, and Barrie was now passing rich on just under a thousand pounds a year. He liked spending the long summer days in the houseboat, writing; there was an agreeable rural scene all round, and he could set off for walks whenever he felt like it. At week-ends the river became gay and lively, when house-parties came down. They themselves often had guests, his and Gilmour's friends with their wives or sisters.

Denis Mackail, in *The Story of J.M.B.*, describes a typical scene on the river in those tranquil days:

Peaceful and delicious glimpses into the eighties. Boats, punts, flannels and straw hats, bustles and parasols, a little waterside inn, paper lanterns again in the evenings, laughter and leisure; such a safe, happy summertime world. Friends coming and going for odd nights, or staying and playing games on a Sunday.

Maggie Barrie came down to London again, and enjoyed being taken to the houseboat; she seems to have been as little concerned over games on a Sunday as was her brother. As for the wives—and especially the sisters—in the week-end parties, Barrie had apparently become reconciled to taking a corner seat when women were present. He was in excellent spirits. He had begun on a new novel, and Robertson Nicoll had agreed to serialize it in the *British Weekly*, even though Barrie had only written a few chapters, and did not know how it was going to develop.

*   *   *

In September, 1887, Gilmour had become engaged to Elizabeth

Keltie, daughter of the librarian of the Royal Geographical Society. He met her through Joseph Thomson, Barrie's explorer friend from the Edinburgh days, and Barrie could now admire as many explorers as he wished, for he, too, knew the Kelties. His early passion to be associated in some way with men of action and adventure had never diminished, and Thomson was as much a hero to him now as he had been when he had taken unknown paths through the Central African bush.

It was in this year that Barrie founded his private cricket team, which came to be known as the Allahakbarries. The team came into being in typical Barriesque fashion. He had been walking in the Surrey countryside with Gilmour and Marriott Watson, and had stopped to watch a village cricket match at Shere, a beautiful little hamlet near Guildford. The cricketers were elderly and leisurely, and Barrie conceived the idea of getting up an eleven of his own and bringing them down to Shere to challenge the locals to a match. Barrie tells the story—or his version of it—in *The Greenwood Hat*:

Anon was appointed captain (by chicanery it is said by the survivors) and he thought there would be no difficulty in getting a stout XI together, literary men being such authorities on the willow. On the eventful day, however, he found out in the railway compartment by which they advanced upon Shere that he had to coach more than one of his players in the finesse of the game: which was the side of the bat you hit with, for instance. In so far as was feasible they also practised in the train. Two of the team were African travellers of renown, Paul du Chaillu of gorilla fame and the much loved Joseph Thomson of Masailand. When a name for the team was being discussed, Anon, now grown despondent, asked these two what was the African for 'Heaven help us,' and they gave him 'Allahakbar'. So they decided to call themselves the 'Allahakbars', afterwards changed with complimentary intention to the Allahakbarries.

Gilmour and Marriott Watson were in the first team, which changed its members in succeeding years but which probably did not have the tearing high spirits of the first match—in which the home team, elderly as they were, soundly beat the Allahakbarries.

Barrie's association with Robertson Nicoll, and therefore with Hodder and Stoughton, was leading to more than a regular supply of articles. It was suggested to him that he might choose a selection from past articles which had some kind of connection, and make them into a book. This was regularly done with essays and articles, and there was always a sale for them.

It was a good idea to put to an author who had not been successful with his first book. The difficulty was one of choice, a difficulty that was quickly resolved when Barrie thought of 'those Scotch things' which had proved so popular in the *St James's Gazette* and other papers. The tales of the Auld Licht Community would do very well, strung together by the dominie-narrator in the form of recollections. It would not take him long to find the Auld Licht articles in the various files and copy them out.

Auld Licht Idylls—he had gone back to the original title—was published by Hodder and Stoughton in April, 1888. There was a public for the author's 'pawky'—the word was now coming up in reviews—sense of humour, the people he wrote about were quaint and unusual, and the language foreign enough to be funny yet not too difficult to understand. Still, the *Idylls* did not create a sensation in London. There was plenty of competition: Anthony Trollope, Charles Reade and Walter Besant of the older generation were still writing best-sellers, which naturally got long reviews; and new novelists like Rhoda Broughton and Barrie's friend, Marriott Watson, were attracting attention.

Barrie worked on his novel, which was based on his experiences on the *Nottingham Journal* and which he was calling *When a Man's Single*. He went on writing articles, which he sold without trouble, and also began a series of studies which he intended to call *An Edinburgh Eleven: Pen Portraits from College Life*. These were to be about some of his professors at Edinburgh, with articles on Joseph Thomson, R. L. Stevenson, Dr Walter Smith and Lord Rosebery making up the eleven.

With it all, Barrie had time for social life, which he much enjoyed. He went to the theatre, visited the Kelties at their home in north London with Gilmour, playing parlour games there and at the homes of other hospitable friends. He accepted praise and admiration with becoming modesty when the *Idylls* were commented upon, and, back in his rooms, ceaselessly made notes for the novel he intended to write next.

Hodder and Stoughton published *When a Man's Single* in 1888, and *An Edinburgh Eleven* a year later. Neither book made more than a ripple on the waters at their first appearance, but the author was not unduly cast down: he had complete faith in his own star.

Gilmour and Miss Keltie were married in 1889, and Barrie now lived alone in comfortable lodgings in Old Quebec Street, near the Marble Arch. He had written yet another book on the lines of the *Idylls*, calling it *A Window in Thrums*, and this was quickly published by Hodder and Stoughton, as well as *My Lady Nicotine*, which came out in 1890. Barrie had gone to Scotland to work on his 'big' novel; he rented a house in Glen Clova, and took his parents and sisters there for a month, together with the Alec Barries, so that Margaret Ogilvy, now over seventy, could have sons and daughters and grandchildren round her. As for himself, it was holiday enough to go fishing and take long walks; most of the time he was writing.

It is probable that Barrie did not trouble to read all the reviews of his books, or that his publishers did not send on any adverse notices. Plenty of the other kind came along: effusive, full of superlatives. There were, however, growing numbers of people who were revolted by the Auld Licht books. Anger had been building up in Scotland ever since the appearance of the *Idylls*, and there were sour notes in some of the reviews of *A Window in Thrums* when it appeared. In Kirriemuir, friends and acquaintances of the Barries had not been slow to show their disapproval of Jamie Barrie's putting his own folk into a book and making game of them. It was quite clear to them that Jess in *A Window in Thrums*, though based physically on Bell Lunan, the Barries' crippled next-door neighbour, was Margaret Ogilvy; while Leeby, the daughter in the book, was obviously Jane Ann, and a caricature at that. As for the inhabitants of 'Thrums', the sly digs at their manners and clothes and inquisitiveness and all the rest—it was indecent! What Margaret Ogilvy and Jane Ann themselves thought is not known, but *A Window in Thrums* was not displayed on the bookshelves in the living-room at Strathview, along with Jamie's other works.

Outside Kirriemuir, the acid criticism of the books had no personal note in it, but was the expression of rage at what was considered to be a slur on the national Scots character in general. It came from reviewers, from schoolmen and other professional men, and it was to lead to a widespread dislike—among at least a literate and realistic minority—of the Kailyard School, of which Barrie was accused of being the founder. The indignation against the kailyarders, 'selling to the world a saccharine conception of the Scot all the more damaging because of the half-truths in it', is well summed up by two critics of a later date, who describe exactly many of

Barrie's contemporaries' fierce reactions against his Auld Licht offerings.

The phrase 'the Kailyard School' was, according to J. H. Millar,[1] invented by W. E. Henley, and was derived from a sentimental grass-roots American novel, *Mrs Wiggs of the Cabbage Patch*, which had enjoyed enormous popularity in the United States. The Scottish term was more pejorative, for kail—curly kale—ranks even lower in the vegetable kingdom than the humble cabbage. Millar wrote: 'It is a fact that J. M. Barrie is fairly entitled to look upon himself as *pars magna* if not *pars maxima* of the Kailyard movement.'

An even more trenchant anti-kailyarder, George Blake,[2] was infuriated at what he considered to be the essential falseness of Barrie's picture of 'Thrums'.

He really wrote in the first place of Kirriemuir as it was in 1840 or there-abouts. The use of the first person deluded the innocent Sassenach into believing that all this was a report on current conditions . . . The Scottish reader has the unhappy feeling of being betrayed to make a Roman holiday. Scots people are legitimate figures of fun in certain aspects of their behaviour, relative to that of other races, but fun is only fair when it is sympathetic. One thinks to perceive in Barrie's Kailyard writings either a positive dislike of his own people or a blatant desire to gratify the prejudices of other peoples. He very readily sold the pass . . . This element in the work is pervasive, fundamental.

Blake was bitter about Barrie's exposition of character—or lack of it. He found it exceedingly superficial:

The novelist's fundamental concern is with the human soul . . . The Auld Licht folk are seen from without, usually as persons of glum countenance and bleak minds; very rarely is an attempt made to interpret them from within . . . When the tale is sad, on the other hand, the pathos is apt to be laid on with a trowel, and very little is sacred to this showman . . .
It is perhaps the most puzzling thing about Barrie from first to last that the expert toucher of emotions, the weaver of charmingly whimsical webs . . . had in all his dealings as a writer with such topics as death and sepulture and grief and suffering the way of a sadist.

This critic did not deny that Barrie wrote exceedingly well, and appreciated his powers in narrative as 'beautifully attractive in a clean, telling prose. The purely visual descriptions of scenes are

1. University lecturer, author of *A Literary History of Scotland*.
2. Author of *Barrie and the Kailyard School*.

admirable.' It was when Barrie described people that the change came:

The Barrie trick of holding out his characters at arm's length, as it were, and making them perform their antics to our sardonic, even sadistic delight, was an early symptom of his instinctive sense of theatre. He never seemed to have lived with and among real people; everybody else was a marionette, floodlit but capable of the most amusing antics. He saw himself in the same light.

Blake went on to lambast two other kailyarders who had taken advantage of the new genre. The Reverend John Watson, D.D., writing under the pseudonym of Ian Maclaren, produced a grass-roots novel called *Beside the Bonny Briar Bush*, set in another Thrums called 'Drumtochty'. It was a collection of blameless sketches with a complete absence of plot, 'thinner in both physical and literary substance than Barrie's *Auld Licht Idylls*, like it only in giving the modern reader a faintly unpleasant impression of a collection of rustic oddities being exposed to the laughter of foreigners.'

Samuel Crockett, Barrie's contemporary and a much inferior writer to both him and Maclaren, had his readers wiping an eye and shaking their heads nostalgically, and his publishers rubbing their hands, over a confection called *The Lilac Sunbonnet*, described by George Blake as being 'too gloriously bad to be true'. The heroine is called Winsome Charteris, and she has 'fair hair, crisping and tendrilling over her brow, swept back in loose and flossy circlets till caught close behind her head by a tiny ribbon of blue—then again, escaping it, scattering and waving over her shoulders, wonderingly, like nothing on earth but Winsome Charteris's hair.'

Ian Maclaren and Crockett were also discoveries of the astute Robertson Nicoll, who saw an ever-widening market for writing of this kind. J. M. Barrie could never sink to Crockett's level, but his critics were convinced that if he had not written about 'Thrums' in a deliberately calculated, dishonest fashion, Ian Maclaren and Samuel Crockett and their even more inferior imitators would not have attempted to copy the style.

*   *   *

Any adverse criticisms of his work, had he noticed them, would not have disturbed Barrie in that splendid year, 1891. He was becoming increasingly prosperous: everything he wrote, he sold. He had begun a play. His greatest work so far, his big novel, would be published in the autumn under the title *The Little Minister*, and he felt justified in joining the Authors' Club and the Incorporated Society of Authors, Playwrights and Composers.

The play had been in Barrie's mind for a long time, and there are numerous notes about it in his notebooks. He called it *The Houseboat*; it was set in a houseboat on the Thames, similar to the one he had once shared with Gilmour. It was not his first play; he had collaborated with Marriott Watson on a play about the eighteenth-century poet, Richard Savage, which had achieved a matinée performance at the Criterion Theatre in April of that year, but had not been taken up by a management. He had also written a skit for J. H. Toole called *Ibsen's Ghost*, which Toole 'improved' but could not make into a success.

Barrie had got to know Henry Irving at the Garrick Club, and Irving encouraged him to go on writing for the stage. This author did not need prodding. He had loved the theatre since his schooldays, and he found that he had a facility for comic dialogue and situation. *The Houseboat* quickly took shape, and he offered it to Toole, who was doubtful about its possibilities at first but decided to take another chance on a Barrie play, and bought all the rights for two hundred pounds.

There came family news from Kirriemuir. Maggie was getting married. She had been friendly with a young minister for several years, but nothing had ever seemed to come of it. Now, apparently, he had 'spoken'.B arrie was pleased. He had got quite fond of his younger sister on her visits to London; she had always been interested in his articles and books, often confessing her own repressed ambitions to do something 'in the same line', but very willing that the glory should be Jamie's. Now she would have something that was right and proper to be ambitious about— marriage.

Maggie's fiancé was the Reverend James Winter, whom, as it happened, Barrie had known in Kirriemuir; he also knew James's older brother, William, who had been a Senior Wrangler and coached young men for University entrance. It was a most satisfying connection. Margaret Ogilvy would be as pleased as he was. Apart from her natural hopes for her daughter's happiness, she would be proud that there would now be a manse in her own family. The Reverend James had not, in fact, yet got a kirk and a manse; at present he was assisting other ministers. As soon as he was assured of a parish, the date of the marriage would be fixed.

*   *   *

The Little Minister was published in October by Cassell's, Barrie having left Hodder and Stoughton for some reason. It is an unlikely tale of a 'little' minister—Gavin Dishart's lack of height is stressed—who falls in love with a gipsy, is hounded by the good people of the town, and triumphs in the end by a noble gesture of self-sacrifice. Originally published, like the others, by Nicoll in serial form, it came out first as a three-decker novel. Some of the reviewers called it a book of genius and went on to say that Mr Barrie had wit, gaiety, charm, 'humour the quaintest and oddest', and a singular command of certain sorts of character—but they had difficulty in reviewing the actual book itself.

Robertson Nicoll wrote to a correspondent: 'I agree with you that The Little Minister is wildly improbable, but is it not a rich book, with many pretty little things in it?'

The novel sold in large numbers, *A Window in Thrums* benefited by the publicity and went on selling, and *Auld Licht Idylls* was remembered afresh. Mr James Barrie was being taken notice of by a large number of people now: his chimneypiece was often lined with invitation cards. He was also being noticed by women. No more sitting in corners. For he was now the amusing Mr Barrie, the charming Mr Barrie, Mr Barrie with that delicious sense of humour.

He enjoyed it all. Why not? The lower rungs of the ladder had been difficult to climb, but the upper rungs were getting easy, and would be easier still with each new success. The only real worry he had was news of his mother; she had not been too well—she was a little better—not so well again—better, a thought better. The faithful Jane Ann wrote regularly, and Jamie wrote as regularly in return.

News came that the Reverend James Winter had been appointed to the kirk in the village of Bower, in Caithness, so Maggie could now look forward to her wedding. James had moved into the manse at Bower, and the marriage would take place in the summer. The young minister intended to get the manse furbished up for his bride, but he had not a great deal of spare time, as he was finding it difficult to visit all his flock in a widely scattered parish. Barrie had a splendid idea. He sent money for a horse for Maggie's fiancé, who could then ride round his parish. It gave Barrie great pleasure to present the couple with this handsome gift: he was with Maggie in imagination as she opened the letter, heard her cry of surprise and delight, stood looking over her shoulder as she wrote off post-haste to her James, stood in James's sparsely furnished manse while the minister read the letter, also with a cry of surprise and delight. Barrie savoured every moment.

Meanwhile, there was *The Houseboat*, for which casting had already taken place. Barrie had been to the auditions, and though he approved of Irene Vanbrugh, an established favourite, for one of the two leading ladies, he was not so sure about Toole's choice for the second.

The play is about an impostor, a barber, who poses as a man of substance. On the point of being exposed, he decides to make a quick exit. He is asked to give his telegraphic address, and as he disappears calls out: 'Walker, London!' The vogue word at the time applied to someone who was trying to hoax one was 'Walker!' The play had to have a new title, as it was found there was already a piece called *The Houseboat*, so Barrie called it *Walker, London*.

Still doubtful about the casting of the second leading lady, Barrie asked Jerome K. Jerome, who had been a friend for some time, whether he could think of someone who was 'very pretty, a good actress, and who could flirt'. Jerome suggested a Miss Mary Ansell, who had been quite good in one of his own plays on tour, and had had some experience in London productions, too. She was in London, and Jerome would arrange a meeting.

Barrie accordingly met Miss Ansell, and found her ravishing. He had always been fond of pretty actresses, and this one was prettier than most. She should have the part. It was a promise. Miss Ansell was naturally very pleased, and smiled radiantly. Barrie had never before had such an adorable look directed full at him, and it is unlikely that he realized he was being given a sample of the second and third qualifications he had told Jerome were desirable for the rôle.

At the next audition, he told Toole that Miss Mary Ansell had been engaged for the second lead. Toole was astonished, and also annoyed. The part was as good as filled already!

'Miss Ansell plays it,' said Barrie.

Chapter 7

MARY

MARY ANSELL is described by a contemporary who knew her as being slim, quick-witted, determined, ambitious. There were some people who thought her face rather hard, but she was so pretty, few people looked beyond her attractive appearance.

Now twenty-nine, she had been on the stage for several years, playing small parts, mostly in the provinces. Her father, who had been a licensed victualler in Bayswater, was dead. Mary didn't get on very well with her mother, who was more interested in her sons, and there is some evidence that the girl was lonely and neglected in her youth. She had never known a happy and secure family life, and as she had been given a scrappy education—the Ansells had not believed in spending good money on high schools for girls—she had come to rely on her undoubted good looks and artistic inclinations. She knew that if she was going to get anywhere in life, she would have to depend on herself.

At one time Mrs Ansell kept lodgings in a south coast resort, but Mary was not then living at home; she had decided to go on the stage, and had obtained a few walking-on parts in stock companies which visited the southern towns. There was a little money in the family, and Mrs Ansell raised no objection when her daughter asked if she could have some of it to back a touring company. This, Mary knew, was the only way for an actress to get into a professional company and play parts worth having. It was nearly impossible to break into the London theatre without knowing people who had influence. If she could be seen in a touring company, there was always a possibility that she might attract the attention of a London manager's scout.

She did not make a great deal of money with her company, but her looks and lively personality at last brought offers of parts in London; as she had hoped, she had been seen and mentioned to

London managers. Her rôles were small but individual: the Player Queen in Hermann Vezin's production of *Hamlet*, a part in *Harbour Lights*, another in the anglicized version of an American farce, *Saratoga*, which had been re-named *Brighton*. She was also a member of Norman Forbes's company at the Globe Theatre for a time, and played for Charles Hawtrey at a charity matinée.

A leading part in Mr Barrie's play meant a great deal to Mary Ansell. Miss Irene Vanbrugh was not pleased when she found out that the second lead was getting a bigger salary than the star herself, but that was not Miss Ansell's fault; Mr Barrie had said it must be so, and Miss Vanbrugh and the rest of the cast and Mr Toole himself were finding out that the little playwright, standing in the background watching, smoking his pipe, and occasionally making suggestions, intended to have his own way when he felt like it.

He was often at the theatre, both at rehearsals and during the run. He escorted Miss Ansell to her lodgings. They dined out, had supper at fashionable restaurants. Barrie liked being seen with a pretty woman—and he also liked the sensation of holding Miss Ansell's sole attention. He knew quite a few Young Ladies, but he was well aware that they wanted to be seen with Mr Barrie. This charming girl obviously liked him for himself.

Mary, in fact, did like him. He was such a good listener when she talked of the theatre, and that was the subject which interested her most. She confided her hopes to him, told him how she intended to become a really good actress and make a name for herself. Barrie was sympathetic and admiring. He liked her pluck and independence, he told her, and as they smiled at each other over a supper table, with theatrical London round them, heads turned and whispers began to rustle. A budding romance?

Perhaps the whispers reached Barrie. He still escorted her, still took her to supper after the theatre, but there were times when he would become quite silent, and would not even answer questions. It was disconcerting. But then his mood would suddenly change, and he made up for everything by such outrageous flattery that she had to tell him to stop, for people near by were listening. He was certainly an unusual man, decided Mary.

Miss Ansell, attractive as Barrie found her, was still but a small star in the widening firmament of his pleasant existence. He had become friendly with many leading figures of the day, including

Conan Doyle, and Quiller Couch, whom he found very congenial. He visited 'Q' at Fowey, in Cornwall, and at the London house where Quiller Couch and his wife stayed on Campden Hill, not far from Kensington Gardens. He was also taken by friends to Broadway, the beautiful village in Worcestershire, where he met *their* friends who quickly became *his* friends; including the legendary actress Mary Anderson, married to Antonio de Navarro and practically queen of the place. The village had attracted a colony of artists, and Madame de Navarro's drawing-room was always full of interesting guests. Barrie was discovering a stratum of cultured, well-bred, sophisticated people which was as different from his own background as could be imagined.

* * *

Maggie and the Reverend James Winter were to be married at the end of May, and Barrie went up to Kirriemuir early in the month. For once he put work aside, and spent a great deal of time with his mother, telling her about his London life, happy in her rejoicing over Maggie's forthcoming translation to the status of a minister's wife. Maggie herself was transformed, and hurried exuberantly about, assisting Jane Ann with preparations for the wedding. Jane Ann, as usual, was quietly efficient, taking, again as usual, her wonted place in the background of the family.

On May 9th, Barrie's thirty-second birthday, came a tragedy which shattered the joy in that household. A telegram arrived from Bower to say the bridegroom had been thrown from his horse and killed.

The horse had been Barrie's gift to James Winter. That was the first thought which came to Barrie, and it plucked relentlessly at his nerves in the terrible days that followed. If he hadn't given James the horse . . .

Maggie was completely prostrated. She did what her mother had done many years ago when grief had descended with the suddenness of doom: she lay on her bed, unable to speak to anyone, refusing food. Barrie slipped into her room and sat by the bed, overcome with misery, remorse, guilt. He had given James the horse—he had given James the horse.

There was only one way in which he could make amends for wrecking Maggie's happiness. He would look after her for the remainder of her life. He told her so, again and again, but she would not answer. He took her hand and repeated his vow. He would

. M. Barrie. Painting by an unknown artist dating from the period when
Barrie signed himself 'Anon'.

Mary Ansell and
J. M. Barrie about
the time of their
marriage.

never leave her. He would look after her. She would have him to lean on.

Guests who had been bidden to a wedding travelled, sombrely clad, to Caithness for a funeral a few days later. Maggie did not go; she lay in the dark, shuttered room, worn out with weeping. Jamie stayed with her. He had written a letter for the minister to read out to the congregation at the funeral service:

To the Session and Congregation of the Free Church of Bower:
To you, at the grave of him who was in three weeks' time to become her husband, my sister sends her love. She has not physical strength to be with you just now in body, but she is with you in spirit, and God is near her, and she is not afraid. You are her loved ones, for it was you who, under God, called him to Bower, and gave him the manse to which he was about to bring her, and, as he loved you, she loves you. God, who gave his Son for the redemption of the world, has told her that He had need of the disciple's life also, and that he died to bring his people of Bower to God's knees. So God chose his own way, and took her Jim, her dear young minister, and she says, God's will be done; and she thanks him for taking away so suddenly only one who was ready to face his Maker without a moment's warning. His great goodness, she says to you, in not taking someone who was unprepared, is her comfort and should be yours. And she prays that Mr Winter's six months' ministry among you, and his death among you while doing his duty, has borne and will continue to bear good fruit. And always she will so pray, and she asks you to pray for her. And she says that you are not to grieve for her over-much, for she is in God's keeping.

This is a word from her brother, who cannot leave her to come to the funeral of his dearest friend, the purest soul I have ever known. It is a word about her. You have never seen her but you knew him, and they have always been so alike in the depths of their religious feelings, in their humility, and in many other things you knew about him, and loved him for, that you may always think of them as one. There were four years and a half of their love-story, and it began the hour they first met. It never had a moment's break; there was always something pathetic about it, for they never parted, and they never wrote but solemnly and tenderly, as if it might be for the last time. The wistfulness of his face, which you must all have noticed, meant early death. They both felt that the one would soon be taken from the other, though he thought that he would be the survivor. Theirs was so pure a love that God was ever part of it. Let all the youth of Bower remember that there is no other love between man and woman save that.

J. M. BARRIE.

Barrie sent copies of this extraordinary address to the *British Weekly* and to the *Pall Mall Gazette*, of which Marriott Watson was literary editor, and it was published in both papers on May 19th. He intended his friends and well-wishers to know how deeply he felt about his sister's tragedy.

He was not so resigned to the will of God as his letter to the congregation indicated. He was very, very angry with God. He thought a thing like this should never have happened, either to Maggie or to him. It was unfair! But outward appearances had to be kept up. The faithful of the Free Church truly believed that all misfortunes sent by the Lord were for one's ultimate benefit, and one must submit patiently. Barrie sincerely felt that he was helping the congregation to accept whatever misfortunes might come to *them*. When it came to himself—he could have written a moving article on the beauties of submission and patience, but he found the reality exceedingly harassing. For one thing, he had undertaken to look after Maggie, and he was already wondering how that was going to be fitted in to his full and varied existence.

Barrie stayed at Kirriemuir for six weeks, and there was no doubt that he was a comfort to the family. Margaret Ogilvy could hardly bear to let him out of her sight. He did not see so much of his father. David Barrie was well over seventy, and had been retired some years from the linen factory. His natural taciturnity had increased with age, and he spent most of his time reading. Though he was ready to put down his book and listen to Jamie's talk, the two did not have much in common, and Jamie too often found himself immersed in one of his own silences.

There was more room for them at Strathview. The downstairs tenants had long gone, and they had the whole place to themselves. Margaret Ogilvy's brother had bought the house and rented it to the Barries; the plan was that when he retired he would come and live with them. Sara, now thirty-seven, had been adopted by Dr Ogilvy; she had not shown any inclination to marry, and appeared to be quite happy as companion to her uncle and housekeeper at the Motherwell manse. Mary had been Mrs John Galloway for some years. Another daughter should have been starting a new life up in Caithness. . . .

The horse, the horse. If only he had not given James the horse. Barrie did not attempt to exorcise the insidious spectre of guilty remorse in his mind: every time he looked at Maggie he thought of the horse. But there were other things to think of, too. He must go south again soon. He would take Maggie with him—had he not promised?—and they would live together, and he would devote himself to her and help her to forget her sorrow.

If Miss Mary Ansell ever came into his mind, he thrust the recollection away. There is no mention of her in the notebooks or in his letters to Gilmour and other friends. He kept his thoughts firmly on Maggie. He had had a note of sympathy from Robertson Nicoll, and now there came another letter, suggesting that Barrie might like to borrow Anchor Cottage, a small house which Nicoll rented at Shere, in Surrey. Shere was a village Barrie liked, and he accepted for himself and Maggie. He parted mournfully from Margaret Ogilvy, and travelled down to Shere with Maggie in late June.

Maggie, with her brother's prompting, 'took care of herself'—in other words, he would not allow her to do anything for herself that he could do. Maggie was not averse to being waited on—something she had never experienced at Strathview—and she accepted his attentions without demur. They went for long walks, but these became dull for Maggie because her brother would not talk for long periods. Sometimes they would be out for an hour without a word coming from him. Maggie told herself that he must be thinking about his writing.

Barrie had never stopped thinking about his writing from the day they had come to Anchor Cottage. It was an ideal place in which to work, and presently he began to sit down after breakfast and put pencil to paper. It was really time he got started again. He had promised to write a play for Henry Irving. An offer had come from an American publisher, Charles Scribner, asking for the serial rights of his next novel. The next novel itself was floating through his head, though he had not written anything yet. He wanted to look after Maggie, and he intended to go on doing it, but he could not turn his mind off. Ideas came so insistently that he had to get them down on paper, or at least into his notebooks. The morning sessions at the writing-table grew longer, and Maggie had to occupy herself as well as she could while her author-brother worked in the sitting-room, completely immersed.

There came one day an unexpected letter which stopped Barrie's busy pencil. A letter from Robert Louis Stevenson! One of his early literary heroes. Stevenson wrote from Vailima, Samoa, his

letter being dated February, 1892, so it had taken many months to
come:

Dear Mr Barrie,
This is at least the third letter I have written you, but my correspondence
has a bad habit of not getting so far as the post, that which I possess of
manhood turns pale before the business of address and envelope, but I
hope to be more fortunate with this; for, besides the usual and often
recurrent desire to thank you for your work, you are one of four that have
come to the front since I was watching and had a corner of my own to
watch and there is no reason, unless it be in these mysterious tides that
ebb and flow, and make and mar and murder the work of poor scribblers,
why you should not do work of the best order. The tides have borne
away my sentence of which I was weary at any rate, and, between authors,
I may allow myself so much freedom as to leave it pending. We are both
Scots besides, and I suspect both rather Scotty Scots; my own Scotchness
tends to intermittency but is at times erisypelitous—if that be rightly spelt.
Lastly, I have gathered we had both made our stages in the metropolis of
the winds: our Vergil's 'grey metropolis' and I count that a lasting bond.
No place so brands a man.

  Finally, I feel it a sort of duty to you to report progress. This may be an
error, but I believed I detected your hand in an article—it may be an
illusion, it may be one of those industrious insects who catch up and
reproduce the handling of each emergent man—but I'll still hope it was
yours—and hope it may please you to hear that the continuation of
'Kidnapped' is under way. I have not yet got to Alan, so I do not know if
he is still alive, but David seems to have a kick or two in his shanks. I was
pleased to see how the Anglo-Saxon theory fell into the trap: I gave my
Lowlander a Gallic name and even commented on the fact in the text; yet
almost all critics recognized in Alan and David a Saxon and a Celt. I know
not about England; in Scotland at least, where Gallic was spoken in Fife
little over a century ago and in Galloway not much earlier, I deny that
there exists such a thing as a pure Saxon, and I think it more than
questionable if there be such a thing as a pure Celt.

  But what have you to do with this? and what have I? Let us continue to
inscribe our little bits of tales and let the heathen rage!
          Yours, with sincere interest in your career,
                    ROBERT LOUIS STEVENSON.

It is a mannered letter, with a certain amount of affectation, but
genuine liking and admiration run through it, and receiving it gave
Barrie enormous pleasure. He sent a reply at once, saying he was
sending Stevenson a copy of *Auld Licht Idylls*.

There was another letter, one from his mother.

My dear beloved Jamie,
My heart keeps blessing and thanking you, but no words can say my love. My heart fails words for my first birthday gift.

My dear beloved son, God bless you and prosper you. You are a precious God-given son to me, the light of my eyes, and my darling Maggie is safe with God and you till we meet.

Your loving mother.

Barrie was now writing in good earnest, working on a play he had promised Irving, which was to become *The Professor's Love Story*. He had also begun to go up to London. A letter to Quiller Couch dated August begins: 'I am still at Shere,' but was written from the Garrick Club. He says: 'I am writing plays to keep myself from thinking.'

In September Barrie left Shere and returned to London, taking rooms for himself and Maggie in Gloucester Walk, a street on Campden Hill. He was still very attentive to his sister, but now that the play was finished he was beginning a novel, and he was glad when Maggie expressed a wish to see a few friends.

It was a shock when Irving turned down the play which Barrie had written especially for him. The actor-manager had wanted a strong, unusual rôle for himself—and a lesser one for Ellen Terry, though he had not put it quite like that. Professor Goodwillie was not exactly—well, not quite Lyceum style. He did not go into further reasons or explanations for his refusal.

Barrie hid his chagrin and considered other managements. Charles Hawtrey at the Comedy—no. George Alexander at the St James's—yes, a possibility. He sent it to Alexander, who turned it down. The Trees at the Haymarket? No. There was, of course, Toole, who was doing well with *Walker, London*, which was still playing to full houses. Toole refused the play, too. John Hare, another possibility, said he could not read the author's handwriting. *The Professor's Love Story* was accepted in the end by Edward Smith Willard, who had made a reputation in villainous parts in plays like *The Lights o' London* and *The Silver King*. He toured America every year with a successful repertory, and was looking for a new play—a new kind of play, if possible—to take back with him to the States this season. In a conversation with Henry Irving at the Garrick Club, J. M. Barrie's latest play was mentioned, and Irving recommended it—possibly out of compunction for his own rather shabby treatment of the author. Willard read it, was very taken with the unvillainous part of Professor Goodwillie, and offered Barrie under a hundred pounds for the American rights. Barrie was now glad to get it accepted at all, and agreed. Willard took the play to America and played the Professor, with Maxine Elliott in the leading feminine rôle. Barrie put the whole thing out of his mind for the present and turned to other work in hand. There was always work in hand.

There was also the resumption of a relationship which had been interrupted by the tragic event in Scotland. Miss Mary Ansell was still playing in *Walker, London*, and when Barrie dropped into the theatre, he found the second leading lady looking prettier than ever. And she was so openly pleased to see him that the little playwright was touched, his spirits rocketed, and he immediately asked her out to supper.

The supper parties became regular engagements. At week-ends they would drive out to Richmond Park, or stroll in the green glades of Kensington Gardens, which they both agreed were as good as the country. Barrie took her to visit Maggie, who was gracious and just a thought possessive where her brother was concerned. Mary Ansell disliked her but didn't show it; outwardly she was friendliness itself. She knew that Maggie was watching her with a wary eye, and she did not want to antagonize Mr Barrie's sister at this stage, at any rate, especially as the dear little man needed a great deal of sympathy, and was turning to her more and more.

Barrie attempted to keep a stiff upper lip, but he was glad of the sympathy which the charming girl gave him without stint. He did not feel at all well. His headaches were getting worse, and he was suffering from bronchial trouble, partly inherited but made worse by his constant smoking. He did not think of giving up smoking; it was now part of the *persona* he showed to the world, a Barrie symbol. The pipe-smoking went on and so did the cough. He was also working at top pressure. Richard D'Oyley Carte had commissioned him to write the libretto for a musical play, and Barrie had begun it. A play and a novel jostling for attention in one large, well-formed head.

He could do them, of course: he could do anything he wanted where imagination and industry were concerned. The trouble was real life, where half of him very often wanted one thing and the other half another. In later life he was to call one half M'Connachie and make humorous speeches about him, but M'Connachie had been inside his skin ever since he had come to London, and sometimes pushed him in one direction when every instinct of self-preservation was pushing him as far away from M'Connachie's insistence as he could get.

Barrie was not well enough to finish the libretto for D'Oyley Carte in time, and Conan Doyle came in to collaborate on it. Barrie had given it the title: *Jane Annie, or the Good Conduct Prize*, and it ran for several weeks, then sank without trace. Barrie was more disappointed for Conan Doyle's sake than his own, and went on making notes for the novel. He also decided to go to Scotland to see his mother. He did not get any farther than Edinburgh, where he was taken ill with chest trouble. Maggie at once prepared to go up to him, and Miss Ansell offered to accompany her. It was difficult to refuse. So Mary left the cast of *Walker, London* and accompanied Maggie to Edinburgh.

The invalid, who was at an hotel, was much moved by this act of kindness—his mind veered away from calling it anything else. When he was better, Mary Ansell returned to London, and he and Maggie went on to Kirriemuir. An invitation had come for him to present the prizes at Dumfries Academy, and he prepared his speech with great care. Also his *persona*. A cigar. A mannerism which had begun as a schoolboy trick while competing in face-contorting, and which was now a useful provoker of laughter: one eyebrow going up, the other down. Pauses in the right place. Stories about his schooldays, but not too many.

One of the first faces he saw in the audience was that of Wellwood Anderson. Wedd! Barrie was back with *Bandelero the Bandit* in a flash. It was a good moment. But they had little time to talk when the prize-giving was over, for everyone wanted to speak to the distinguished Old Boy of the school. Wedd told him that he was now a professional actor, and Barrie talked of future meetings, but he knew, as Wedd did, that their ways lay apart.

Another function: opening a bazaar for the Auld Lichts, who were replacing their barn-like structure with a new kirk. Ironic moment! Forgiven and apparently forgotten were past strictures on his writings which had held them up to the public gaze; he was famous, and the bazaar was crowded and sold out. Margaret Ogilvy was a proud woman that day.

At Strathview, a visitor was beginning to call rather often. This

was William Winter, the University coach who was on holiday in
Kirriemuir. He would have been Maggie's brother-in-law, but now,
astoundingly, he appeared as her suitor. Barrie, who had known him
for a long time, made him specially welcome when he saw the way
things were going. This would be the best solution of all to a situation in which he had involved himself, but which was increasingly
becoming a grave embarrassment. He would look after Maggie all
his life, if necessary, just as he had promised, but if she and William
Winter made a match of it, that would be the happiest way out for
her and for everyone else. Himself included.

Maggie and William Winter were married in the summer and
departed to live in Hampshire, where William had his coaching
connection with a large number of pupils. Barrie returned to
London, and went on with the novel, visited his friends, looked in at
his clubs. There was also cricket. The Allahakbarries were still
going strong, and he found it thrilling to be captain of a team of
authors and artists who gave him the best of comradeship. He loved
the matches—against Shere, against an eleven at Broadway, against
other village teams—and he was at his most scintillating at the
supper-parties which followed, where the laughter and fun grew
uproarious.

Then there was Mary Ansell. Supper *à deux*. His friendship with
Miss Ansell was developing in a direction where the signals stood at
danger. He did not want to go on, and he did not want to turn back.
He had begun to fall in love with her in earnest, but it was getting
confusing. What he really wanted was for Miss Ansell to be in love
with *him*, so that she would not allow other admirers to take her out,
and pay her compliments. That was *his* privilege.

Mary seemed content to let things go on as they were, but both of
them knew that no relationship of the kind could remain indefinitely
in a state of suspended animation. Mary's friends were frankly
curious. In reply to their discreet questions, she made it clear that
she was quite ready to marry Mr Barrie. She did not add that she was
beginning to wonder what his motives were. He was always taking
her out, ostentatiously paying her compliments in public. Why did he
act in that way if he wasn't serious? The newspapers were putting
in little paragraphs. Journalists called on her, ostensibly to get
her opinions on fashions and interior decoration—her good taste
was well known. Their questions were not so easy to parry.

Mary's smile must have grown a little strained as she evaded direct replies.

Then Barrie received a telegram to say his mother was very ill with bronchitis, and he took the first train he could to Scotland. Alec had come, too. Margaret Ogilvy was like a wraith, but she had a strong will, and with Jamie and Alec beside her, she hung on. It was Jane Ann's appearance that shocked the two men even more than the mother's weakness. Jane Ann was about forty-seven, but she looked like an old woman, completely worn out. Perhaps they both realized at last what this sister's life had been, spent entirely in the service of her mother, more than a nurse, more like a ministering angel, a saint.

Margaret Ogilvy slowly recovered, and Barrie stayed on for a time, working at his new novel. When his mother was well enough to be left, he returned to London.

There were several letters from Vailima: one was dated November of the previous year. Stevenson thanked Barrie for a letter, and said that the *Auld Licht Idylls* had not yet reached him:

I wish it had. And I wonder extremely whether it would not be good for me to have a pennyworth of the Auld Licht pulpit. It is a singular thing that I should live here in the South Seas under conditions so new and so striking and yet my imagination so continually inhabits that cold, old huddle of grey hills from which we come.

He went on to describe his methods of writing:

You should never write about anybody until you persuade yourself, at least for the moment, that you love him, above all anybody on whom your plot revolves. It will always make a hole in the book; and, if he has anything to do with the mechanism, prove a stick in your machinery. But you know all this better than I do, and it is one of your most promising traits that you do not take your powers too seriously. 'The Little Minister' ought to have ended badly; we all know it did; and we are infinitely grateful to you for the grace and good feeling with which you lied about it. If you had told the truth, I for one could never have forgiven you. As you had conceived and written the earlier parts, the truth about the end though indisputably true to fact, would have been a lie, or, what is worse, a discord in art. If you are going to make a book end badly, it must end badly from the beginning. Now your book began to end well. You let yourself fall in love with and fondle and smile at your puppets. Once you had done that, your honour was committed—at the cost of truth to life, you were bound to save them. It is the blot on 'Richard Feverel', for instance, that it begins to end well; and then tricks you and ends ill. But in that case there is worse behind, for the ill ending does not inherently issue from the plot—the story *had*, in fact, ended *well* after the great last interview between Richard and Lucy—and the blind illogical bullet which smashes all has no more to do between the boards than a fly has to do with the room into whose open window it comes buzzing. It *might* have so happened; it needed not; and unless needs must, we have no right to pain our readers . . .

Write to me again in my infinite distance. Tell me about your new book. No harm in telling *me*; I am too far off to be indiscreet; there are too few near me who would care to hear . . .

And in the inimitable words of Lord Kames, Faur ye weel, ye bitch.

Yours very truly,
ROBERT LOUIS STEVENSON.

Stevenson was writing again within a month:

Dear J. M. Barrie,
You will be sick of me soon; I cannot help it. I have been off my work for some time, and reread 'The Edinburgh Eleven', and have great mind to write a parody and give you all your sauce back again and see how you would like it yourself, and then I read (for the first time—I know not how) 'A Window in Thrums'; I don't say that it is better than The Minister; it's less of a tale—and there is a beauty, a material beauty of the tale *ipse*, which clever critics nowadays long and love to forget; it has more real flaws; but somehow it is—well, I read it anyway, and it's by Barrie, and he's the man for my money. The glove is a great page; it is startlingly original and as true as death and judgment . . . Tibby Birse in the Burial is great, but I think it was a journalist that got in the word 'official'. The same character had a word to say to Thomas Haggart. Thomas affects me as a lie—I beg your pardon; doubtless he was somebody you knew, that leads people so far astray. The actual is not the true . . . There are two of us now that the Shirra might have patted on the head, and please do not think when I thus seem to bracket myself with you that I am wholly blinded with vanity . . . I am a capable artist; but it begins to look to me as if you were a man of genius. Take care of yourself for my sake, it's a devilish hard thing for a man who writes so many novels as I do that I should get so few to read, and I can read yours, and I love them.

He goes on in a long postscript to try to persuade Barrie to come out to Vailima to visit him: 'We would have some grand cracks! Come, it will broaden your mind and be the making of me.'

Barrie was elated to receive such long letters from Stevenson.

Yes, he would go one day to Vailima, and meet this writer who above all others understood and appreciated him. He talked about Stevenson and the letters to Mary Ansell, who was, as always, interested and sympathetic. She really was a most intelligent girl, Barrie thought. Exceedingly pretty and very intelligent: it was a pleasure to take her out, to be seen with someone so gracefully dressed, stylishly, but with excellent taste.

The little suppers continued, as did the walks in the Gardens, the excursions to Richmond and sometimes to the Surrey countryside in the neighbourhood of Shere. She liked walking, too. She liked the country and gardening—at least, she would love gardening if she ever had a house and garden. There was not so much talk these days about her career; she was doing well in *Walker, London* and her ambitions seemed to have advanced no farther than that popular success. She would rather listen to Mr Barrie and *his* ambitions.

Alexander Barrie came down to London on a visit. Alec was now over fifty, a grave man, still full of sound good sense. He reminded Jamie of their father: he was the same build, and possessed the same kind of calmness. The old, bleak sense of frustration came over Barrie once or twice: he came not much higher than Alec's shoulder. But he was too fond of his brother to be jealous on those lines—he'd done well enough himself without the extra inches.

Alec was taken along to meet Miss Ansell, and soon was finding opportunities to talk to the attractive young woman alone, for he guessed which way the wind was blowing. He also saw that things were not going as straightforwardly as they should. Mary, sensing his sincerity, talked to him frankly. James was thirty-four, she herself was turned thirty. Did Alec think it was any use going on waiting, and hoping?

Alec considered the matter in his calm way, and told her that he was sure his brother was greatly taken with her. But Jamie could not be hurried: he had always been like that. Alec realized that this continual procrastination was keeping other suitors away, but if Mary really cared for his brother, and would go on being patient a little while longer, all would come right in the end. Perhaps when the novel was finished, his mind would be more free.

Mary knew that when one novel was finished, another was soon boiling up in that restless brain, but Alec meant to be kind, and she hoped that all would, indeed, come right in the end.

Jamie and Alec went down to Hampshire to visit Maggie and her husband at Medstead, where William was teaching. Maggie seemed happy enough; William was obviously a most considerate husband. Barrie had already visited them several times, and had done a good deal of work on his novel at Medstead. It was to be called *Sentimental Tommy*, and was about a sister and brother who had been left motherless—the father was not spoken of, except when necessary. What mattered was the way the little sister almost worshipped her brother, and the wonderful way he looked after her. He was by no means a perfect boy, but he had promised to care for his sister, and care for her he did . . .

The novel went racing on. Back in London, Barrie spent hours at his writing-table, but he managed to fit a growing list of social items into his day. He went to the Garrick Club, where he met his friends. There were gatherings of the Allahakbarries. He had been elected to the Reform Club, and he looked in there sometimes. His days were full, his life was full. But there came a moment when he must face the fact that there was Mary Ansell.

He knew she wanted to marry him, and, in a way, he longed for the stability of a home where he could entertain his friends with an attractive wife at the other end of the table. But he hesitated, as he had hesitated for months. Heaven knows what dark night of the soul James Matthew Barrie went through at the idea of a union with a flesh and blood woman. He would never again be able to escape into romantic images when life brought his high-powered imagination into conflict with the realities of marriage.

How much did Barrie know about himself? Did he know, or did he suspect, that he lacked virility and should not marry at all? It is difficult to believe that he never thought about sex, with that imagination; but, equally, it is not difficult to understand why he still flinched away from any full-blooded approach to women. Margaret Ogilvy had put her thumbmark on him in his most impressionable years, and subconsciously he still accepted her appalling puritanical attitude to a man's relations with his wife as being 'regrettable but necessary'. It is probable that the only way he could resolve the complexes which this attitude set up was by sublimating his natural desires—turning them into a kind of romantic worship which he knew in his inner heart was false, but which he was not able to help. His pathological shyness must also have been a factor.

There is no evidence that any woman had ever excited him in the way other men were excited by attractive women. His worship of them did not go deeper than admiration for their beauty. Why, then, did he pursue Mary Ansell with his attentions? It is possible that he did indeed recognize what had happened to him: that he hoped marriage would help him to become normal, that with a seductive wife there would be a change. But this can only be surmise, for he never discussed it with anyone, and nobody can possibly know what went on in that massive head.

The nearest one can get to him is to read *Tommy and Grizel*. With hindsight, one can begin to understand something of the tragedy which later compelled Barrie to seek romantic compensation for what was denied him as a man. In *Sentimental Tommy*, and especially in *Tommy and Grizel*, Barrie looked ruthlessly into himself and created Tommy Sandys. He drew much of Tommy from life—his own. In Chapter Thirty-one of *Tommy and Grizel*, Grizel has been taken mentally ill because she has found out Tommy's duplicity:

'Have done with heroics,' he [David] said savagely, when Tommy would have spoken.

'. . . I can marry her, and I'm going to do it . . . I shall do it willingly.'

And then it was the doctor's turn to laugh.

'You!' he said with terrible scorn. 'I was not thinking of you . . . I was thinking how cruel to her if some day she came to her right mind and found herself tied for life to the man who had brought her to this pass . . .'

'You have the key to me. You know I am a man of sentiment only . . . it has its good points. We are a kindly people. I was perhaps pluming myself on having made a heroic proposal, and though you have made me see it just now as you see it, I shall probably soon be putting on the same grand airs again.'

Later in the book, Tommy having married Grizel solely to look after her, comes another revealing passage in Chapter Thirty-three:

He could not make himself anew. They say we can do it so I suppose he did not try hard enough. But God knows how hard he tried.

He went on trying . . . He told her all that love meant to him, and it meant everything that he thought Grizel would like it to mean . . .

It was just the same when they returned to Double Dykes, which they added to and turned into a comfortable home, Tommy trying to become a lover by taking thought, and Grizel not letting on that it could not be done in that way . . . He was a boy only. She knew that, despite all he had gone through, he was still a boy. And boys cannot love. Oh, is it not cruel to ask a boy to love?

There is no record of when or where Barrie proposed to Mary Ansell. She does not mention it anywhere in her letters or books, and Barrie, usually so full of detail when writing about these romantic situations, is equally silent about the beginning of his own romance—if one can call it so. All one knows is that he asked Mary Ansell to marry him, and she accepted.

Chapter 8

MARRIAGE

WHATEVER James Barrie's private battles may have been, having taken the irrevocable step, he immediately began to lay down conditions. No announcement must be made: the engagement was to be kept secret, even from their friends. He would break the news to his mother himself. His family were used to the idea of Jamie being associated with the theatre, but—actresses! In Margaret Ogilvy's eyes, at least, they were a different species from other people. Jamie had mentioned Miss Ansell at home, as he had mentioned other people in his London life, but without any special emphasis. He knew it would be a shock.

He went home, but whether he told Margaret Ogilvy then about his intended marriage or not is unknown, for he caught a bad cold which turned to a chill on the chest, and soon, with terrible suddenness, to pneumonia and pleurisy. He was so ill that Dr Murray left his own practice in the hands of a *locum tenens* and came up from Bristol post-haste, to assist the local doctor. The patient was not out of danger for some time, but at last the crisis was passed, and the long, slow haul back to health began.

Mary Ansell anxiously travelled to Kirriemuir to help Jane Ann, who already had one semi-invalid to look after. There had been items of news about the playwright's illness from the beginning, and now additional paragraphs appeared, noting Miss Ansell's departure for Scotland, and making speculations. On July 1st, 1894, Barrie was writing to Quiller Couch:

I could make a long letter of it but am shaky with a pen, though was holding a golf club firmly yesterday. My lungs are quite right again, and I have only to pick up strength now. Miss Ansell, who has an extraordinary stock of untrustworthy information on diseases of the human frame, knows all about quinsey, and says she can sympathize in full. Yes, it is all true though it was in the papers [the news of their engagement] and I am just recovering from the pleasure of having a letter on the subject—yours—which is not comic. Even so long ago as when I was going to you in Bedford Gardens I was beginning to hope that this would come about, and I am not in a position to deny, as the Speaker would say, that the obvious happiness of you two seemed to me a most enviable thing. We have worked hard to get married unbeknown to the lady journalists but vainly. In about a week it will be—up here, so that we can go off together straight away, she to take charge. We go across the channel first for a month, and fully mean to come your way soon thereafter. Vague talk of winter quarters, one idea to come to Fowey for a month or two into rooms. I want Miss Ansell and your wife to be friends, and feel so sure they would be, and it would be a good place for me—and consider the causeries we'd talk! We are both against London life for permanency.

James Barrie and Mary Ansell were married quietly at Strathview on July 9th, 1894; the bridegroom was thirty-four, the bride thirty-two. They went to Switzerland for their honeymoon. Barrie was still not strong, and there were no tiring walks, but the weather was perfect and they were able to visit many beautiful places. At Lucerne, they saw a litter of St Bernard puppies that delighted Mary so much, Barrie bought one of them for her. He had never possessed a dog, but Mary adored animals, and as they intended to live in the country when they returned to England, there would be plenty of space for a large dog to gambol about. They arranged for the puppy to be sent to them when it was a little older, and came back to London to begin their new life together.

They intended to take their time over finding the perfect cottage, and moved into lodgings. They might even have two homes, one in town and the other in the country. Barrie was earning a good income, which looked like being substantially increased as he had been persuaded by his literary friends to put his work into the hands of a good agent.

It was a sensible decision. Barrie was hopeless at negotiating a contract; he would accept a figure and grumble privately about it, but would not talk it over first in a businesslike way. Addison Bright was a good agent, and he set about putting his client's affairs on a sound basis. There was *The Professor's Love Story*, to begin with. E. S. Willard had had such a great success with it in America that he wanted to produce it in London. Barrie had imprudently sold him the American rights outright, but the English rights were still free. Addison Bright was able to vary the contract and negotiate a proper agreement with Willard which included royalties. The play was put on at the Comedy Theatre, and though it wasn't an immediate success, it had enough appeal to stay on, and presently it was playing to capacity audiences. Willard said later that he was always safe with *The Professor's Love Story*; it had the right ingredients for popular success—romance, sentiment, a little sly satire, a happy ending. The royalties which were soon rolling in were useful to a newly married man. *Sentimental Tommy* was nearing completion, too, and already other ideas were jostling for attention.

There was a very long letter from Vailima. Stevenson had written a kind of journal in the form of a letter, beginning it in July:

My dear Barrie,
This is the last effort of an ulcerated conscience. I have been so long owing you a letter, I have heard so much of you fresh from the Press, from my mother and Graham Balfour, that I have to write a letter no later than today, or perish in my shame, but the deuce of it is, my dear fellow, that you write such a very good letter that I am ashamed to exhibit myself before my junior (which you are, after all) in the light of the dreary idiot I feel. Understand that there will be nothing funny in the following pages. If I can manage to be rationally coherent, I shall be more than satisfied.

The letter rambled on, not always rationally coherent; about taking photographs, recollections of an early fishing holiday near Kirriemuir, stories of his youth. Then it broke off, and was continued on July 29th, after he had seen accounts of Barrie's illness in newspapers which had been sent to him:

No, Barrie, 'tis in vain they try to alarm me with their bulletins. No doubt you are ill, and unco' ill, I believe; but I have been so often in the same case that I know pleurisy and pneumonia are in vain against Scotsmen who can write. You cannot imagine probably how near me this common calamity brings you . . . Keep your heart up and you'll do . . . and by the way, if you're at all like me—and I tell myself you are very like me—be sure there is only one thing good for you, and that is the sea in hot climates. Mount, sir, into 'a little frigot' of 5,000 tons or so and steer peremptorily for the tropics; and what if the Ancient Mariner, who guides your frigot, should startle the silence of the ocean with the cry of Land Ho!—say when the day is dawning—and you should see the turquoise mountain tops of Upolu coming hand over fist above the horizon? Mr Barrie, sir, 'tis then there will be larks! And though I cannot be

certain that our climate would suit you (for it does not suit some) I am
sure as death the voyage would do you good.

Stevenson's health was deteriorating, and he knew it. Lonely,
homesick for the city he found 'snell, blae, nirly and scowthering',
he longed for a fellow-spirit to whom he could talk and talk, and for
first-hand news of the world of letters from which his malady had
exiled him:

I tell you frankly you had better come soon. I'm sair failed a'ready; and
what I may be, if you continue to dally, I dread to conceive. I may be
speechless; already, or at least for a month or so, I am little better than a
teetoller—I beg pardon, teetotaller. It is not exactly physical, for I am in
good health, working four or five hours a day in my plantation, and
intending to ride a paper-chase next Sunday . . . The obligation's poleetical,
for I am trying every means to live well with my German neighbours—
and, O Barrie, but it's no' easy! To be sure, there are many exceptions, and
the whole of the above must be regarded as private—strictly private.
Breathe it not in Kirriemuir; tell it not to the daughters of Dundee! What
a nice extract this would make for the daily papers!

On August 12th he finished this journal-letter with:

And here, Mr Barrie, is news with a vengeance. Mother Hubbard's dog is
well again—what did I tell you? Pleurisy, pneumonia, and all that kind of
truck is quite unavailing against a Scotsman who can write—and not only
that, but it appears the perfidious dog is to be married. She went to the
graveyard to see him get buried, And when she came back, the deil had
got married. It now remains to inform you that I've taken what they call
here 'German offence' at not receiving cards, and that the only reparation
I will accept is that Mrs Barrie shall incontinently upon the receipt of this,
Take and Bring you to Vailima, in order to apologise and be pardoned for
this offence.

Barrie intended to go to Vailima one day, to follow the directions
Stevenson had once given him: 'You take the boat to San Francisco,
and then my place is second to the left.' Mary liked the idea, too, if
only they could get away: there was so much to do. But Robert
Louis Stevenson died in 1895, and Barrie was never able to see the
turquoise mountain tops of Upolu coming hand over fist above the
horizon.

*   *   *

The St Bernard dog had now arrived from Switzerland, and was at first called Glen, then Porthos, after the St Bernard in *Peter Ibbetson*, a book Barrie admired. He was brown and white and very large, a dog of character, who, when he was a little older, was trained to stand on his hind legs and box with his master. They both loved him from the beginning; Mary washed and combed and fed him, Barrie took him for walks and played endless games with him at home.

After various lodgings and a stay in a residential hotel, Mary at last found a house at 133, Gloucester Road, South Kensington. It had a room on the first floor over the front door, which Barrie took as his study; the rest of the house was Mary's concern. She had a real talent for making a comfortable home, and the house was soon a pleasant place for their friends to visit. George Meredith dined with them; he was in poor health and came to London to consult specialists, but an evening with the Barries put him in good spirits. He and Mary got on excellently together, and she felt completely at ease with him, in spite of his awe-inspiring reputation.

Barrie had again collected an eleven of the Allahakbarries to play against Shere, and several of them stayed at Gloucester Road. Gilmour and Marriott Watson were two of the original members, and new friends had been roped in: Bernard Partridge, the artist, and a 'real' cricketer, Henry Ford, who was illustrating Andrew Lang's fairy books, were among them.

In July, the Barries went up to Kirriemuir to see Margaret Ogilvy before going off for a holiday themselves, again to Switzerland; Barrie had to assure himself that his mother was well, or he would not leave the country. Margaret Ogilvy was not ill—apart from growing weakness, and a tendency to talk to herself, she seemed cheerful, holding Jamie's hand and occasionally nodding and smiling at Mary. Now that she had met her daughter-in-law several times, Margaret Ogilvy had had to revise her opinion of actresses, for Jamie's wife was ladylike, and, what was more important, had had an obviously respectable upbringing.

Porthos had come, too, and the sight of the famous son of Kirriemuir, his pretty wife in her London clothes, and the great St Bernard dog with his sagacious face and gentle manners, brought many a face to the windows.

A fortnight passed and it was time to leave. Barrie could hardly bear the look on his mother's face when the moment for parting came, but goodbyes had to be said. Jane Ann promised to write to Switzerland every day, and Barrie and his wife set off for the

Engadine, where they had engaged rooms at the Maloja Hotel. This would be a holiday, and so it turned out to be—at least where physical comfort was concerned, for they could afford the best of everything. Mary found, however, that her husband never took a holiday in his mind, and there were the inevitable notebooks in his bag.

Addison Bright had suggested some weeks before that *The Little Minister* would make a good play, especially after the great success of *The Professor's Love Story*. Barrie did not think it would, and had given Bright permission to dramatize the novel himself. (This did not prevent his jotting down possible ideas for the play in a notebook.) Barrie was now working out the shape of a sequel to *Sentimental Tommy*, which was finished and in the publisher's hands.

Jane Ann wrote regularly as she had promised, so Jim—Mary could never call him Jamie—was free from anxiety about his mother. In spite of her husband's constant preoccupation with the notebooks, Mary was enjoying the Engadine. On mountain paths, Barrie walked ahead with Porthos, silent—he could be silent for hours, even on holiday—while Mary looked for wild flowers and alpine plants, and thought of the day when they would find their ideal country cottage, and she at last could make a garden.

On September 1st the daily letter came from Jane Ann. It was followed, a few hours later, by a telegram from Kirriemuir, telling them that Jane Ann had suddenly died.

Mary was a rock of strength in the three terrible days that followed, for it took them that time to reach Scotland. Alec and the other sisters were already at Strathview, waiting for Jamie with deepening dread. For Margaret Ogilvy had only survived her daughter by those three days. She had been lying in bed in a world of her own, talking to herself, ever since Jane Ann's collapse, and when the travellers reached Kirriemuir all was over.

Jane Ann had died of cancer. Nobody had known of it; perhaps she had not known herself, for she had never complained of pain. Had Margaret Ogilvy guessed that her prop, her stay, the arms which had sustained her, had been withdrawn? No one had dared to try to make her understand why Jane Ann was no longer there, but in the shadowy world in which she had been sinking for the past week, she somehow knew. And the watchers knew, too, that it was best this way.

Jamie and Alec took charge, both stricken, but Jamie did not show it. No letter to be read to the congregation this time: no image of grief to hold before the face. He and Alec made arrangements for the funeral, and for their father, who was now over eighty and more withdrawn than ever. He was to go and live with his brother-in-law at Motherwell, where Sara, his only unmarried daughter, would look after him as well as his uncle.

Margaret Ogilvy, aged seventy-six, and Jane Ann Adamson, aged forty-nine, were buried in the cemetery on the Hill of Kirriemuir, and Barrie knew that he would never go back to the town for many a long year. Dr Ogilvy owned Strathview, and when he retired he intended to live there, but now it was to be shut up, and James Matthew Barrie left it without looking back. That chapter in his life was closed.

* * *

Kensington Gardens was the green centre of London for the Barries at 133, Gloucester Road. They took Porthos there every day; it was easy to dodge the horse-buses and infrequent carriages and drays on the main road, and the walk was quite a short one. Children and nurses in the Gardens soon came to know the St Bernard, walking between the little man in the bowler hat and overcoat, and the fashionably dressed lady with him. Mary, still in blooming good looks, might have passed for twenty-five instead of thirty-three.

Porthos was a great attraction. Once he was let off the leash in the Gardens, his master would play with him, and then the children watching would be spellbound, for the huge dog, up on his hind legs, was as tall as the little man in the bowler hat. Man and dog boxed, circled, and stopped to go off running, then walked on again, with the lady, to play hide-and-seek among the trees.

At home, Mary played with her pet: she would hold his paws and dance, or give him toys to turn over and push about. She tried not to mind when he preferred his master's study, relaxed and with paws outstretched, content to stay there without moving while her husband sat at the table, smoking, or walked up and down, up and down, and sat down again to write. She had learned not to ask him what he was writing about—he did not care to discuss his work. But his note-books still exist, and there are odd entries. One, concerning his old friend, Joseph Thomson, the explorer, who died earlier that year:

On Oct. 31, '95, I dreamt that going into Thomson's old rooms I found him there. Cd not doubt that it was he, but said I had been to his funeral. He became hysterically angry, & I felt it wd not do to mention subject to him again. A character like Sara was much with him. In house belonging to T. I saw signs of foul play, curious servant, &c. Heard jeering laughs. Vague feeling that this man was personating T. to get his effects, that Sara shielding him for characteristic reasons. Began to play detective & woke.

Sentimental Tommy was now being published serially in America in Scribner's magazine, and Barrie, still thinking about a sequel, also turned his thoughts to *The Little Minister*. Addison Bright had finished his dramatization and gave it to Barrie to read. Bright had made ruthless cuts in the novel, and had sharpened up the action so as to lead to good theatrical climaxes. Barrie was impressed with his agent's draft, and saw the possibilities of an effective play. He began to dramatize it afresh; Bright made no objection, for he knew that the Barrie magic was what audiences wanted.

Charles Scribner wrote from New York with a suggestion. He was publishing *Sentimental Tommy* in book form in the autumn, and he proposed that he should bring out a uniform edition of Barrie's works, with the texts slightly revised, and each with a new preface by the author. This would enable them to take advantage of the American 1891 Copyright Bill, which at last protected authors from literary pirates. Rogue publishers had, from the time of Dickens and before, been producing unauthorized editions of books without paying royalties or any fees. Dickens had complained indignantly about the practice, but in his day he had not been able to get any redress, as there was no copyright law in America. The Copyright Bill now protected authors, and Barrie's prefaces would be sufficient to ensure that everyone knew Scribner's held the sole rights to the authorized new edition, which he proposed to call the Thistle Edition.

Barrie agreed, and proceeded to plan the prefaces, but mundane daily life insisted on breaking in. Not Mary, who seemed quite content with Porthos to spoil, a house to run, friends to visit or to entertain. Money matters were simple. Mary saw to it that cheques were paid into the bank, and she settled the bills. If she was extravagant that did not matter; there was plenty coming in, and Gilmour, now a barrister and interested in stocks and shares, invested any surplus when the unbusinesslike Barrie thought of such a thing.

Now there was an unpleasant series of letters from the income tax authorities. Barrie had never attempted to evade income tax—he simply did not pay any. Forms, incomprehensible in phrasing and demands for information, went into the fire. Letters on the subject were pushed aside. But officialdom, if slow and patient, was also inexorable when patience came to an end. Mr Barrie was requested to put his tax affairs in order, and soon. Barrie turned to the friend who understood these maddening matters. He wrote from Gloucester Road on February 15th, 1896:

My dr Gilmour,
I meant to consult you about this last night. The fiends of the income tax are on me for what I am liable for. Do I pay income tax to them therefore from the year when I had a banking account (beyond that I don't know what my income was and don't want to know), or is there a limit of years beyond which they can't claim arrears?

Yours ever,
BARRIE BARNATO.

Gilmour came to the rescue; the standard rate of income tax was eightpence in the pound, and the total sum payable did not reach a hundred and fifty pounds. Thereafter, Gilmour took on his little friend's increasingly complicated financial affairs, and Barrie turned with relief to his writing-table.

*   *   *

A preface to any book with a Thrums background inevitably meant references to Margaret Ogilvy. He began obliquely at first, but soon found that it was not painful to write about his mother—quite the reverse. It was some kind of release, one that he did not attempt to understand though he was quite aware of it. The years fell away, and he was once more safe in that world of the little girl in the magenta pinafore, as she carried her father's dinner across the fields to the quarries.

Again, the Auld Lichts. They could not touch him, but he could not take his mind away from them. He remembered the dire authority of the Kirk Session in those days, their power to sit in judgment on sinners and rebuke them in the face of the congregation, the minister calling down hell-fire on those who found the flesh to be weak. He remembered how Margaret Ogilvy had wanted him, her son, to be a minister, and her grievous disappointment when he had gone another road.

The preface grew, and became a chapter. Another chapter
followed. Margaret Ogilvy shone on every page, filtered through the
net of his imagination. He told how, once she had accepted that
literature was to be his game, she had begun to enlarge her reading:

Biography and exploration were her favourite reading, for choice the
biography of men who had been good to their mothers . . . Explorers'
mothers also interested her very much: the books might tell her nothing
about them, but she could create them for herself and wring her hands in
sympathy with them when they had got no news of him for six months.
Yet there were times when she grudged him to them—as the day when
he returned victorious. Then what was before her eyes was not the son
coming marching home again but an old woman peering for him round
the window curtain and trying not to look uplifted. The newspaper
reports would be about the son, but my mother's comment was 'She's
a proud woman this night.'

More recollections began to edge in, and more and more. He could
remember whole conversations, and it was an aching joy to set them
down. No image now. The thick, clotted dialect of the Thrums
books had disappeared, and he wrote in the straightforward Scots-
English which had actually been spoken in his home:

'You stand there,' my sister would say with affected scorn, 'and tell me
you don't think you could get the better of that man quicker than any
of us?'
     'Sal, I think I could manage him,' says my mother with a chuckle.
     'How would you set about it?'
     Then my mother would begin to laugh. 'I would find out first if he had
a family, and then I would say they were the finest family in London.'
     'Yes, that is just what you would do, you cunning woman! But if he
has no family?'
     'I would say what great men editors are!'
     'He would see through you.'
     'Not he!'
     'You don't understand that what imposes on common folk would
never hoodwink an editor.'
     'That's where you are wrong. Gentle or simple, stupid or clever, the
men are all alike in the hands of a woman that flatters them.'
     'Ah, I'm sure there are better ways of getting round an editor than
that.'
     'I daresay there are,' my mother would say with conviction, 'but if you
try that plan you will never need to try another.'

A skilfully presented piece: the man recollecting it instinctively shaped reality as he shaped fantasy. Yet the passage stays in the mind. Chapter succeeded chapter: it was far beyond the length of a preface and was growing into a book. Unplanned, subtly giving the impression of intimacy—but true? The author himself would have shied away from that direct question. What was truth? What had actually happened, or what had partially happened? How much was there, hidden by the image?

It was a short book, and when it was finished, Barrie and Mary went to Paris for two weeks. They had been before on several occasions, sometimes alone together, more often with friends. Barrie loved Paris, and Mary was always happy there, for the notebooks were left in the luggage if he was enjoying himself. He was generally in bubbling high spirits within an hour of getting to the city, responsive to the gaiety which was in the very air as they strolled along the sparkling boulevards—especially if they were with friends. Barrie detested sightseeing, but time could be agreeably filled driving in the Bois and out to Versailles and Fontainebleau, dining at exclusive restaurants, going to the theatres. His knowledge of French was limited, but he could appreciate superb acting and witty staging, and the sheer *élan* of the French when they were out for an evening's pleasure brought a smile to that usually unsmiling face.

Home again, and a careful revision of *Margaret Ogilvy* before sending it to the publishers. He altered very little: he could not improve it. If anyone had whispered in his ear that the book was, essentially, the story of an emotional boa-constrictor, he would have recoiled in the utmost horror. It was, in fact, a little masterpiece of its kind, a kind never before attempted. Real sentiment merged with sentimentality all the way through: man and image. Yet the whole was compulsive reading when it came out, just as it had been compulsively written.

Cassell's were publishing *Sentimental Tommy* but Robertson Nicoll, having seen the manuscript of *Margaret Ogilvy*, was so overcome by its 'beauty and pathos' that he determined his own firm, Hodder and Stoughton, should bring it out. The book was under fifty thousand words, little more than half the length of an ordinary novel, and it did not fit into any known category. A memoir? A tribute? An autobiography? Barrie refused to describe it in any way. What he had written, he had written. He turned to other work in hand.

There were still the prefaces to do, and there was *Tommy and Grizel*—he had decided on this title for the successor to *Sentimental Tommy*, which would have the same characters as the first book: sweet little dependent sister, the equivocal Tommy, the ideally lovely Grizel. Already he was making notes, numbered and set out, in a new notebook.

Chapter 9

AMERICA

ROBERTSON NICOLL was going to America on business connected with his numerous publishing ventures, and he suggested that Barrie should go with him. Addison Bright was enthusiastic about the idea when he heard about it, as he worked closely with a well-known American dramatic agent, Elisabeth Marbury, and Miss Marbury did a lot of professional business with one of the most powerful American theatrical magnates, Charles Frohman. Bright wrote to her. Elisabeth Marbury replied by return, assuring him that she could interest Mr Frohman in a play based on *The Little Minister*. Addison Bright wrote again; he thought that a meeting between playwright and impresario was desirable, and if he, Bright, could persuade Mr Barrie to go to New York, would Miss Marbury arrange matters? Again Miss Marbury replied by return, saying she would.

Addison Bright took the precaution of talking to Mary Barrie first. Mary was delighted at the idea of a trip to the States, but she knew better than to urge her husband to go when he would be certain to react unfavourably at first. It still needed an effort on Barrie's part to overcome his congenital shyness at the prospect of meeting people he knew nothing about, so she and Bright approached the matter carefully. Barrie reacted as she had expected. He dreaded what he had heard of American reporters, who would ask embarrassing questions and try to ferret out his private life. And he loathed personal publicity.

Mary thought it would be nice to meet Mr Cable in the flesh. Barrie stopped being obstructive, and turned this new idea over in his mind. He had for long admired and been in correspondence with the Southern novelist, George Washington Cable, who had written stories of Creole life in Louisiana in much the same way as Barrie had written of life in Thrums. Cable now lived in New England, which was not far from New York. Barrie took the bait, and agreed to the trip, his mind on Cable. Mary bought a wardrobe of fashionable clothes and prepared to be received in the New World as the wife of a famous writer.

It worked out very well. They sailed from Liverpool on the *Campania* in late September, 1896, and arrived in New York early on October 3rd. A posse of reporters was waiting to receive them, and after the usual high-powered interviews, with Mary and Nicoll shielding Barrie as much as they could, they were driven to the Holland House, a hotel where celebrities stayed. Frohman had put a box at their disposal at the Empire Theatre for that evening, and after resting and dining, the party went along to see the play. The piece was called *Rosemary*, and the rôle of the heroine was taken by a charming young actress called Maude Adams. The party from England admired her very much.

Barrie had brought with him to America the dramatized version of *The Little Minister*, though it was still unfinished. Next day, Elisabeth Marbury collected it and took it along to Charles Frohman to read.

The actual sequence of events was related by Robertson Nicoll in letters to his fiancée, Catherine Pollard, whom he was to marry the following year. He told her that Frohman had put a box at their disposal on the day they arrived, and after resting, they went to the theatre, and added: 'We saw *Rosemary*, which was well acted, especially by the heroine, one of the best young actresses I have seen for some time.'

Elisabeth Marbury gives a different account in her book of reminiscences, *My Crystal Ball*. She says that Charles Frohman summoned her to his office after he had read the script, said he liked it, but could not use it as it was a man's play, and he was looking for a vehicle for Maude Adams. Whereupon Miss Marbury declared that she would get the author to re-write the play and make Lady Babbie the leading part. When she tackled Barrie, he refused outright: 'I pleaded, I coaxed, I argued. Barrie consented to make the necessary changes, and Frohman rejoiced at the result of my diplomacy.'

An even more piquant account is given in the official biography of Charles Frohman, *Charles Frohman: Manager and Man* by Isaac F. Marcosson and Daniel Frohman:

Under Frohman's influence he [Barrie] had begun to consider a dramatization of *The Little Minister*, but the real stimulus was lacking because, as
he expressed it to Frohman, he did not see anyone who could play the part
of Babbie. Now came one of those unexpected moments that shape lives.
On a certain day Barrie dropped into the Empire Theatre [New York]
to see Frohman, who was out.

'Why don't you step downstairs and see *Rosemary*?' said Frohman's
secretary.

'All right,' said Barrie.

So he went down into the Empire and took a seat in the last row. An
hour afterward, he came rushing back to Frohman's office, found his
friend in, and said to him, as excitedly as his Scottish accent would
permit:

'Frohman, I have found the woman to play Babbie in the Little
Minister! I am going to try to dramatize it myself!'

'Who is it?' asked Frohman, with a twinkle in his eye, for he knew
without asking.

'It is that little Miss Adams who plays Rosemary.'

'Fine,' said Frohman. 'I hope you will go ahead now and do the play.'

No decision could be made because the play was still unfinished.
Barrie had been impressed by Miss Adams, but there, for the time
being, the matter rested.

The real importance of the American visit was his meeting with
Charles Frohman, and the strong and true friendship which grew
between these two dissimilar men. Charles Frohman, about Barrie's
age, was the Jewish type which makes a mark in the world of
entertainment: far-seeing but ready to take chances, buoyant,
quick-minded, decisive. Charles Frohman could also be obstinate,
but he was generous-minded, too. He was trusted by everybody.
Barrie liked him at their first meeting, and he never changed his
opinion of Frohman as 'my kind of man'. It was Wedd all over
again. Here was a man who was totally absorbed in the theatre, and
that was something James Barrie could understand. The two men
did not have much time together then, but they knew that this was
the beginning of an association. Barrie would have liked some kind
of definite opinion on the play, unfinished though it was, but he did
not press Frohman. He would hear in good time.

The party moved on to Northampton in Massachusetts, where
they spent a week-end at George Washington Cable's home—Barrie
feeling absurdly pleased because Cable turned out to be hardly
taller than himself. There was a party, and Cable sang Creole songs,

and Barrie gave an imitation of Irving as Matthias in *The Bells,* and
Mrs Barrie's good looks drew admiration from all eyes, and the
whole visit was very pleasant.

The rest of the crowded trip was a triumphal progress; Boston and
other New England towns, Washington, on to the Deep South to
see New Orleans, back to New York, and then, thankfully, home.
They had had a wonderful time and made a number of friends—but
Barrie knew that he would have to re-write the play if Frohman was
going to produce it in America.

Meanwhile, *Sentimental Tommy* had been published, and was
selling well. In December, Hodder and Stoughton brought out
Margaret Ogilvy. The reviews were favourable in England; in
Scotland, there were several shocked critics. Many considered the
book a violation of privacy. The Scots are often inarticulate where
their deepest feelings are concerned, and this kind of anatomical
opening up of family life offended their sense of fitness. J. H. Millar,
again summing up the reaction of these critics, says that Barrie's
discriminating admirers would not readily forgive the writing of this
book, 'an exercise compared with which the labours of the resur-
rectionist are praiseworthy, and which many men (I believe) would
rather lose their right hand than set themselves to attempt.'

George Blake wrote: 'No reader of Barrie's earlier fiction can
escape the painful sense of being privy to an exposure. Whether or
not *Margaret Ogilvy* amounts to a positive act of indecency is still a
proper subject of debate.' He goes on:

Barrie really wrote throughout his Kailyard period for, out and from his
mother. The complex was more than maternal; it seems to have been
positively foetal . . . One may very well wonder why *Margaret Ogilvy* was
ever written, except for private circulation, but Barrie threw the portrait
of his mother into the whirlpool of commerce: in cold fact cashing in on
his own popularity. Not many men would deliberately expose their own
domestic affairs in this fashion, but Barrie was one of the few; and we can
only conclude that commercial success, after a chilly boyhood, had turned
his head . . . For all his reputation for the understanding of women and
children, we have to deal here with what seems to be a case of refined
sadism.

Praise outran criticism and the book sold forty thousand copies
within weeks. In America the tale was the same, laudatory reviews
and immense sales. And J. M. Barrie's stock rose higher than ever.

The cheques grew larger. Barrie, already deep in his work, left all
that to Mary and Gilmour, now acting as his broker. Turning
money into more money was of no interest to him; he had a play to
re-write.

It was not all work, however. In the spring Barrie and Mary, who
had been learning to ride bicycles—the latest craze—ventured on a
cycling trip to Broadway, and were made much of by the de Navarros
and their friends. Madame de Navarro was interested in what she
called 'crickets', and there was much laughter when Barrie suggested
that the Allahakbarries should challenge a Broadway team under her
captaincy. Madame accepted the challenge; she did not play 'crickets'
herself, but she would get together a team, certainly.

Charles Frohman came to London, and Barrie met him again.
The Little Minister had been re-written and was ready, with more
emphasis on the rôle of Lady Babbie. Frohman liked the play, but he
wasn't yet ready to produce it; Maude Adams had other commitments for the near future, and Frohman intended to wait until she
could take the part.

Addison Bright decided to try the managements for a London
production, but it was Barrie himself who got the play taken.

Cyril Maude describes how it came about in his book, *Behind the
Scenes with Cyril Maude*:

It was in the summer of 1897 that James Barrie first came into my life. I
had at the time played in a piece written by him and Marriott Watson,
called Richard Savage, at the Criterion, in which I played Sir Richard
Steele, and we had become to a certain extent friends through that, but it
was that summer when one day he told me that he was ready to write a
play founded on his delightful book The Little Minister. He told me this
while we were playing billiards at the Garrick Club. I missed several fine
cannons, and rushing over to the Haymarket, told Harrison [Frederick
Harrison, manager of the Haymarket Theatre] and sooner than we could
have hoped for, we had the play and put it into rehearsal.

I loved every minute of the work on it. Barrie sat with me on a little
platform we had rigged up in front of the stage and worked and helped
in every minute of the stage-management, and we lunched and tea'd
together and nursed the lovely thing into the perfection everybody seemed
to consider it six weeks later . . .

The cast was *perfect*. Winifred's[1] Babbie was exquisite. Why shouldn't
I say so?—everyone said the same!

1. Winifred Emery, Cyril Maude's wife.

The Allahakbarries went down to Broadway for the match against Madame de Navarro's team. Barrie's men included Conan Doyle, Gilmour, and Bernard Partridge, the artist, while Madame de Navarro put in her husband—no cricketer, but he was reading a book about it and at least knew the rules—and two singers, Kennerley Rumford and Plunket Greene. There was also a tall, unassuming figure of a man, Charles Turley Smith, a writer of schoolboy stories, one of which, *Godfrey Marten*, had become very well known. 'Turley' was one of those people of whom it can truly be said that he had a genius for friendship. He was described as 'charming and delightful, sincere and simple—a man whose character was as upright as his own fine body in its prime.' Turley was to become one of Barrie's most cherished friends.

The Broadway team won by a single run, much to the delight of Madame de Navarro, who, though not a participant in the victory, was ready to assist her team in every possible way. Even Barrie had to grant that her methods were not always scrupulous: 'She had a way of wandering round the field with the Allahakbarries' top scorer, who, when he came back, would sheepishly tell his captain that he had promised to play for Broadway in the second innings.'

After the match, the de Navarros entertained the teams to supper. It was a rollicking evening. Barrie was at the top of his form, jolly, joking in his deep, rumbling voice, one of the band of comrades round the dining-table but actually its focal point. It was always so, when he exerted himself to make it so. The laughter and good talk flowed out from his place at the table, wherever he happened to be sitting, and no one knew how it happened.

There was dancing after dinner, and even Barrie went on to the polished floor of the drawing-room with Mary. She was not much taller than her husband, but she tried to keep herself down to his level as they danced, knowing how sensitive he was about his height. It irritated Barrie. Many things about Mary irritated him, and when this happened at home he felt guilty and tried to make up for it by urging her to buy clothes or jewellery. At Broadway, among these sophisticated, brilliant people, Mary was apt to shrink in spirit, though outwardly she was calm and cool. Jim's new friends made her intensely aware of her origins as the daughter of a Bayswater publican. Her mother still kept a boarding-house. Did they know? Had Jim mentioned that they had both been down to see Mrs Ansell on several occasions, and had even stayed in the boarding-house? Hardly. He seemed able to fit into their world without effort. Mary's instinct was to efface herself. It was different in London, where ease and poise came naturally to her when they were with their mutual friends, however high-born or well-known. At Broadway, she felt outside the charmed circle of painters, musicians and other clever people with whom their hostess surrounded herself. Madame de Navarro was graciousness itself, but Mary was glad when the time came to go home.

Home meant Gloucester Road, but she was now looking in earnest for a cottage in the country, and was on the books of the principal agents. They sent her particulars of many houses, and she spent days taking the train to villages in the counties round London, inspecting, considering, rejecting. She particularly wanted enough ground for a spacious garden, where Porthos would have plenty of room and she could plan flower beds and shady walks. Her husband left it entirely in her hands; when she found exactly what she wanted, he would go down and see it. Meanwhile, *The Little Minister* was taking up his thoughts.

Frohman had written to say that he was now ready to put on the play, and rehearsals were in progress in New York. He thought that Miss Adams's part was a little thin and would like more added to it. He thought some of the parts were superfluous. Frohman would have liked the title changed to *Lady Babbie* so as to give his young star more prominence, but he knew the author would not agree to that. Still, there was room for improvement; he sent cables with suggestions, cables that Barrie did not always answer. Frohman wrote that the cast were 'learning Scotch'. He told Barrie not to worry: 'You wouldn't recognize it, but the American public will.'

The play opened in September in Washington for a try-out. Audiences and critics were puzzled at first, and then it settled down to a capacity success, playing for six months in New York, followed by tours all over the States. Maude Adams had become a star of the first magnitude. Frohman was jubilant. They had a winner.

In London, rehearsals were in progress at the Haymarket, with the playwright walking up and down in the dark auditorium, drawing on his pipe and occasionally stopping to make suggestions. Winifred Emery played Babbie as if she had been born to the rôle of the wild, fearless, glorious gipsy girl, and Barrie was enthralled. He wrote her notes declaring his fervent adoration; he came up to the edge of the stage during a break in rehearsal and paid her jewelled

compliments, her husband standing not three feet away and Mary
Barrie sitting in the front row. Winifred Emery laughed lightly at
his more extravagant flights and exchanged looks with her husband.
They glanced at Mrs Barrie, but she was smiling. Mary was a good
actress.

The play ran for many months. Another money-maker. There
were times when Mary Barrie wondered where it was all leading.
Barrie didn't need any more money: there was no necessity whatever
for him to work so continuously. In any case, he took little interest
in money for its own sake. Was he happy? She did not think so, but
they never discussed a subject so fundamental and important as
happiness. They never discussed anything. When Barrie was not
shut up in his study, writing, he was filling up every moment of his
time—at his clubs, with his friends, entertaining at his own dinner-
table. The only hour they had alone together was when they took
Porthos to Kensington Gardens, and even then he often went alone
with the dog.

Why was he not as other men? What did he want from life? She
did not know, but she was quite sure of what *she* wanted. The
secure, stable existence that other women enjoyed with their
husbands: a life where she would not feel an outsider. And, more
than anything else, she wanted children.

There were moments when she felt despair. She had many friends,
but none very close—no one to whom she could talk about her
intimate private life. Her mother was friendly enough, pleased to see
her daughter rich and leading what she called 'an interesting life with
the best in the land'. Mary sometimes wondered just how long she
could go on leading this 'interesting life'.

Then she shook off the dark thoughts and resumed her search for
the country cottage.

Chapter 10

THE DAVIES FAMILY

THERE now comes the most extraordinary period in James Matthew Barrie's life, one which was to affect his deepest emotions. It was to have even more lasting effects on the lives of a whole family, the Llewelyn Davieses, totally unrelated to him by kinship, with an entirely different background and code.

According to family accounts, Barrie first met Sylvia Jocelyn Llewelyn Davies at a dinner party at Sir George Lewis's house in Portland Place in 1897. Lewis was a fashionable solicitor, and had acted for Barrie for some time; they were friends as well as professional man and client, and Barrie liked Lady Lewis, who was a notable hostess. Margaret Llewelyn Davies, who became Sylvia's sister-in-law, remembered Barrie telling her that he found himself sitting next to the most beautiful creature he had ever seen, and being overwhelmed. He was also intrigued by the way she put aside some of the various sweets which were handed round at the end of dinner, and secreted them in her silk reticule. When he asked her why, she replied, 'For Peter'.

A different account is given by H. J. Ford, the artist, who was a friend of Barrie's and had been in the Allahakbarries. In a letter to Peter Llewelyn Davies he said that it was at his studio in Edwardes Square 'that at a tea J. M. Barrie first met your mother, who was dressed in a corduroy jacket made by herself. He saw, fell a victim, and was instantly conquered. Hence Peter Pan and all the rest of it.'

In many memoirs and letters of the time, there is mention of Sylvia's loveliness. She did not possess classical features, but a contemporary described her:

Without being strictly pretty, she has got one of the most delightful, brilliant sparkling faces I have ever seen. Her nose turns round the corner—also turns right up. Her mouth is quite crooked, her eyes are very pretty—hazel and very mischievous. She has pretty black fluffy hair, but her expression is what gives her that wonderful charm, and her low voice.

Sylvia was the second daughter and third child of George du Maurier, and a sister of the actor, Gerald du Maurier. Arthur Llewelyn Davies was one of the six sons of a clergyman, John Llewelyn Davies, who held the living of Kirkby Lonsdale. His mother had been a Crompton, and both sides of the family were very well known.

Arthur, a brilliant scholar, had won exhibitions and scholarships to Marlborough, and scholarships to Cambridge, where he took a First Class in the Classical Tripos in 1884, an international law scholarship, and a law scholarship in the Inner Temple in 1889. One of his friends at Cambridge was Hugh Macnaghten, who became a master at Eton. Arthur went there as an assistant master while he was reading for the Bar. There was very little money behind the young barrister: he would have to make his way.

It was this knowledge, together with natural diffidence, which inhibited him when he fell in love with Sylvia du Maurier after only two meetings. The first was at a dinner party at which, according to the host, Miss du Maurier sat on the handsome barrister's right hand and 'displayed liberally the most beautiful neck, shoulders and bosom to an admiring world', and the second time at a charity ball, where they 'danced and danced', apparently without eyes for anyone else, and when Sylvia decided that he was the man she was going to marry. A friend who shared chambers with him remarked later that suspicions of Arthur's attachment were aroused because he was constantly singing 'Who is Sylvia?' in chambers.

Sylvia's mother, Emma du Maurier, did not care for Arthur Llewelyn Davies; she probably thought he was not a good enough match for her daughter, in spite of the fact that he came from an impeccably respectable and respected family. The young couple had to wait several years. Sylvia was twenty-six and Arthur twenty-nine when they were finally able to get married. Arthur had been less than three years at the Bar, and was making a very small income from regular legal work. A legacy of three thousand pounds from his maternal uncle, Charles Crompton, decided the question of marriage. Mrs du Maurier had to come round to the match.

They aimed to live on four hundred pounds a year, which was not a large income but which made marriage possible. Sylvia was determined to earn some money if she could, and went to work with Mrs Nettleship, a well-known theatrical dressmaker. It was good training for someone with taste and imagination, and Sylvia, who possessed both in good measure, became adept at turning out smart clothes at low cost.

The marriage took place in 1892. After a honeymoon in Cornwall, the couple took a house at 18, Craven Terrace, in Paddington. George, the first son, was born there in 1893, and Jack, the second son, in 1894. The family had an increased income a year or two later, following the death of George du Maurier, Sylvia's father, in 1895; he had made a great deal of money, mainly due to the enormous success of *Trilby*. George du Maurier left a typically French will, providing for the interests of his family to the second generation. It did not appear to the young people at Craven Terrace that there would be any serious money difficulties in the future, especially as Arthur was making his way, slowly but surely, at the Bar.

*   *   *

On Barrie's walks with Porthos in Kensington Gardens, he would often see two small boys in red berets in charge of a nurse, who also had a perambulator to push in which there was a baby. The boys were George Llewelyn Davies, aged four and a half, Jack, just over three, and Peter, the latest arrival, nearly a year old: he had been born in 1897.

The large brown and white dog attracted their attention, and soon the dog's owner was making friends with them. When he learned their name, he told them that he knew their mother. The man with the dog was different from anyone the children had ever met; he could lift one eyebrow while he dropped the other, and he knew a lot of stories. George and Jack had books read to them by their mother nearly every bedtime, but never stories like these. Adventures. Adventures that went on and on; and the man often pretended to forget what came next, and asked them to help him out.

Sometimes a lady would be there, as well as the dog, and presently the stranger became Mr Barrie and the lady Mrs Barrie. Sylvia Davies heard all about them, and she invited the Barries to lunch at her house, now in Kensington Park Gardens, the one in Craven Terrace having become too small. The Barries entertained the Davieses in turn. Mary liked Sylvia Davies; they had a great deal in common, both being artistic and fond of clothes.

The growing friendship was soon being noticed by a good many of their acquaintances. There was no overt comment, but it became natural to talk of the Barries when the Llewelyn Davieses were mentioned; they were together a great deal, just as if they had been very old friends instead of rather new ones.

Arthur began to find this state of affairs not much to his liking. He did not care a great deal for the strange little Scotsman, in any case; they had nothing in common. He could not understand why Mr Barrie should show such a sentimental partiality for children who were not connected with him in any way. There was scarcely a day now when Barrie did not come back with them from the Park, and as he was generally in the midst of some tale, the boys would beg him to come in. Mr Barrie would then remain, without a by-your-leave, until the children went to bed. It was extraordinary. Arthur was exceedingly fond of his boys, and the only time he saw them at leisure was in the evening. He wanted to shut the door on the outside world and enjoy their company in his own way. Never having been faced with a situation of this kind, he did not quite know how to handle it. There was nothing he could do. Mr Barrie continued to haunt the house, and the children showed that they were very willing to listen to his endless stories, told in that deep, curious burr which struck the public school Englishman at times as being quite incomprehensible.

There was something else. Barrie, who was obviously of a very generous nature, was ready to buy them anything that was mentioned in conversation. Arthur Llewelyn Davies had a fiercely independent nature, he was a struggling barrister, and he had to watch expenditure. It was very kind of the little man—but Arthur wished heartily that he wouldn't be so possessive. Yes, possessive was the word; Mr Barrie seemed to think that it was the most natural thing in the world to come to 31, Kensington Park Gardens without question, day after day, whether the boys had been in the Park or not.

There were acquaintances who must have wondered why, if Barrie was so fond of children, he had none of his own. He had been married for several years, and nobody had heard either of the Barries mention a possible family, nor was there any hint that doctors had been consulted. If anyone had said anything at all on the matter, however tactfully, both Barrie and his wife would have changed the subject immediately.

People did not gossip about the friendship—there was nothing definite to gossip about, as yet—but it began to be noticed that Mr Barrie's devotion to the Davies family now began to extend to their mother. He made no secret of his admiration of her beauty, and seemed totally unaware of the looks that followed him when he sat next to her at any social gathering, and tried to claim her sole attention. Sylvia, secure in Arthur's love and her own love for him, responded with friendly amusement and gave him no encouragement, but Arthur was not amused.

Mary Barrie occupied herself in beautifying her home, buying pretty clothes, going down occasionally to see her mother at the sea, looking for a cottage. She was perfectly aware of Barrie's romantic infatuation for Sylvia Davies, but she kept her head. She had been through all this before, mostly with actresses. Nothing ever came of it: the infatuations had always died down, and this one would probably fade, too. She knew that there was a great deal in her husband's emotional make-up that she must accept, for there was no way of altering it.

Barrie was writing *Tommy and Grizel*, and there must have been many friends of the Davieses, reading that book when it was published, who realized which model Barrie had chosen for Grizel:

She was nineteen, tall and graceful, and very dark and pale. When the winds of the day flushed her cheeks she was beautiful, but it was a beauty that hid the mystery of her face; the sun made her merry, but she looked more noble when it had set, then her pallor shone with a soft radiant light, as though the mystery and sadness and serenity of the moon were in it . . . Her eyes at least were beautiful, unusually far apart . . . such clear, grey searching eyes . . . And she had an adorable mouth . . . screwed up provokingly at one side . . .

In one of Barrie's notebooks, where he put down revisions, he makes Grizel's nose tip-tilted, and adds: 'A woman who will always look glorious as a mother . . . a woman to confide in (no sex, we feel it in man or woman). All secrets of womanhood you felt behind those calm eyes.'

No sex! A woman who would always look glorious as a mother. Back to Margaret Ogilvy, with a vengeance.

*   *   *

The earliest letter from Barrie to Sylvia is a typical piece of absurdity.

It was written in 1897, just before Sylvia's fifth wedding anniversary, but Barrie dated it August 14th, 1892, pretending that he had been acquainted with her at the time of her marriage:

Dear Miss du Maurier,
And so you are to be married tomorrow! And I shall not be present. You know why.

Please allow me to wish you great happiness in your married life. And at the same time I hope you will kindly accept the little wedding gift I am sending you. It is not a hinge, but if you wear it, it will be part of one. It reaches you somewhat late, but that is owing to circumstances too painful to go into.

With warmest wishes to you and Mr Davis [*sic*]
Believe me, dear Miss du Maurier,
Yours sincerely,
J. M. BARRIE.

Peter Davies[1]: This characteristic whimsicality is written on the back of a piece of 133 Gloucester Road notepaper; the envelope, unstamped, is addressed to Miss Sylvia du Maurier, 31, Kensington Park Gardens. No doubt it was delivered by hand on the 14th August, 1897, and is the earliest letter from J.M.B. in my possession. What gift it enclosed I know not.

Fame as well as fortune had now established J. M. Barrie as one of the leading authors of the day. He was asked everywhere: everyone wanted to know him. In March, 1898, he was given an honorary degree by St Andrew's University, and travelled to that ancient town to be capped by the Vice-Chancellor and cheered by the students. Mary went with him, and they stayed for a few days in Edinburgh to see old David Barrie and Dr Ogilvy, who was now an honorary Doctor of Divinity. David Barrie's health was failing but he was still able to read a great deal. Sara had instructions to let Jamie know if any extra money was needed for more comforts in that small household.

A few weeks later, Barrie wrote from Gloucester Road to Arthur Davies:

24th May, '98
My dear Davies,
Mrs de Navarro has issued her challenge for the match at Broadway for Saturday, June 11, and wants us to go down on the previous day, for

1. Peter Davies's comments are given immediately after each letter from now on. See Preface, page 11.

which she is arranging sports of an undignified character. She also invites us to supper and a ball. I hope you will contrive to make this suit you and that Mrs Davies will come too as she is particularly wanted and is said to be good at managing boys.

Let me know as rooms have to be booked.

Return on Sunday.

Yours ever,

J. M. Barrie.

Peter Davies: Did Mr and Mrs Davies go to Broadway on this occasion? History is silent on the point, but it is a fair comment that the occasion would not have been A.'s cup of tea.

The Barries went to Scotland for their summer holiday, taking a house on the Tay so that Barrie could do some fishing. The house was large enough to have guests, and Cyril Maude and his wife were invited for a stay, their two young daughters being included in the invitation. *The Little Minister* was closing temporarily for the summer break, so the actor and his wife would be free for a few weeks.

One of the little girls, Pamela, recollected that visit when she was grown up and married herself:

He [Barrie] was a tiny man, he had a pale face and large eyes and shadows round them. We only stayed with him once, in Scotland, but he had always been in our lives, like Mr Gilbert. Our parents called him Jimmy. He was unlike anyone we had ever met, or would meet in the future. He looked fragile, but he was strong when he wrestled with Porthos, his St Bernard dog. Porthos was also called Glen, he had two names. Mr Barrie talked a great deal about cricket, but the next moment he was telling us about fairies, as though he knew all about them. He was made of silences, but we did not find these strange, they were so much part of him that they expressed him more than they could say.

'Jimmy didn't say one word during the whole of lunch,' we heard Mam say to our father. 'It is difficult for poor Mary.' But it seemed to us that his silences spoke loudly.

The Maude children were also asked to parties in the Barries' house, and Pamela mentions a play given there, *The Greedy Dwarf*, which is described in detail by Mary Barrie:

It was a play for children, and took place in the drawing-room and was acted by his [Porthos's] master and missis and many now famous authors and actors. Porthos's part was one of those that plays itself, at least that is how the actors who are not playing it speak of it. It was a showy part, not a great deal to do, but every action to the point. I was the heroine,

escorted every morning to her school in the woods by her big dog. The
point here was that he got a biscuit before leaving her, and when, as had
happened on this occasion, he didn't get it, he refused to budge. He
would neither shake hands nor go back home, until the mistake was
rectified. All this he did to the life, especially the biscuit part of it. In the
2nd act he defended the hero from the devilry of the villain—his master.
This was done by holding him in the wings until a given signal, when he
was let loose. Then he rushed on to the stage, sprang upon the villain,
and wrestled with him until he was overthrown. It was a consummate
performance, and the curtain came down to thunderous applause. Again
and again he was called before the curtain, and ended by walking across
the footlights among the children, who then discovered that he was a real
dog, not a man.

George and Jack Davies were now going to school, a large day
school for girls and very young boys. It was easy for their father to
take them, catching his horse-bus to the Temple as soon as he had
safely delivered them. It is possible that the thought may have
crossed Arthur Davies's mind that now the two elder boys were at
school, and Peter still in the nursery, James Barrie would not have
so many excuses for coming to their home without warning and,
indeed, without invitation. But Barrie did not need excuses. He had
established a firm relationship with the children and their parents—
at least, with their mother—and he considered the entire Davies
household to be his own territory. He also took it for granted that
any suggestions he made should at once be given priority over any
plans they might have of their own.

133, *Gloucester Road, S.W.*
22 *June*, '99.

My dear Sylvia,
Do come to the cricket match at Broadway and help me to win by doing
crooks in the pavilion. Friday week (30th) afternoon till Sunday is only
two nights. You would be my guest of course, and Mary and I are longing
to have you. Also there are twenty-two wickets for you to take, and you
need not pretend (musketeers or no musketeers) that you don't like
bowling at them.

You know how hugely delighted I shd. be if Arthur could come also
but I suppose that is hopeless.

I thought you were to ask us to dine with you. Are you trying to get
out of it?

Yours ever,
J.M.B.

Peter Davies: So the Christian name stage has now been reached. 'Doing crooks in the pavilion' [whatever that may mean] is as Barriesque a phrase as could be found. *Vide* Grizel's smile in *Tommy and Grizel,* on which he is now at work. (She had not had it in *Sentimental Tommy*)
  I don't know the significance of 'musketeers or no musketeers'.

Charles Frohman came to London and entertained Barrie and Mary sumptuously in London restaurants, and Barrie invited him to Gloucester Road. Mary had grown almost as silent as her husband, except when they had guests, and then she suddenly lit up into her old liveliness. She liked Frohman and he treated her with the right mixture of respect and teasing. And then her husband would interrupt with some quip, and an invisible shutter would come over Mary's animated face and she would sit back, silent again.

The cricket season came round, and Barrie divided his time between the Allahakbarries and filling his notebook. Broadway provided irritation as well as fun and friendship: the reporters and photographers had discovered where Mr Barrie's famous team played, and their privacy was at an end. He was glad to get away— this time abroad, to Germany for a holiday. On their return they took a furnished house at Rustington, in Sussex. The Llewelyn Davieses were there. George Meredith was also staying in the neighbourhood, and Barrie visited the old man, whom he had not seen for some time. It was not difficult to pick up the relationship where it had left off: George Meredith had a special affection for the man who had once been a pilgrim to his shrine on Box Hill.

On March 8th (probably) 1900, the two eldest Llewelyn Davies boys wrote to Barrie from Kensington Park Gardens:

Dear Mr Barrie,
Please will you come to the Lizard at Easter. We are going in the train to Helstone, and the next day we drive to the Lizard. If you can come do bring Porthos. Please will you have some lovely storrys ready for us.
             Yours Faithfully,
                         GEORGE LLEWELYN DAVIES
                              and
                         JACK LLEWELYN DAVIES.
Mother left some of her precious purple jewels at your house, please gard them safely for her.

Peter Davies: I suppose the 'lovely storrys' may be called the first surviving hint of the germination of P.P. It was in the following summer that, during our first Tilford holiday, the photographs were taken in the woods round Black Lake Cottage which crystallized into *The Boy Castaways* . . . the 'storrys' being held back for further elaboration.

And, in the interval (Jan. 7, 1901) another P.P. germ—*The Greedy Dwarf*—was produced at 133 Gloucester Road, with S. as Prince Robin— 'Enormous engagement of Miss Sylvia du Maurier who has been Brought Back from the year 1892 in a Hansom to play the Principal Boy . . .' S., 'modestly draped, and hardly attempting to act, smiled exquisitely at the onlookers with an air of bewildered apology.' A. was an onlooker, and I shd think an uncomfortable one. I have a copy of the programme, with a photograph of myself, as author, on the cover.

Chapter 11

PETER PAN

THE search for a country cottage came to an end at last. Mary Barrie found just the place she wanted near Farnham, in Surrey. It was a house set in a neglected garden to the south-east of the town, on the Tilford Road. There were thick pinewoods all round, and no other house near; not far away was a small lake with herons standing on the shore. Here was a perfect setting, and Mary knew she could make Black Lake Cottage into a perfect country house.

The house inside was, to her, the very abomination of desolation. The furnishings were suffocating; plush, tangles of draperies, fringes everywhere, ugly wallpaper and uglier chimney-pieces. Mary returned to London feeling happier than she had done for years; now she could turn her thoughts to transforming the house and making a lovely garden.

Barrie was pleased that she had found a place that she liked, but—very unusually for him—jibbed at the price which had been asked for it. Mary was immediately irritated, and declared that she would buy the lease of the cottage herself. Gilmour had helped her to invest money favourably, so she had some capital. Barrie was uninterested: he had not seriously intended to make an issue of where the money was to come from. In any case, he was always glad when Mary found plenty of occupation. They had very little to say to each other nowadays.

Barrie was becoming obsessed by the Davies family. He worked at home with his usual fanatical concentration, but there was hardly a day when he did not meet the boys in Kensington Gardens, or call at their home. He had begun a new saga about the Gardens, bringing in a winter palace for the fairies which haunted its dells, and elaborating stories about the Birds' Island in the middle of the Serpentine, presided over by old Solomon Caw. It was, he said, on Birds' Island that all the birds were born who became, in due time, baby boys and girls. The Llewelyn Davies boys heard a great deal about the Birds' Island, and presently another name slipped in, Peter Pan. No one knew where he came from, least of all his creator. Barrie was in the habit of naming his imagined characters after children he knew, and Peter Davies was there, handy. The Pan part tacked itself on quite naturally. Peter Pan. The boys soon got to know him as if he actually existed.

At home, Barrie was working on several ideas at once: a play based on the Hanky School of his youth and which appears in his notebook as *Phoebe's Garden*, another play jotted down which was to be about the *Smart Set*, and a novel which he intended to call *The Little White Bird*. This last was already shaping as a collection of short pieces written round a boy called David, but it inevitably gravitated towards Kensington Gardens, and it wasn't long before fairies were making an appearance.

Meanwhile, in the practical world outside his teeming imagination, Black Lake Cottage had been made a charming week-end retreat to which the Barries could ask their friends, and they bought a car, very high off the ground, driven by steam. A chauffeur called Alfred was engaged, but he could not prevent it from breaking down and having numerous punctures. A Lanchester and a chauffeur called Frederick replaced the previous models, and Mary was now able to go down to Black Lake in grand style.

At Kensington Park Gardens, a happy family event had taken place. Barrie wrote to Sylvia from Gloucester Road on 21st June, 1900:

My dear Jocelyn,
It is very sweet and kind of you to write me from the throne, which is what I take your present residence to be. He is a gorgeous boy, is Delight, which was your own original name for him in the far back days of last week or thereabouts when you used to hug Peter with such sudden vehemence that I am sure he wondered whether you were up to anything.

I don't see how we could have expected him to be a girl, you are so good at boys, and this you know is the age of specialists. And you were very very nearly being a boy yourself.

May he always be a dear delight to you and may all your dreams about all of them come true.

Ever yours,
J.M.B.

Peter Davies: A pretty irresistible affair, when you come to think of it, and

serving appropriately to record here the birth, on 16 June, of Michael
Ll. D., at 31, K.P.G.

Though I remember nothing naturally of the alleged vehement hugs,
I seem to recall the birth of M. and being taken in to see the new baby.
But I am more likely confusing this recollection with that of N.'s birth
three years later.

This is the earliest instance I have of J.M.B.'s use of S.'s second name,
by which no doubt he elected to call her, and did ever afterwards, because
(so far as I know) no one else used it.

In November, 1900, Barrie wrote two verses on the back of a piece
of card which had on the other side of it the remains of the name of
a Bond Street jeweller's:

> To a Crooked Lady
> on her 33rd Birthday.
> At thirty-three she's twice as sweet
> As sweetest seventeen could be,
> At sixty-six I'm sure she'll beat
> The record made at thirty-three.
>
> So sure am I her crooked ways
> Will baffle Time and all his tricks,
> Impatiently I count the days
> Till Jocelyn shall be sixty-six.

Sylvia took George, Jack and Peter to the Isle of Wight for a month
at Easter in 1901, leaving Michael, the baby, in the charge of Mary
Hodgson, the nurse. Mary was an important member of the Davies
household. Peter Davies says:

Of her goodness and devotion to us all for twenty years and more, and of
the absolute trust placed in her by S. Ll. D. despite certain occasionally
awkward idiosyncrasies in her character—perhaps inseparable from and
traditional to her calling—there will be better opportunities to speak
further on, as and when she is mentioned.

On Sylvia's return home, Mary Hodgson went for a holiday herself
to her home in Morecambe, where Sylvia wrote to her, giving news
of the children. Michael had another tooth through, and 'Jack was
seedy for two days and afterwards Mr Barrie took him to spend an
afternoon at Earl's Court. Peter wished to go too but I thought it
would be wiser to let only one, so Peter is to go alone one day
later on.'

Sylvia wrote to Mary Hodgson a week or so later:

We have taken a charming cottage at Tilford, near Mr Barrie's, instead of Burpham. When you come back I will go down and settle about rooms.

Do you think you could make a sort of plan for the new work. Bessie thinks you would do it best ... I am sure Anna had better do the nurseries once a week and anything else upstairs you think best. What about Monday's washing? You see it would be very nice for the new girl to have some time for sewing. The dining room and hall are to be taken away from the cook. If Nancy will not come ... Bessie will take Nelly's place till we go away, and Mrs Vallender will stop on from then till we come back in September. Then I shall find a country housemaid for the time we are away.

Peter Davies: 4 maids to Tilford! It's uncanny! ... Where did they sleep in that truly charming old cottagy farmhouse—or at 31, K.P.G. either, for that matter? All in one room, and two to a bed, I shouldn't wonder ...

One has no notion of what A. Ll. D.'s average income from the Bar may have been at this stage, but it certainly couldn't have been large. What made this enormous gang of servants possible was, I think, not only the almost non-existent taxation and the cheapness of the servants themselves and of things in general, but also the simplicity of the way the family lived: hardly any drink (an occasional bottle of claret from Hedges & Butler in Regent Street and a glass of beer or so for A. Ll. D.), no car or carriage, practically no restaurants to eat and drink expensively in, of course no wireless or refrigerators or other gadgets, and no serious school bills. I think A. Ll. D. always had lunch at an A.B.C. for about 6d., and I take it S. made most of her own lovely clothes. This isn't at all a clever or penetrating analysis, but what emerges is that they concentrated on essentials—and no doubt managed to save something every year!—and evolved, on a small income, something as near perfection in the way of family life as could be wished.

During that summer holiday at Tilford, the Barries and the Davieses were inseparable. Michael was still in his pram, but George, Jack and Peter were off with their friend every day. If Arthur Davies, who saw little enough of his sons at home, wondered if he was going to see even less of them on holiday, he could hardly say anything. They were obviously very happy and excited at the new stories Mr Barrie was spinning for them. The stories had come alive. The three boys now acted out wonderful adventures in the most perfect setting which could have been devised. The Black Lake became a South Seas lagoon, the pinewoods were tropical forests in which enemies lurked. George, Jack and Peter were transformed into pirates, Redskins and other rumbustious characters, with Mr Barrie

Sylvia Llewelyn
Davies.

Arthur Llewelyn
Davies.

J. M. Barrie: portrait by William Nicholson.

directing the proceedings. Long, magical days in the sunshine, and a playfellow who entered into the games so completely that they forgot he was a famous man in London: here, he was one of themselves.

Barrie was a good photographer, and he took scores of snapshots of the boys and of Porthos, who was cast for the rôle of any wild animal required by the continuous verbal script. Day after day the adventures went on, and when the end of the holiday came at last, Barrie had a great sheaf of photographs to take home. Sorting them out later, he had the idea of making them into a book, with descriptive chapter headings but no text, only the photographs in sequence. Thirty-five photographs were finally chosen, and a printer called in to make two copies, one for Arthur Llewelyn Davies and the other for Barrie. The author purported to be Peter Davies:

THE BOY
CASTAWAYS
OF BLACK LAKE ISLAND
BEING A RECORD OF THE TERRIBLE
ADVENTURES OF THE BROTHERS
DAVIES IN THE SUMMER OF 1901
FAITHFULLY SET FORTH BY
PETER LLEWELYN DAVIES
LONDON
Published by J. M. BARRIE
in the Gloucester Road
1901.

The Preface runs:

I have been requested by my brothers to write a few words of introduction to this little volume, and I comply with pleasure, though well aware that others may be better acquitted [*sic*] for the task.

The strange happenings here set forth with a *currente calamo* are expansions of a notebook kept by me while we were on the Island, but I have thought fit, in exercise of my prerogative as general editor, to omit several observations with regard to *flora, fauna*, etc. which, however valuable to myself and to others of scientific bent, would probably have but a limited interest to the lay mind. I have also in this edition excluded a chapter on *strata* as caviare to the general.

The date on which we were wrecked was this year, on August 1, 1901, and I have still therefore a vivid recollection of that strange and terrible summer, when we suffered experiences which have probably never before been experienced by three brothers. At this time the eldest, George, was eight and a month, Jack was approaching his seventh *lustrum*, and I was a good bit past four. Perhaps a few words about my companions on the Island will not be deemed out of place.

George was a fine, fearless youth, and had now been a term at Wilkinson's.[1] He was modest withal. His chief fault was wanting to do all the shooting, and carrying the arrows inside his shirt with that selfish object. Jack was as brave as a lion, but he also had many faults . . . and he has a weakness (perhaps pardonable) for a pretty face (bless them!) Of Peter I prefer to say nothing, hoping that the tale, as it is unwound, will show that he was a boy of deeds rather than of words, which was another of Jack's blemishes. In conclusion, I should say that the work was in the first instance compiled as a record simply, at which we could whet our memories, and that it is now published for Michael's benefit. If it teaches him by example lessons in fortitude and manly endurance, we shall consider that we were not wrecked in vain.

There followed a list of chapters in the style of those employed in popular boys' tales by Marryat, Ballantyne and Jules Verne:

1. A famous preparatory school in Orme Square, Bayswater to which all the boys went in turn.

them-down and Jack of the Red Hatchet—a Holocaust of Pirates—
Rescue of Peter.

The photographs which follow the chapter headings show three
small boys in knickerbockers and berets playing out these high
adventures on the shores of the lake and in the woods. Porthos was
Captain Swarthy's dog, and enjoyed the proceedings as much as did
his master and the boys.

Barrie had two copies of *The Boy Castaways* made, one of which he
gave to Arthur Davies (who left it in a train and never saw it again).

*   *   *

Barrie's latest two plays were nearly finished: *Phoebe's Garden* had
become *Quality Street*—a name he had once seen between Leith and
North Berwick—and the *Smart Set* idea of the notebook had
developed into *The Admirable Crichton*. *Quality Street*, set in the
period of the Napoleonic Wars, is about two spinster sisters, the
younger of whom has a romance with a dashing army captain. He
goes off, however, without 'declaring himself', and the disappointed
Miss Phoebe puts on spectacles, hides her ringlets in a muslin cap,
and determinedly looks forward to being an old maid. The captain
returns in two years' time, invites Miss Phoebe to a ball, but is asked,
instead, to escort her 'niece'—no less a charmer than Miss Phoebe
herself, without her muslin cap and spectacles. Of course the gallant
captain 'declares himself' this time and is suitably impressed by the
extraordinary deception.

The Admirable Crichton has a stronger theme. Crichton, a butler,
proves himself a natural leader and virtual dictator when he and
other domestic staff are wrecked on a desert island with his employer,
a noble lord, and the latter's haughty family. Back again in civiliza-
tion, Crichton reverts to butlerdom, and all—or nearly all—goes on
as before.

Barrie was also working, at this time, on *The Little White Bird*, where the character which fascinated him most, Peter Pan, was taking over the story of his own accord. Barrie altered and revised the chapters, but when he came to the volatile Peter Pan, the boy seemed to slip through his fingers. He had a life of his own. This excited Barrie, and he worked on the later chapters with intense concentration.

At Christmas, he took Jack, George and Peter Davies to see *Bluebell in Fairyland*, a 'Musical Dream Play' which Seymour Hicks had written. Hicks was a gay young actor with an extremely attractive wife, Ellaline Terriss, and he had tailored his play to show off their united talents. Bluebell, a little flower-girl, goes to fairyland; it all turns out to be a dream, but it has been a very pretty dream. There were songs and dances, and the play was a success. Barrie was taken with Seymour Hicks's stage personality, and would later remember him.

Barrie's days were as full as he could pack them. His social acquaintance was growing even larger; he was invited to make after-dinner speeches, he met other authors at his clubs. He and H. G. Wells had got to know each other a few years before, and they occasionally corresponded. Wells and his wife came down to Black Lake Cottage; Barrie and Mary dined with them now and again.

It was the Davies family, however, which meant most to Barrie, and he made no secret of the fact. His shyness did not operate where they were concerned; he just took them over, as if he had every right to do so.

Arthur Davies wrote to his father from Garden Court, Temple, E.C., on November 28th, 1902:

Dearest Father,
I don't know what your arrangements are for Christmas, nor if you are likely to have the Vicarage very full. I should like to come, if possible, bringing one boy, or perhaps two . . .
Sylvia is at present on a trip to Paris with her friends the Barries, by way of celebration of the huge success of Barrie's new plays and new book. The party is completed by another novelist, Mason, and they seem to be living in great splendour and enjoying themselves very much. They left on Monday and return tomorrow. Barrie's new book, The Little White Bird, is largely taken up with Kensington Gardens and our and similar children . . .

My work is moderately prosperous but no more. I have a son of Mrs Humphrey Ward as a pupil.

Your affec. son,

A. Ll. D.

Peter Davies: Her friends the Barries is a suggestive phrase; the Daviases and Barries had known one another now for some five years. Was A. a little put out by S.'s visit to Paris? I think it pretty clear that A. was a shade vexed and thought it all rather a bore. On the other hand, how S. must have enjoyed it, and why not? And Jimmy was, in his own odd way, an excellent Parisian and most delightful of hosts, and it would have been hard to imagine a more satisfactory addition than Alfred Mason, a new and devoted admirer and one of the most romantically minded men of that day who put all beautiful women on a pedestal, and a most attractive, amusing and romantic figure himself.

The hugely successful plays of which the Paris trip was a celebration were *The Admirable Crichton,* produced on November 4th, and *Quality Street,* which preceded it by only a little more than a month. They ran for ten and fourteen months respectively. And a few days before the party left for Paris *The Little White Bird* had been published. What a year for Mr Barrie!

Barrie had decided that the lively Seymour Hicks should be offered the leading part in *Quality Street,* a chance which the young actor seized with enthusiasm. Hicks had a gift for improvisation, and it wasn't long before he received a letter from the author of the play. Barrie could not abide his words being altered by actors. He took immense pains over rehearsals, and though he would listen to suggestions for altering lines, he would seldom agree to changes. He had written the play: he knew best. If anyone reported 'misconduct' in this respect once the run had started, he took immediate action:

My dear Hicks,
I am told by people who were at the theatre on Tuesday that you inserted a line about Liz being under the bed. I am supposing it slipped out by accident, as you promised me not to say it, but please don't say it again. I am wondering if this is what Frohman referred to. I have had letters about it from strangers, and was told there was a letter on the subject in some paper.

A few weeks later he was writing even more forcefully:

My dear Hicks,
I find that a good deal both in words and business have crept into the

latter part of the 4th act of Q.S. which was not in it when produced. You say a good deal more than is in the part when you are talking about the cloak. The fact is that in this part of the play (and not in any other, for I think you better than ever in the serious parts) we have got out of the spirit of the piece, and what I meant for comedy has become farce. I am anxious that Frohman should see the production at its best, and I wish you would have a rehearsal of this half of the last act and cut out all the words and business that were not in the piece as I left it. If you would like me to come down to go over it with you I shall do so with pleasure. You see, a play of this kind, if the delicacy goes, the [illegible] story is gone.

Early in 1903, Arthur Davies moved his family to a 'grand new house' at 23, Kensington Park Gardens, almost opposite his old house; they needed more room, and Sylvia was expecting another child. Arthur was still finding life hard financially, but he was very happy otherwise. He wrote to his sister, Margaret, that they were much enjoying their new home, 'except when the time comes to pay rent and rates'. He was still 'moderately busy' and had two pupils in chambers.

The Davies boys had come to accept Mr Barrie as one of the closest friends of the family. On April 23rd, 1903, Jack wrote from 16, Royal Crescent, Ramsgate, a house which belonged to his grandmother, Emma du Maurier:

Dear Mr Barrie,
We are all coming back on Monday and we are longing to see you. We are having a very jolly time at Ramsgate. We wish you were here. We spend most of our time on donkeys and the sands, so when George and I are riding donkeys it makes four altogether. Uncle Gerald and Aunt Muriel are coming down on Sunday and Uncle Guy says they are always looking into each other's eyes. I hope you enjoyed yourself at BLACK LAKE COTTAGE. Is the new motor-car finished yet? I've put Black Lake Cottage in capital letters because wherever you live must be a very celebrated place. Mother has got rummertism in her shoulders. I hope Clare Mackail is better. Did you think Aunt Muriel looked beautiful at the wedding? Mother said you were in the church. Father said you have got a topper! I didn't know it before.
                                    Your story-listener,
                                                        JACK LL. DAVIES.
P.S. I expect a letter.

Peter Davies: It is the earliest Ramsgate letter I have, and I take this to have been our first of so many Easter holidays there, in the house which had been left to Emma du M. the year before by her aunt Susan Caught.

Gerald du M. and Muriel Beaumont had been married a few days before this letter was written—on 11th April. Guy was recently home from the long-drawn-out South African War and would soon be going abroad again. Clare Mackail: younger sister of Angela (Thirkell) and Denis.

Guy du Maurier, brother of Sylvia and Gerald, was a regular soldier and spent three years in South Africa, commanding first a mounted infantry company of his regiment, and later a mounted infantry regiment. He was a man of considerable character. Peter Davies describes him:

The impression one gets of Guy du M. himself is of a regular soldier, more or less reconciled to his lot, but with a shade too much temperament to be altogether contented in a rather hidebound profession. Temperament—what a sod it is, unless the possesser of it is in a walk of life where it can be made capital of! It rears its head rather particularly in his caustic remarks about generals and peacetime Army life, but such feelings are usual towards the end of a campaign.

The Barries now lived on the north side of the Park, the same side as the Davieses. Gloucester Road had suited them quite well, but Mary wanted a London house with rather more character, and she had found it at the corner of Leinster Terrace, adjacent to Lancaster Gate. It was a pleasant Regency house, facing due south, with views over to Kensington Gardens, and the old stable, now a garage, had a room over it which was exactly right for Barrie's study. Mary called the house Leinster Corner, and at once began to have it painted and papered, and furnished as only she knew how. Soon they were entertaining—the Allahakbarries, theatre friends, Frohman when he came over, fellow-writers and others.

Jamie Barrie still kept in close touch with his family, but death was cutting them off, one by one. His sister Isabella had died in Bristol the year before, leaving Dr Murray with a son and four daughters to look after. Barrie went to the funeral and told his brother-in-law not to hesitate to call upon him if in need—and one of the daughters, Madge, was to come to London later and be glad of the help of her influential uncle, as she intended to go on the stage.

David Barrie was also dead. At the age of eighty-seven he had returned from Edinburgh to Kirriemuir, where Dr Ogilvy had decided to settle for good, with Sara to look after them both, as she had done in Edinburgh. The ghosts at Strathview had been laid for them, and they looked forward to a few years of peace. But David Barrie was knocked down by a cart in the High Street, and died a few weeks later. Another journey north, then back to Leinster Corner, to the different world which he had conquered and made his own.

There was a cricket week that year at Black Lake Cottage, with the Allahakbarries playing matches against Shackleford and Frensham. Mary's garden was a picture, the house a delightful background to the festivities. Mary showed all her talents as a hostess: the guests who couldn't be accommodated in the house were found comfortable rooms in Farnham, with the Lanchester to transport them. There was golf-croquet on the lawn, and walks in the pinewoods, and tea in the garden, and good talk and much laughter as they sat round the large table and talked about scores, and made cricketing jokes.

But there was no Porthos any more. He, too, had died; it was his successor, Luath, a Newfoundland dog, who gambolled about, a large black and white ball of fluff, so shaggy that you could never tell which end of him was looking at you, both were so alike. When they first got him, Luath was dull and apathetic, and Mary, realizing that he was ill, spent a great deal of time getting him well. She became especially fond of him because she had nursed him back to health. She wrote:

I became a child with him. We played ridiculous games with him. What races we ran in Kensington Gardens, hiding behind trees . . . I am quite aware that my games, even at their wildest, were not a patch on those he had with his master, for he was an adept at games, but I didn't worry about it . . . He hated those walks when friends joined us and we got separated. Backwards and forwards he ran, trying to make us see that something was wrong, quite like the child in the melodrama, who, at the end of the play, joins the hands of mama and papa. He was always that kind of dog. He never probed into the complexities of life. Life to him was a very simple affair. Home, food, and a walk out every afternoon all together: what more could you want?

Barrie wrote to Peter and Michael from Leinster Corner on May 11th, 1903:

Dear Petermikle, i thank u 2 very much 4 your birth day presents and i hav putt your portraitgrafs on mi wall and yourselves in my hart and your honey lower down.

i am your friend, J. M. BARRIE

Peter Davies: Worth putting in for its own inimitable sake, as well as because it is the earliest surviving letter from its author to the writer of these lines (half of it, anyway).

Lady Ponsonby, a great friend of the family, writing to Peter many years later, gives an evocative picture of Sylvia and Arthur Davies during the summer of that year, 1903. The Davieses had taken Rustington Mill and the adjoining cottages on the northern limit of Rustington Village. Lady Ponsonby and her husband had come to call on their friends, and stopped for a few moments outside: 'Sylvia looking divine, but really the picture of them from the road through the open lamp-lit cottage window was the loveliest I ever saw, Arthur reading, with his Greek coin profile, and Sylvia with her beautifully poised head and Empire hair, sewing in a gown of white and silver.' She described the Davies boys, with their father and a friend out in her own father's yacht, the *Humber*, 'swarming up the rigging like monkeys, and George, with the assistance of ropes, bathing off the boat though unable to swim.'

Barrie was not with them on that holiday. He was occupied in writing a new play, one which had been absorbing him for months past. It was based on *The Little White Bird*, and the chief character was, inevitably, the boy who had dominated the book—Peter Pan. Barrie did not tell anyone about it yet, but continued to move as close as possible into the family life of the Davieses. He still insisted on calling Sylvia by her second name, Jocelyn. It was clear that he wanted to establish a special relationship with her, and if her husband minded—but there was nothing Arthur Llewelyn Davies could have said without sounding foolish in his own ears. Barrie wrote on October 23rd, 1903:

My dear Jocelyn,
I shall come round for the revellers tomorrow about two. I hope Arthur can turn up at the theatre. We have two boxes flung into one, so there is plenty of room for Mary [Hodgson] and Michael.

Yours ever,

J.M.B.

Peter Davies: Anyone might be forgiven for thinking this was *Peter Pan,* but in fact it antedates that terrible masterpiece by some fourteen months. In October 1903 *Crichton* had just come off and *Quality Street* was still running—in its thirteenth month. *Little Mary* had begun its run the month before. It may have been either of these plays to which the revellers were bidden; perhaps the balance tips in favour of *Little Mary*.

Barrie received an unusual honour later that year. Viscount Esher, an enthusiastic theatregoer, had become acquainted with him, and suggested that as the author had written so enchantingly about Kensington Gardens in *The Little White Bird*, he should have his own private key to the Gardens. Barrie did not particularly want a private key—he was not in the habit of wandering about the Gardens after they were closed at night—but he did like being singled out for a privilege that nobody else was likely to get. Lord Esher was Secretary to His Majesty's Office of Works, and he was able to persuade the Ranger of the Gardens, the Duke of Cambridge, to grant this unique request. The key was cut and presented to Mr J. M. Barrie.

A few days later there was sad news from Kirriemuir. His sister Sara had died suddenly. She was not yet fifty, and Barrie, always strongly affected by family bereavement, was greatly upset. Mary went with him to Kirriemuir for the funeral, and both found the experience painful, for Dr Ogilvy was over eighty, and now had no companion. They stayed long enough to make sure that the old man would be properly looked after, and returned to London.

Mary, was still enveloped in silences when they were alone. Barrie never discussed his plays or any ideas with her. The only time she regained her old vivacity was when they were entertaining their friends. If Barrie noticed how quiet she had become, he made no comment. He would spend whole days in complete silence himself. He was completely engrossed in the fairy play; he had made hundreds of notes, and was at last thinking of beginning the first act.

*   *   *

By 1904 the friendship between the Barries and the Davieses had grown even closer, though they would no longer be within walking distance of each other's houses, as the Davieses were moving to the country. Arthur was becoming a little more prosperous, and had decided on Berkhamsted, as he felt the country air would be better for the boys. Also, his finances did not warrant his sending them to an expensive public school, and they could go to Berkhamsted School as day boys. This was an ex-grammar school of ancient foundation which had been worked up by a distinguished headmaster, the Reverend T. C. Fry, to the status of a good public school.

They found a charming house in Berkhamsted, which Peter Davies describes:

The house was a mighty nice one, in its unassuming way; Elizabethan, standing a little back from the broad High Street, covered over, it's true, with rather unattractive roughcast, but not much altered or restored . . . That garden, with its plum trees on the walls, and luscious mulberry tree, and lovely pale wistaria by the stable, and the little orchard at the end . . . the big fir-tree which grew on the bank at the back of the lawn . . . A good deal had to be done to the house in the way of interior decoration and furnishing, all no doubt a delight to S., who had a talent far in advance of her day for such things, hardly less conspicuous, indeed, than her talent—which I think amounted to genius—for clothes. And all done with very little money; simply by the exercise of *flair*. So that in one way and another, while the house, viewed from the outside, was a very pleasing example of English Tudor architecture, it revealed itself, when you went in, not in the least as a museum or 'period' affair or a place to make you catch your breath at its exquisite beauty, but as a gracious, happy, pretty, comfortable home.

Sylvia was soon busy with the move, and in order to make things easier, Mary Hodgson went to Ramsgate with the two younger boys; George and Jack were at Leinster Corner, the Barries having gone to Black Lake Cottage.

Barrie had almost finished the new play. He had thought of several titles, but he was calling it *Peter and Wendy*—for there was a girl in the elaborate plot. A motherly, out-of-this-world little girl, and if she did not wear a magenta pinafore, she still had a strong resemblance to another little girl who, long ago, had been built into James Barrie's mind.

When he had finished the script, Barrie took it along to read to Beerbohm Tree, who was known for his elaborate productions at His Majesty's Theatre. *Peter and Wendy* required a company of about fifty, and five sets, which meant a large theatre and a manager prepared to spend money. Tree did not like the play at all. He agreed that it was original, and thought privately that it was too original—a farrago.

Barrie decided to wait until Charles Frohman came over for his annual visit. Meanwhile, he wrote another play, which he called *Alice-Sit-By-The-Fire*, a whimsical-sentimental piece centred on the relationship between the mother-heroine, Alice, and her daughter, Amy. Barrie had Ellen Terry in mind for Alice, and had already decided on the line he would take with Frohman over the two plays.

The American impresario retained a suite at the Savoy, and when he arrived on his next visit, Barrie called on him and laid his cards on the table. He knew that *Peter and Wendy* would be a very expensive production and might even lose money, but if Frohman cared to take the risk, there was this other play, *Alice-Sit-By-The-Fire*, which would probably recoup any loss. He left both scripts with the American.

Charles Frohman never did things by halves. *Alice* would fit Miss Ellen Terry like a glove, he was sure, and as for *Peter and Wendy*, he was enchanted with it. Here was something completely new in the theatre. Enthusiastically he declared that he would put it into production, and spend as much money as was needed. He wasted no time. Dion Boucicault, son and namesake of a famous Victorian playwright, had established himself as a producer—then a new figure in the world of the theatre, where productions had usually been put together by an actor-manager playing the leading part. Boucicault had already proved in other productions that a skilful co-ordinator of all that went on in a play was of immense value, and Frohman was the man to encourage a new talent of this kind. Boucicault would produce. His sister, Nina Boucicault, was exactly right for the part of Peter Pan. Barrie's first choice for Captain Hook was Seymour Hicks, with Hicks's wife, Ellaline Terriss, as Wendy. Miss Terriss, however, was expecting a baby, and Hicks did not want to play without his wife.

Hilda Trevelyan was chosen for Wendy, and Gerald du Maurier for Captain Hook. The character was based on Captain Swarthy of *The Boy Castaways*, but Barrie had injected more character into the swaggering Swarthy, and du Maurier created him in the round. Daphne du Maurier, in her book about her father, *Gerald: A Portrait*, says:

He was a tragic and rather ghastly creation who knew no peace, and whose soul was in torment; a dark shadow; a sinister dream; a bogey of fear who lives in the grey recesses of every small boy's mind. All boys had their Hooks, as Barrie knew; he was the phantom who came by night and stole his way into their murky dreams. He was the spirit of Stevenson and of Dumas, and he was Father-but-for-the-grace-of-God; a lonely spirit that was terror and inspiration in one. And, because he had imagination and a spark of genius, Gerald made him alive.

William Nicholson was invited to design the costumes and the sets, and he could make them as elaborate as he wished. Frohman intended this to be a production which would be remembered: Barrie was a genius, a marvel! Charles Frohman was as capable of hero-worship as his own little hero, and money was to be no problem where the artistic integrity of this wonderful play was concerned. Nicholson was a portrait-painter as well as a scenic artist, and he painted Barrie that year. The author was forty-four and still very thin—a wisp of a man. The large forehead and deep-sunk, shadowed eyes were the most striking features in the face, where the mouth was hidden by the drooping moustache he had worn for many years.

Rehearsals began; but Barrie was revising *Alice* at the same time. His energy and powers of concentration were astounding. He and Frohman went to Smallhythe in Kent to visit Ellen Terry at her cottage. Barrie did not take the script of *Alice* with him, as the revision was not complete, but, as the actress wrote in her auto-biography, 'he told it better than he wrote it.' Ellen Terry had not had any good parts lately, and she agreed to do the play.

There were six exhausting weeks of rehearsals for *Peter Pan*, as the play was now called. A very pretty American actress, Pauline Chase, played the First Twin in the production; she was later to play Peter for eight years running. Barrie came to most of the rehearsals, following every detail, and endearing himself to the Lost Boys by gathering them round him during the intervals and telling them story after story. The dog Nana was a constant delight: never had such a dog been seen on the stage before. The actor who played the part, Arthur Lupino, came to Leinster Corner at Barrie's request to study Luath. They had a session in the dining-room. Luath walked when bidden, wagged his tail, barked, beat his feet on the floor—one of the tricks which Mary had taught him.

Arthur Lupino studied the dog's movements carefully, and rehearsed so assiduously that he was able to reproduce them with amazing fidelity. Mary took Luath and Lupino to a studio in Drury Lane where experts specialized in making-up actors to look like dogs for the stage. They sketched Luath, and took a sample of his thick, furry coat; the dog-covering they produced later was exactly like the original.

Peter Pan, or the Boy Who Wouldn't Grow Up was produced at the Duke of York's Theatre on December 27th, 1904. It was a shorter version than that seen in later years; the lift which was to raise The Little House to the Tree Tops was not ready, and one of the flying devices was not considered safe. But even in its truncated form, it set all London talking. The _Morning Post_ called it 'not so much a play as a spree', the _Daily Telegraph_ found it 'so true, so natural, so touching that it brought the audience to the writer's feet and held them captives there'. But Anthony Hope, a friend of Barrie's, was heard to murmur as he left the theatre: 'Oh, for an hour of Herod.'

A cable went off to Frohman, who had gone back to America, giving news of the success, and he cabled back his congratulations. When he came over to London later, he saw that here was a vehicle for Maude Adams in the States. And he foresaw that the play would make money, a great deal of it, until well into the future.

He took _Peter Pan_ off in April, in order to begin rehearsals at the Duke of York's for _Alice-Sit-By-The-Fire_, but he announced at the same time that _Peter Pan_ would be revived in December, and that seats could be booked throughout the year for the revival.

Ellen Terry did what she could with _Alice_, but it had what one critic called a ludicrously stupid plot, and not even this legendary actress could make it a success. After a few months' run it went on tour: Ellen Terry needed the work. In America, Ethel Barrymore was persuaded by Frohman, with great tact, to try _Alice_, but she had no more fortune with it than Ellen Terry had had. It was never one of Barrie's favourites among his plays, and he put it out of his mind and went on with the next thing, as usual.

*   *   *

The Davieses now had five sons; Nicholas was born in 1903. The home at Berkhamsted was perfect for the family, and Arthur Davies must have reflected with some relief that Leinster Corner was a long way away, and that the insistently friendly playwright who had been thrusting himself into their lives for several years would now be too much occupied with his successful plays and proliferating commitments to invade his, Arthur's, privacy so often.

He was mistaken. Distance made no difference to James Barrie. He wrote to Sylvia from Black Lake Cottage on September 15th, 1904:

My dear Jocelyn,
If K[illegible] is right I think you should get her. She sounds promising. The thing to do is to have her sent to you on trial, so do that. I think the fact of her being a pony will comfort you. I'm writing our friend 'Mart' that you are having a pony, also writing to Windover to hurry the cart. I suppose there's no reason agnst having the pony before the cart comes. If K [illegible] doesn't suit you might try the roan. This is a very horsey letter. Yoicks, gee whoa, there.

Your loving,

J.M.B.

At the end of the letter there is a scribbled representation of a horse in full gallop, bearing a female figure with an infant in her arms, and four male figures of decreasing size behind her.

Peter Davies: I imagine the lavish gift of a pony and cart—a sort of governess cart, as I recall it—was bestowed as a tangible recognition of indebtedness to 'Sylvia and Arthur Llewelyn Davies and their boys (my boys)' for their contribution to *The Little White Bird* and *Peter Pan*. It must have been rather difficult for A . . . note the signature. The pony with the illegible name was either re-christened, or, more probably, rejected in favour of the roan; at any rate the animal finally selected was called Crichton.

I wonder if any sharp words passed between A. and S. before this gift was accepted? One of the many things which conspire to lend a certain unreality to childish recollection is that it is almost impossible to me to conceive a quarrel between these two. But on the other hand it is equally impossible to believe that relations weren't strained, and at pretty frequent intervals, too, by the infiltrations of this astounding little Scotch genius of a 'lover'.

Barrie wrote to Peter Davies from Leinster Corner on November 3rd:

My dear Peter,
Sometimes when I am walking in the Gardens with Luath I see a vision and I cry Hurray, there's Peter, and then Luath barks joyously and we run to the vision and then it turns out to be not Peter but just another boy, and then I cry like a water cart and Luath hangs his sorrowful tail.

Oh, dear, how I wish you were here, and then it would be London
again.

Goodbye.

Write soon.

Your loving
godfather

J.M.B.

Peter Davies: Luath reached immortality as Nana in *Peter Pan* . . . J.M.B.
was never technically my godfather, perhaps because I was never
christened, and I daresay this is the only occasion on which he so signed
himself.

*   *   *

In April, 1905, Barrie was the moving spirit in organizing a banquet
in honour of Frederick Greenwood's seventy-fifth birthday.
Greenwood was no longer one of the leading London editors; his
departure from the *St James's Gazette* had been the beginning
of a long decline in his fortunes, and he was unknown to the
new generation of newspaper men. Barrie, however, had not forgotten what he owed to Greenwood, and gathered together an
influential committee which included Thomas Hardy and Andrew
Lang.

The banquet was a great success; there were speeches from the
eminent, and Barrie told the story of 'the Greenwood hat'. He was
adept at projecting his image by now: he knew what his audiences
expected, and he gave it to them. No, no, no, he would say to eager
seekers after lions to grace the top tables of dinners, he was no
speech-maker, he begged to be excused. But he could relent with
splendid modesty when pressed, and a delightful evening would be
had by all, including the guest of honour.

Although Barrie worked very hard, he made time for social
occasions with men he liked. He descrbied his first meeting with
Thomas Hardy:

Hardy I first met at a club in Piccadilly where he had asked me to lunch.
It's a club where they afterwards adjourn to the smoking room and talk
for a breathless hour or two about style. Hardy's small contribution made
no mark, but I thought 'How interesting that the only man among you
who doesn't know about style is the only one among you who has got
one.' Style is the way an artist paints his pictures—no, it can't be as easy
as that . . . Hardy could scarcely look out of a window in the twilight
without seeing something hitherto hidden from mortal eye. That must

The Llewelyn Davies boys—'The Five': *left to right* George, Jack, Peter, Michael, Nicholas.

Duke of York's Theatre.

ST. MARTIN'S LANE, W.C.

Proprietors ... ... Mr. & Mrs. FRANK WYATT.

Sole Lessee and Manager ... ... CHARLES FROHM

EVERY AFTERNOON at 2.30, and EVERY EVENING at 8.30,

CHARLES FROHMAN

PRESENTS

PETER PAN

OR

THE BOY WHO WOULDN'T GROW UP.

A Play in Three Acts, by

J. M. BARRIE.

Peter Pan	Miss NINA BOUCICAULT
Mr. Darling	Mr. GERALD du MAURIE
Mrs. Darling	Miss DOROTHEA BAIR
Wendy Moira Angela Darling	Miss HILDA TREVELYAN
John Napoleon Darling	Master GEORGE HERSE
Michael Nicholas Darling	Miss WINIFRED GEOGHEGA
Nana	Mr. ARTHUR LUPIN
Tinker Bell	Miss JANE WRE

Tootles		Miss JOAN BURNET
Nibs		Miss CHRISTINE SILVE
Slightly		Mr. A. W. BASKCOM
Curly	(Members of Peter's Band)	Miss ALICE DUBARR
1st Twin		Miss PAULINE CHAS
2nd Twin		Miss PHYLLIS BEADO

Jas. Hook ... ... (The Pirate Captain) ...	Mr. GERALD du MAURIE
Smee		Mr. GEORGE SHELTO
Gentleman Starkey		Mr. SYDNEY HARCOUR
Cookson		Mr. CHARLES TREVO
Cecco	(Pirates)	Mr. FREDERICK ANNERLE
Mullins		Mr. HUBERT WILL
Jukes		Mr. JAMES ENGLIS
Noodler		Mr. JOHN KE

Great Big Little Panther	(Redskins)	Mr. PHILIP DARW
Tiger Lily		Miss MIRIAM NESBIT
Liza ... ... (Author of the Play)	Miss ELA Q. MA

Beautiful Mothers, Redskins, Pirates, Crocodile, Eagle, Ostrich, Pack of Wolves, by Misses Mary Mayfren, V
Addison, Irene Rooke, Gladys Stewart, Kitty Malone, Marie Park, Elsa Sinclair, Christine Lawrence,
Maddison, Gladys Carrington, Laura Barradell, Daisy Murch. Messrs. E. Kirby, S. Spencer, G. Malvern, J. Gra
Masters S. Grata, A. Ganker, D. Ducrow, C. Lawton, W. Scott, G. Henson, R. Franks. E. Marini, P. Gicardo, A. B

ACT I.—OUR EARLY DAYS.	**ACT III.—WE RETURN TO OUR DISTRACTED I**
Inside the House. (*Mr. W. Harford*).	Scene 1.—The Pirate Ship. (*Mr. W. Harford*).
ACT II.—THE NEVER, NEVER, NEVER LAND.	Scene 2.—A last glimpse of the Redskins.
Scene 1.—The House we built for Wendy. (*Mr. W. Hann*).	Scene 3.—How to know your Mother.
The Curtain will be lowered for a few moments.	Scene 4.—Outside the House.
Scene 2.—The Redskins' Camp. (*Mr. W. Hann*)	Scene 5.—The Tree Tops. (*Mr. W. Hann*.)
Scene 3.—Our Home under the Ground. ,,	

The Play produced under the Direction of Mr. DION BOUCICAULT.

General Manager ... ... (For CHARLES FROHMAN) ... ... W. LESTOCC

The Esquimaux, Pirates and Indian Costumes designed by Mr. W. NICHOLSON, and executed by Messrs. B. J. SIMMONS, 7, Kin
CoventGarden. Miss Boucicault's Dress designed by HENRY J. FORD. Miss Baird's Costumes by Madame HAYWARD 64, New
Miss Trevelyan's Dresses designed and executed by SHEBA, 17, Sloane Street. The Beautiful Mothers' Dresses designed and exe
Madame J. BLANCQUAERT & Co., 38 & 39, South Molton Street. The Dances invented and arranged by Mr. W. WARD
The Music composed and arranged by Mr. JOHN CROOK. The Flying Machines supplied and worked by Mr. G. KIRBY.
supplied by Mr. LOUIS LABHART. 12, Queen's Square, W.C. Stage Mechanist, Mr. H. THOMPSON. Electrician, Mr. C. HAMB
Property Master, Mr. W. BURDICK.

Stage Manager	DUNCAN McRAE	Musical Director ...	JOHN CR
Business Manager	... ...	JAMES W. MATH

Extract from the Rules made by the Lord Chamberlain

(1.) The name of the actual and responsible Manager of the Theatre must be printed on every play bill. (2.) The Public can leave th
at the end of the performance by all exit and entrance doors, which must open outwards (3.) The fire-proof screen to the p
opening will be lowered at least once during every performance to ensure its being in proper working order. (4.) Smoking is not perm
Auditorium. (5.) All gangways, passages and staircases must be kept free from chairs or any other obstructions, whether permanent or t

ICES TEA AND COFFEE can be had of the Attendants.

Programme for the first production of *Peter Pan*.

have helped his style. He has been called a pessimist. Surely pessimists are people without any root to them. Was he that? . . .
Hardy could be easily hurt by not-ill-intended-pens. He never desired his fame. If it could have been separated from his poesy he would have given it to any beggar at the door.

At Easter, 1905, Sylvia Davies with two of her sons, Jack and Michael, went to Normandy with the Barries, while her husband took George and Peter to his parents' home at Kirkby, and the baby Nico remained with Mary Hodgson. Peter Davies wrote:

It has always seemed to me, looking back, that this split holiday can hardly have been agreed to without a good deal of argument and protest . . . contemporaries thought the whole business pretty odd by this time. But after all, what do we know? I have no letters referring to the Normandy visit, which Jack remembers well.

If contemporaries thought the whole business 'pretty odd', some of the comments may have reached the ears of Mrs James Barrie. She was, as usual, her cool, pleasant self, and, in her way, as unapproachable where her inmost thoughts and feelings were concerned as her husband. She had found something besides Black Lake Cottage to occupy her; after a short training in fine hand-crafts, she had rented a studio in Kensington and was doing some artistic enamel-work. There were several artists' guilds in London; the influence of William Morris and others had raised the standard of hand-crafted work of all kinds, and good metal and enamel work found a ready sale in the expensive shops. Mary did not need the money but she did need something to do. She spent a great deal of time in her studio when she was in London, until warmer weather sent her down to Black Lake Cottage and the house-parties and the cricket matches where she was required to play the rôle of hostess.
In America, *Peter Pan* had opened its run in Washington, going on to Frohman's Empire Theatre in New York. Maude Adams, in a tunic and breeches of her own devising, a hat with a feather in it, and a boyish touch of white at the throat which was to become known to the future as the Peter Pan collar, brought her own special quality to the part. The play was an enormous success. In the American magazine *Outlook* on November 21st, the dramatic critic wrote:

After the indecencies of a Zaza and Sappho, the scarcely less veiled and

J.M.B.   K more insidious indecencies of the plays presented by Mrs Patrick Campbell, the horror of 'Ghosts', the tropical passions of 'Monna Vanna', the sinister cynicism of 'Man and Superman' and of 'Mrs Warren's Profession', Mr Barrie's 'Peter Pan' now being played at the Empire Theatre, is like a breath of fresh air. It is not to be judged by the ordinary standards of drama, it is a bit of pure phantasy by the writer who, since the death of Robert Louis Stevenson, has most truly kept the heart and mind of a child.

After a seven months' run at the Empire Theatre, Frohman started the play on a series of tours which lasted for most of the year. Maude Adams identified herself completely with her part: she was acclaimed in every city, and the theatres were sold out at most performances. Frohman was, of course, delighted. Money was flowing in a never-ending stream to his and Barrie's coffers. Frohman liked making money as much as he liked spending it freely on ventures which he believed in, but what pleased him most about *Peter Pan*'s success was the fact that his famous little friend was growing even more famous.

And Barrie? It is doubtful whether he thought about either the money or the fame. He was re-writing again. He had already altered and improved the original script, but still he was not satisfied. Work —action—*doing* something all the time—that was the motive power of his existence. Finding something to fill up sixty seconds in the minute, sixty minutes in the hour. That was what life had become.

Preparations were going on in London for the December revival of *Peter Pan*. Nina Boucicault, who had expected to play Peter again, found to her dismay that she had been replaced by another young actress, Cecilia Loftus. No reason was given: Mr Barrie had made the change, and Mr Barrie's word was law. An impulse? Barrie could make important decisions on the merest whim, and stick to them, no matter how other people were affected. Nina Boucicault's name remains in theatrical history as the first Peter Pan, but she never played the part again.

*   *   *

Peter Davies, aged eight, wrote to his aunt, Margaret Llewelyn Davies from Egerton House, Berkhamsted, on 31st December, 1905:

Dear Aunt Margaret,
I heard that George was kicked off the pony, little boys ought not to be

allowed to do such dangerous things. Michael has a bad cold, but is getting better . . . I have got two guinea pigs from Mother, one is black and the other black and brown . . . Michael got a bird like a canary and it flies about in the nursery . . . Nicholas squeaks to it . . . Perhaps Mother is going to Paris this week, and then perhaps I am going to have dinner with Father, perhaps, for the first time . . .

Barrie wrote to Sylvia Davies from Leinster Corner on January 3rd, 1906:

Dearest Jocelyn,

As if I could be angry with you for caring for your children! I don't think it would have been the thing to leave them just now, and we can go to Paris any time.

I hope Nicholas is getting better and that Michael is obstreperous once again. How I love that boy.

We could not ring you up today, as your line is broken. I should be so glad to know that you are feeling well yourself again.

Whenever they are able for P. Pan, it awaits them.

Your loving,

J.M.B.

Peter Davies: Evidently the Paris trip mentioned in the last letter had to be deferred owing to childish ailments, which were (I think in Michael's case) sufficiently protracted to make the visit to P. Pan impracticable; with the astonishing and most completely Mr Barrie-like consequence that P. Pan came to Egerton House instead.

Peter Davies sent a letter to his grandfather for his eightieth birthday, February 26th, 1906; he wrote on the 25th, his own ninth birthday:

Dear Grandfather,

I hope you will have a nice birthday, it is my birthday today, and although I am not quite so old as you, I hope to be soon. I hope I shall come to Kirkby next summer or Christmas . . . Some actors and actresses from Peter Pan came down on Father's birthday in two large motor cars to act in the nursery. Peter Pan is about a boy ran away from home the day he was born, and lived in the Never-never-never-Land. One day he came back to the house of some people called the Darlings, and in the night took away the three children away [*sic*]. The father was so sorry he had taken the dog, Nana, out of the room that he lived in the kennel. Then one day they came back, and Wendy, the girl, was allowed to go to Peter, every Spring cleaning.

Wishing you many happy returns of the day, from Peter.

P.s. I am sending you a programme of Peter Pan in Michael's nursery.

Barrie wrote to Peter Davies from Leinster Corner on February 25th, 1906:

My dear Peter,
Hurrah for your birthday. Nine years ago the world was a dreary blank. It was like the round of tissue paper the clown holds up for the lady in the circus to leap through, and then you came banging through it with a Houp-la! and we have all been busy ever since.

I expect twenty years from now there will be a half-holiday given at the Berkhampstead [*sic*] School because it is the birthday of the famous pupil, Mr (now Lieut-General) Peter Davies, V.C.

I am to get a knife tomorrow to send you. I expect it will draw blood before you lose it. If you are still on friendly terms with Primus, &c. give them my comps.

Your loving friend,

J.M.B.

Some weeks later, Barrie's professional life was temporarily disrupted by what was for him a desolating experience. The affairs of Addison Bright, the literary agent he had trusted for many years, were disclosed as being in financial chaos.

There had been rumours for some time. Barrie had heard them but had immediately discounted them as malicious gossip; Addison Bright was the last person to do anything dishonourable. Frohman, who had had business dealings with the agent for years, was as indignant as Barrie at the ugly stories being whispered around.

The rumours persisted, and in the end turned out to be true. Hard-working, go-ahead, a bit of a genius in his own way, Bright must also have had a streak of the adventurer in him, for he began juggling with his clients' accounts. He was agent for many of the leading playwrights, as well as for men just making their way in the theatre, and enormous sums passed through his hands. Friendly, bland, confident in manner, he was not one to rouse suspicions of malversation; yet investigations had been quietly going on, and the day came when everything was disclosed. He had misappropriated nearly thirty thousand pounds. The extraordinary part of the whole business was the fact that he had not spent the money: most of it was still in his bank account. His action could only come under the heading of temporary insanity.

Barrie had been one of the chief victims; sixteen thousand pounds of the total had been abstracted from the royalties which Bright handled for him. Barrie was not concerned about the money. He had always liked his agent, and naively assumed that if the unfortunate man returned the money to the authors who had been defrauded, all would go on as before. Some of the other playwrights were not so charitable. Wrong had been committed, justice must be done, and they demanded a prosecution. Nothing that Barrie or Frohman could do on Bright's behalf made any difference. Proceedings were started. Addison Bright could not face what lay before him, and he committed suicide.

Apart from the personal shock, Barrie was now saddled with the appalling prospect of looking after his own financial affairs. Gilmour, though willing to go on assisting him with income tax tangles and investments, could not be expected to deal with theatre accounts, about which he knew nothing. It was with great relief that Barrie learned that Addison Bright's younger brother, Golding Bright, was straightening out the dead man's affairs, and would be launching out himself as a theatrical agent when the debts were paid. There was a gasp from the literary world at this turn of events, but Barrie's only feeling was one of relief: he need no longer do accounts. He thankfully left everything to Golding Bright. (Barrie was with him for over thirty years, and there was never a breath of suspicion against Addison Bright's brother.)

Meanwhile there were notebooks to be filled, speeches to be made at dinners, and, above all, his friends the Davieses.

Chapter 12

TRAGEDY

PETER DAVIES writes in his papers:

If this was a proper book, as opposed to a mere desultory compilation, there ought to be a division here: the end of a section or 'part'. For with the next letter begins the truly morgue-like matter which, besides providing a chief reason why I undertook this job makes me wonder more than any other element in it whether the job is one that was worth undertaking at all. However, I may as well go through with it now.

Most of the very full series of letters which follows, dealing with A's illness and death, came to me from Margaret Ll. D. a year or two before her own death. I may as well quote here her covering letter to me at the time, which sums things up pretty adequately.

'I have lately been going through (and destroying)' she wrote, 'a large quantity of letters and papers, and among them are records of your father at different times of his life. I feel it would not be right to destroy these without giving you the opportunity of saying whether you would like to have them. To me, the knowledge of what Arthur was is one of my most precious possessions, showing one the rare beauty that happiness and suffering may bring out in a life . . . Dear Peter, you may feel you would rather not revive such sadness, and that your life is too full and the world's state too difficult, not to occupy all your time and thought with immediate doings and happenings. If so, do not hesitate to say so. Maurice[1] finds he cannot bear to dwell on what is painful in the old days— but he agrees most strongly with me that you should be asked if you would like me to send you what I have. You may feel you already know the man your father was, and what people thought of him . . . I am sorry not to have put Arthur's letters in better order, but you will understand that the task I have had, and still have, with the accumulations of years, has been a little difficult, especially for a 77-yearer! . . .'

For better or worse, I said I would like to have the letters. I still feel doubtful about the propriety of making copies of them, particularly Sylvia's which have for me a greater poignancy and privacy even than

1. Margaret's brother, Maurice Llewelyn Davies.

A's. But of their deep family interest there is no question, and it seems a pity they should perish utterly after being kept all these years.

In May, 1906, came the first premonition of the tragedy which was to alter the course of several lives. On May 26th, Arthur Davies wrote to his sister Margaret that he had been hoping to manage a visit to Kirkby at Whitsun:

but I am doomed to spend Whitsuntide less agreeably—in lying up for a small operation. I have a slight swelling inside of the face which is beyond the dentist's skill, and on his advice I consulted an expert in cheek and jaw. He is going to perform on Friday, and I shall stay at a nursing place till the following Tuesday. Probably the cause of the trouble is the root of an old dead tooth, possibly a minute fragment of a tooth long pulled out. The surgeon cannot be sure without operating, and he says the swelling will certainly not go away of itself . . . There is no ground for anxiety, but I can imagine pleasanter ways of spending money in June . . . I expect to be more or less recovered after a week.
Sylvia will probably leave with her friends for Paris on Tuesday, June 5, if I am fit to be left.

Sylvia did not go away to Paris with her friends—the Barries—for after the small exploratory operation it was found necessary to perform a more serious operation a week later, and a further minor operation on June 18th. The swelling had not been an abscess, but had turned out to be a growth, and one of a serious kind called sarcoma. It meant removing half the upper jaw and palate. Sarcoma, a manifestation of cancer, was not really curable.

Arthur faced his ordeal with the greatest courage. He wrote to his father that his speech would be very much affected until it was possible to insert an artificial jaw:

It is curious how quickly one's standpoint changes, and one ceases to look at things from the point of view of one who regards all such diseases as incredible and horrible. But still we need all our fortitude. The infinite kindness of all the family and of many friends is a great support. Sylvia, of course, is brave and utterly devoted. If I was not obliged to help her, I could sometimes hardly endure the suspense. Barrie has been wonderful to us—we look on him as a brother. He is here tonight as well as Crompton[1] and Margaret.
Peter Davies: I think it is quite clear that, saddled as he was with a family of five, A. had had no chance of saving money. He was now faced, not
1. Arthur's younger brother.

only with immediate and complete cessation of earning power caused by the operation and slow recovery, and the permanent diminution of earning power which, at best, would result from the impediment to his speech, but with all the ghastly expense of surgeons' and specialists' fees as well. Both J. Ll. D.[1] and Emma du M.[2] helped, and I think I have heard —but have no evidence of it—that contributions were made by various brothers. But it is certain, both on the evidence and from one's own instinctive knowledge of the situation, that from the moment the seriousness of things was revealed, J.M.B. stepped in to play the leading part; and played it in the grand manner. It's not easy to weigh the whole of this matter up. I can sympathize in a way with the point of view that it was the last straw for A. that he should have had to accept charity from the strange little genius who had become an increasing irritation to him in recent years. But on the whole I disagree. We don't really know how deep the irritation went; and even if it went deep, I am convinced that the kindness and devotion of which J.M.B. gave such overwhelming proof from now on, far more than outweighed all that, and that the money and promise of future financial responsibility he was so ready with—and with what charm and tact he must have overcome any resistance!—were an incalculable comfort to the doomed Arthur as well as to Sylvia in her anguish. I have no precise documentary proof as to the financial side, but the circumstantial evidence is crystal clear, and I have little doubt that the resultant ease of mind as to the future of his wife and children did more to make A. Ll. D.'s last months bearable than anything else could have done.

Crompton Llewelyn Davies wrote to his father on June 8th, saying that the operation was over, but they couldn't yet say how things were going, adding: 'His courage and serenity were so great that it gave others courage, I felt—and instead of requiring help he seemed able to give it.'

Barrie was constantly at the house, and visiting the nursing home. Arthur appeared to be getting on well, and though he couldn't speak he was able to write. In a letter to his father on June 11th he told of the favourable progress he was making, and added that Sylvia was constantly with him, and Barrie never wearied in kindness.

Practically the whole of Barrie's time was now devoted to the Davies family. He visited Arthur every day, read the newspapers to him, was always on hand to do anything the sick man wanted. On June 16th, Sylvia wrote to her son Michael, who was having his sixth birthday:

1. Arthur's father.   2. Sylvia's mother.

I don't like being away from you on your dear birthday, but I shall see you in a few hours . . . Father does so want to be back with his sons. He is sleeping now, and I am being very still and writing this letter by his bed . . . Mr Barrie is our fairy prince, much the best fairy prince that was ever born because he is *real*.

Loving

MOTHER.

When Arthur had recovered sufficiently from the major operation, he had another minor one on the glands. On 26th June he was writing to Peter that he had been taken out that morning in a bath-chair 'like a feeble old man, with Mother and Mr Barrie walking by the side. We shall probably come on Thursday afternoon in Mr Barrie's motor-car, if it is fine. I suppose you know that I cannot talk properly yet, and you will all have to try and guess what I am saying.'

Barrie had now become 'Jimmy' to Arthur. Writing to his sister on June 27th, he told her he expected to come to see her on the following afternoon, 'motoring, if it is fine, with Jimmy'. There was a great deal of mention at this period of Barrie's motor-car, the open Lanchester, driven by the elegant chauffeur, Frederick.

On July 5th, Barrie, who had gone down to Black Lake Cottage, wrote to Sylvia from there:

Dearest Jocelyn,

I am conceiving you both in London today and I fear Arthur is having a bad time. If they put something into his mouth what I am afraid of is that it may seem pretty right at the time and gradually become unendurable after he is home. There is a great deal of human nature in Gerald's standpoint which I think is this, that after surgeons and their like have been working their will, we should be allowed to butt at them with our heads. I shall depend on one of you writing tomorrow to let me know what happened today. I seem so far away from you now, and feel as if you are not so safe as when I am by. That is the feeling that makes you in your heart hate all of us who propose to take a few of the five away for a 'season' (as Jack puts it) and it is strange that I should feel so now about Arthur, but I do. When I was in the garden I had no fears, but now I see that gate pushed open softly and rows of operators trying to steal in. I love Roughton [the surgeon] but there are six of us prepared to receive him with cries of Duck and a hard butt on the head. So do write a line often.

It has been a terrible month to yourself. I had so hoped that Jocelyn would always be spared such a time. 'Sylvia in her blue dress.'

My love to Arthur and his brown patch [the patch he wore over his eye] and to dear Jocelyn.

Your

J.M.B.

Peter Davies does not comment on this astonishing letter—perhaps not unnaturally.

George Davies, now thirteen, was being sent to Eton to sit for the scholarship examination at this time. The boys had all been very happy at Berkhamsted, but with Arthur's connections at Eton, they hoped George would have a chance of going there; it would not be possbile, however, unless he was awarded a scholarship. He did not, in fact, get it—he could not reach the required standard.

Peter Davies says: 'I guess—it is no more than a guess—that within a short time . . . both Hugh Macnaghten and J.M.B. came forward with offers to help towards George's Eton expenses as an Oppidan.'

Sylvia wrote to Barrie at Black Lake Cottage from Egerton House on July 21st, 1906:

Darling J.

It *is* such good news, and I know you will be glad—seems almost the old voice. The thing of course is not comfortable yet, but it will be altered from time to time. It was fine to happen on George's birthday . . .

I like to tell you—but only you—as you understand so well! A. has been seeing Lord Justice Vaughan Williams, as V.W. has been talking to the Lord Chancellor about him, but it is all very difficult for Arthur to know what is best for the future. He will like talking to you at Rustington.

Your JOCELYN.

Arthur was well enough for the family to be able to go for a summer holiday. Sylvia's mother had taken a large house at Rustington. Barrie went, too. Jack, who had mumps, was left behind in London in the care of Mary Hodgson. Arthur wrote to his sister on August 6th:

Cudlow House,

Rustington.

I look on this week as an interval between Mumpses. By the end of this week I expect some of these boys here to begin to swell, and then probably we shall arrange for Jack to join us and finish his convalescence here . . . We have plenty of bathing, and the boys play endless cricket and lawn tennis in the garden. Just now we have an invasion by some friends of Jimmy's; Nicholson, an artist and his family, one of them being of an age

with George, and a large game of cricket is going on in the garden . . .
The sea has become thoroughly warm, and we all enjoy the water very
much.

He wrote to Margaret again on August 23rd:

We all, except poor George, bathe with great enjoyment in the warm sea,
Sylvia from a tent, and the rest of us from an adjacent beach . . . Jimmy is
still with us, very good in all the amusements. Mary Barrie is motoring in
France with Molly Muir . . .

Peter Davies: Although A. was able to bathe, I don't think he could take
much part in the lawn tennis and cricket games which went on in the
garden . . .
    The presence of J.M.B. at Cudlow House throughout those holidays
was a queerish business, when you come to think of it: as odd a variation
of the *ménage à trois* as ever there was, one would say. I think by now A.
had surrendered utterly and was reconciled, for all sorts of reasons. But
how strange the mentality of J.M.B., whose devotion to S. seems to have
thriven on her utter devotion to A., as well as on his own admiration for
him. It would be misleading to call his devotion more dog-like than man-
like; there was too much understanding and perception in it—not to
mention the element of masterfulness. And how about Mary Barrie
meanwhile? I suspect that on the whole the state of affairs suited her well
enough, and I say this in no disparaging sense.

On September 6th, Arthur was writing to his sister telling her that
they were at the end of their stay at Rustington.

We have succumbed to an invitation to go to Scotland with Jimmy for the
close of the holidays . . . We are to stay at a small village called Fortingall,
in Glen Lyon, 2½ miles from Loch Tay among high mountains (especially
Ben Lawers and Schiehallion), and surrounded by burns in which the
boys will fish. They are all prodigiously excited at the prospect.

Peter Davies: The week at Fortingall, crowning a summer holiday
throughout which, apparently, J.M.B. had been with us, constituted a
bridge between the old regime, so to speak, and the new. A purely fishing
venture, it was a momentous enough affair to the boys; not viewed, I
believe, with any tremendous enthusiasm by A. who, apart from anything
else, had absolutely no interest in field sports. I think that when he spoke
of 'succumbing' to Jimmy's invitation, it was no mere figure of speech.
The Highland scenery, however, was a considerable compensation to him.
    And so goodbye to Rustington, so long known and loved by A. and S.,
and so well remembered by J. and me.

On their return to Berkhamsted from Scotland, Arthur Davies wrote a letter of thanks to Barrie:

Egerton House,
Berkhamsted,
Sept 16, 1906.

Dear Jimmy,
You have done wonderful things for us since the beginning of June—most, of course, during June and also in the last week—but at Rustington also you made all the difference to the success and pleasantness of the holiday.
We all hope to see you soon and often,

Yours,

A. Ll. D.

Peter Davies: It is easy enough to read all sorts of undertones into this laconic note. One can say that it expresses gratitude but little cordiality; or even feel that there is a hint of resentment against the fate which had brought about the position in which gratitude had to be incurred and acknowledged in that quarter . . . I am strongly inclined to think, myself, that when he wrote this A. already suspected the recurrence which was confirmed by Roughton only two days later, and was in no mood for much letter writing to anyone less intimate than his sister.

This letter makes it quite clear that J.M.B. had begun to assume a major share of the financial responsibility at the time of the operation, besides devoting almost all his own waking hours to A. and S. That he did so purely because he wanted to, and that he made no less than £44,000 during 1907 alone, constitutes no reason for modifying the view I have arrived at after going through all these documents, namely, that he played an incredibly generous part, and that, but for him, A.'s last months would have been far more unbearable even than they were; and that the gratitude felt by A. for the comfort so afforded him far outweighed the resentment which he must also at times have experienced.

[Peter Davies asked his brother Jack to comment on these views. Jack replied: 'I couldn't at all agree that Father did anything but cordially dislike the Bart. I felt again and again that his remarks and letters simply blazoned the fact that he was doing all he could, poor man, to put up a smoke screen and leave Mother a little less sad and try to show her he didn't grudge the Bart being hale and hearty and rich enough to take over the business . . . I've no doubt at all he was thankful, but he was a proud man, and it must have been extraordinarily bitter for him. And altogether too soft and saintlike to like the little man as well.']

* * *

Jack Davies wanted to go into the Navy, and Barrie wrote to his friend, Captain Scott, to ask if he would use his influence to help get the boy an entrance to Osborne.

Barrie had kept his early enthusiasm for explorers and brave men of action. He had met Robert Falcon Scott the previous year, after Scott had returned from his first Antarctic expedition in the *Discovery*. Scott, who had ambitions to write, was doing a good deal of lecturing on the expedition, and was, in the process, meeting writers, publishers, and other men in the literary world. Because of his ambitions, he was just as keen to meet established writers as they were to meet the man of the moment, and he was asked out everywhere.

Barrie wrote a Preface to his friend Charles Turley Smith's book, *The Voyages of Captain Scott*, which begins:

On the night of my original meeting with Scott he was but lately home from his first adventure into the Antarctic, and my chief recollection of the occasion is that having found the entrancing man I was unable to leave him. In vain he escorted me through the streets of London to my home, for when he had said goodnight I then escorted him to his, and so it went on I know not for how long through the small hours. Our talk was largely a comparison of the life of action (which he pooh-poohed) with the loathly life of those that sit at home (which I scorned); but I also remember he assured me he was of Scots extraction. As the subject never seems to have been resumed between us, I afterwards wondered whether I had drawn this from him with a promise that, if his reply was satisfactory, I would let him go to bed.

Barrie met Scott again at a luncheon party given by Mabel Beardsley, sister of Aubrey Beardsley. A young sculptress, Kathleen Bruce, was also there. She later wrote that she sat between Max Beerbohm and J. M. Barrie, and noticed another guest, Captain Scott: 'Not very young, perhaps 40, but looking very healthy and alert, and I glowed rather suddenly when I clearly saw him ask his neighbour who I was.'

Kathleen Bruce, then under twenty, was a lively, independent-minded girl, daughter of a Canon of York Minster. She had lost both parents when young, and had been brought up by a lawyer great-uncle in Edinburgh. Kathleen got away to London as soon as she could, and went to the Slade School of Art, then on to Paris. She was in Rodin's studio for a time, having decided on sculpture as a career. Back in England in 1906, she set to work to earn a living as a sculptress, and was already making a name for herself when she met Barrie—and Captain Robert Falcon Scott—at Mabel Beardsley's luncheon party.

Scott fell in love with Miss Bruce, and a slow and chequered courtship began. He was not in a position to marry, as he had to support his mother, but in the end they became engaged. They tried, for various reasons, to keep the engagement secret, but A. E. W. Mason knew about it. Before long Barrie heard about it, too, and he was very upset because they hadn't made a point of telling him personally—he had had to learn of it through a third party.

This curious kind of jealousy, with its possessive overtones, was another of the quirks in Barrie's character which made him, as well as many other people, unhappy. Kathleen Bruce did not laugh at it; she had a great deal of intuitive understanding. She sent a note to her fiancé: 'We must not hurt so sensitive and dear a person. Please write *quite* by return of post. He is at Black Lake Cottage, Farnham. As nice a letter as ever you can think of.'

The friendship became firm, and when the occasion arose it was not difficult for Barrie to send Captain Scott a letter asking for his interest in the matter of Jack's entrance to Osborne.

*   *   *

News from Berkhamsted had turned grave. Arthur Davies had had a recurrence of the sarcoma, and no further operation seemed possible. He asked Roughton how far off the end would be, but the surgeon could not guess; pressed, he hazarded six months, possibly a year. There might be little or no suffering, only increasing weakness.

Sylvia had to be told. At first she was so upset she could not face seeing her friends, but in the end she gathered her courage together, with Arthur's help, and tried to take up the threads of everyday life. The family had to know, and Barrie. He wrote to her from Leinster Corner on September 20th:

Dearest Jocelyn,
I mean to come down tomorrow. It may not be before seven or thereabout, as Mr Boucicault is pressing for a meeting in the afternoon. I shall bring a bag, and stay the night or not, just as you like. I am thinking of you and Arthur all the time. I am still full of hope.
                                        Your loving
                                                J.M.B.

Dion Boucicault was in the thick of rehearsals for *Peter Pan*, the third annual production of which would be coming on at the Duke of York's theatre at Christmas. Barrie was still adding to and altering the script, so Boucicault's insistence on the author's presence at rehearsals was understandable. At Berkhamsted Arthur was getting steadily worse. He wrote to his father on September 21st:

Whatever may be in store for me, I hope I shall bear it as befits the son of a brave and wise man. I am troubled for myself, but much more for Sylvia. She is brave to a degree that I should have thought hardly possible, busy all day with endless activities and kindnesses for me and the boys, and all the time the burden is almost heavier than she can bear. Besides her sympathy for me, she shrinks terribly from the loneliness after I am gone . . .
    Barrie's unfailing kindness and tact are a great support to us both.

There followed a week or two when things looked more hopeful; the expected spread of the malady did not materialize as they had been warned it would. On September 26th, Barrie wrote from Leinster Corner:

Dearest Jocelyn,
I feel myself with you and Arthur all the time just now; all day I am looking at you and speaking to you, so that I feel I couldn't be closer were I actually in the house. But for all that I shall come down again this week. I do feel we have a right to be calmer now and to look forward with hope to the future, and I see your much loved house going on and in its old way. Of course I am always wondering how Arthur is feeling, and I hope there will be a letter tomorrow . . . With my love to you both and all the five.

Your

J.M.B.

A few days later he was writing to her again, urging her to take a sleeping draught, as she had had so many broken nights; he had fixed up everything with Dr Rendel, who would be writing to her about the draught. On October 11th, Arthur visited Sir Frederick Treves, one of the best-known surgeons of the day, who said that it was impossible to say positively that there was not a fresh growth behind the new swelling now showing itself, and he advised Arthur to take a course of electrical treatment. Arthur went for treatment for an hour twice a week, and though the swelling did not go down, his general health was, in fact, improved; he was able to go daily to the Temple to do a little work in his chambers. He even managed a six-mile walk with Sylvia and Michael over the Common at home, while the other boys were playing football.

He must have had extraordinary courage. He knew that if and when he recovered, he would no longer be able to practise in the ordinary way at the Bar. He had had to resign his lectureship under the Council of Legal Education, and would be looking for a job. Nevertheless, he refused to give up hope that something would come along. There was a possibility of some other kind of work from the Council of Legal Education, but nothing definite as yet.

By the end of the year, the courage had not diminished but hope was wearing a little thin. He knew he was getting weaker. It was time to face the inexorable consequences of what was happening. The brave visits to his chambers had to stop, for now pain was beginning and he had to have morphia. He wrote to his sister:

I think it will be best for Sylvia to leave as soon as possible and with George and Jack away, she will like to be in London I'm pretty sure—a small house in London. I can't talk about these things to her now—she doesn't like it.

I wrote to Hugh Macnaghten today (about George going to Eton)—I think Sylvia wished it.

Peter Davies: There is no indication, in any letter or note I have, of any financial obligation expressly undertaken by J.M.B. Yet it is difficult to see how either Eton for George or a house in London, or, indeed, any financial arrangement at all, can have been contemplated without some such undertaking. This is a mystery I can't solve, and about which one can speculate as much as one likes but always inconclusively.

Barrie was almost constantly at Arthur's bedside, and the dying man pencilled a number of notes to him as he was unable to speak. One was: 'Do write more things other than plays.'

Peter Davies: On the face of it, a peculiar remark to address to J.M.B. and one which the world would be unlikely to endorse. He was at that time in the process of writing 'What Every Woman Knows', produced 18 months later, and was, after all, the most praised as well as the most successful dramatist alive, but I think that, nevertheless, it was intended as a compliment, and may even have been accepted as one. I think that A. had heard so much that was wise and good and true said by that strange little Scotch genius, that he felt his plays, and indeed his writings generally, did less than justice to the brain that conceived them. The whimsicality that so many people have found intolerable in J.M.B.'s work and which was no doubt of the essence of his genius, and primarily responsible for his achievements and success, was something almost beyond his control as soon as he had a pen or pencil in his hand. His conversation was often on a much higher plane, and doubtless rose to its highest in his talks with the dying Arthur.

Arthur Davies died on 19th April, 1907. Even though his death had been expected, there was a numbed feeling of loss and sorrow in the house which nothing could alleviate.

Peter Davies writes:

The following 'directions' are in S. Ll. D.'s handwriting in ink, on three sheets of unheaded notepaper. They do not seem to have been completed, and there is no date; the envelope in which I found them in J.M.B.'s desk has on it in his handwriting: 'Notes for a Will, written by Mrs Davies at Berkhampstead soon after Mr Davies's death. J. M. Barrie.'

'I may die at any time but it's not likely to happen yet as I am strong I think on the whole. However in case it happens (and God forbid because of my precious boys) I will put down a few directions.

'I wonder if my dear kind Florence Gay[1] would care to make a home for them till they are out in the world (if she is still single) as she is so good and kind to them always and so understanding and she could always ask advice from Margaret and J.M.B. and Trixie[2] and May[3] and all the kind uncles—(also of course Mama if she is still alive). With dear Mary Hodgson, and I hope she will stay with them always (unless she marries) Florrie would find it not too unattractive to think of what I ask . . .

'I hope they will marry and have children and live long and happily and be content to be poor if it should have to be, and that they will always be very careful (whatever incomes they have) to live within their means. Also that they will realize that there is nothing so perfect as a true love match and in that no one was ever more blessed than their own mother . . .

'If it is possible for dear Florrie to do what I ask of course a sum of money will be paid her each year but that will be settled by Crompton. Of one thing I am certain—that J. M. Barrie (the best friend in the whole world) will always be ready to advise out of his love for [end]'

Peter Ll. Davies: In J.M.B.'s writing are added the words: 'This paper which ends thus was found after Mrs Davies's death. It was evidently written (as relatives agree) at Berkhampstead soon after Mr Davies's death. J. M. Barrie.'

But for the confident assignments of these 'directions' by J.M.B., and

1. A valued old friend.
2 and 3. Sylvia's sisters.

presumably by Crompton and Margaret and Trixie or May, to the late spring or summer of 1907, I should have felt a little doubtful of dating them so early. I still think it possible that they may have been written two years or so later, when S. felt the first approach of her own fatal disease . . .

It seems clear that, whenever S. wrote these 'directions', it had not occurred to her that we should be so comprehensively 'looked after' by J.M.B. as in fact we eventually were . . . And in point of fact, nowhere in the documents I have, neither in any of the letters, nor in the final 'will', nor anywhere else, is there mention of any definite undertaking on our behalf by J.M.B.

S. had very little money of her own; there must have been a thousand or two of A.'s and there were a (very) few thousands which had been left to her during her lifetime, and thereafter to us, under George du M.'s will. I have always understood that there was a whip-round among the uncles —kind uncles indeed. But on any showing there was precious little out of which to deal with five boys and their education, without J.M.B. in the background. There is a vagueness about the financial future which suggests that she was not very exact in the matter of £.s.d. I don't mean that she was in the least extravagant; on the contrary I am sure that her insistence on the importance of living within one's means was heartfelt and sincere . . . Perhaps to S., as to many women and not a few men, money was something which generally turns up somehow or other, in sufficient quantities to make life tolerable. And perhaps this attitude, which is far from being a greedy or grasping one, made it easy for her to accept the money which J.M.B. was so ready to give.

Life at Egerton House went on somehow. Peter was at Berkhamsted School, and presently Jack went to Osborne, having got his entrance. Peter Davies writes:

Whether J.M.B. from the start made himself responsible for J. at Osborne I don't know, but it seems likely; and I take it that meanwhile arrangements were come to with Hugh Macnaghten to take G. into his house at Eton as soon as a vacancy occurred, i.e. in the coming winter half. By the summer S. had decided to give up Egerton House and return to London —doubtless with financial help from J.M.B.

*   *   *

For the summer holiday that year, Barrie rented Dhivach Lodge, near Drumnadrochit, in a wild part of Inverness-shire. Sylvia and her sons went there—and Mary Barrie. Mary had remained in the background all through the dark days leading up to Arthur's death. Whether her husband had indicated to her that he alone was a close enough friend of the Davieses to be taken into the inner circle is not known; what is clear is that Mary found friends to motor with in Normandy, and clients to consult in her studio, for much of the time Barrie was spending at Egerton House. Her inclusion in the house-party at Dhivach Lodge may have been an undiscussed tactical decision on Barrie's part to avoid gossip. Whatever his motives, Mary accepted the situation and played hostess to Barrie's host.

The boys enjoyed themselves, chasing butterflies and fishing every burn within walking distance. Crompton Llewelyn Davies came for some climbing. Barrie's niece, Madge Murray, the twenty-year-old daughter of Isabella and Dr Murray, also came, 'the most normal and human member of the Barrie family, who sang songs at the piano and . . . introduced a welcome note of natural gaiety into the household', as Peter Llewelyn Davies later wrote.

Other guests during the summer were Captain Scott, and Harley Granville Barker with Lillah, his wife, 'a somewhat overwhelming person'. Peter goes on to remark:

It would be fascinating to know what such guests as these thought of the Dhivach inmates. Plenty of scope for comment, one would say. And however the boys enjoyed it, there must have been uncomfortable moments among the adults . . . The whole pattern of the Dhivach holiday seems to me to have had something rather deplorable about it.

At the end of the holiday George went to Eton, and settled down very quickly. Sylvia and the three youngest boys stayed at Ramsgate, while their new home at 23, Campden Hill Square was being got ready. 'No doubt,' says Peter Llewelyn Davies, 'the cash was partly put up or guaranteed by J.M.B.'

The boys at Ramsgate had come to think of Barrie as one of themselves. Michael wrote to him on October 18th, 1907:

> DEAR MR BARRIE
> I hope you are quite well
> I HAVE SENT YOU A
> Picture of a Pirate he has
> GOT PLENTY OF WEAPONS
> And looks very fierce.   Please
> COME SOON TO FISH
>   from Michael with Love
> FROM NICO   THE END.

Barrie wrote to Sylvia from Leinster Corner the following day:

Dearest Jocelyn,

All right, I'll go down with you on the Wedy or Thursday and meet you wherever and whenever you fix. Mr Mason will come some time also. You might get me a sitting-room and bedroom. I am hoping you are pretty well . . . Mary's intention is to start on Monday but at present she is miserable with neuralgia. Madge is here rehearsing and I suppose I'll have to be up for the first night, about a week hence. I had capital letters from both George and Jack. Jack was 8 his first fortnight, and Captain Scott was so delighted he at once agreed to go with me to see him. S. will be away for a fortnight.

I am writing away at my play, and am just getting among the breakers.

Your

J.M.B.

Peter Davies: Idle, perhaps, to speculate after all these years as to what Mary Barrie's feelings must have been, now that Jocelyn was a widow and her children fatherless. It is at least possible she may have found the situation to her taste, up to a point. This was the month when there first appeared at Leinster Corner, as secretary of a committee formed to do battle with the censor of plays, a good-looking young writer named Gilbert Cannan.

I suppose the first night for which Madge was rehearsing was the annual Peter Pan revival. The play at which he was writing was What Every Woman Knows, produced eleven months later.

Is there a faintly proprietary air about this letter? . . . A bit odd, for example, to be informing S. of her son's place in class at Osborne. However . . .

Chapter 13

A CAMPAIGN

THE literary profession was disturbed in October, 1907, by a decision of the Lord Chamberlain's Examiner of Plays not to issue a licence for Granville Barker's play *Waste*, a play which he considered too outspoken on a subject of social comment. The plot of the play is simple: a promising politician ruins his career by getting involved with a woman. It sounds innocuous enough, but the censor would not pass it, even though the dramatist had treated the subject seriously and responsibly.

Granville Barker was able to collect support from the leading writers of the time. Gilbert Murray and John Galsworthy organized a campaign for the abolition altogether of the office of censor, and Galsworthy drafted a letter to *The Times* which was signed by seventy dramatists. Barrie was among the campaign's strongest supporters, and there were meetings of the committee at his house. He sent a letter to every dramatist of the day:

Dear Sir,
We ask you as a dramatic author to lend the weight of your name to the enclosed protest, too long delayed, against the Censorship of Plays.
The following authors, amongst others, have already promised their support.
G. Meredith
W. S. Gilbert
T. Hardy
Bernard Shaw
Henry James.
It is proposed to send this protest to the Prime Minister, and the most important papers.
As set forth in the protest, the Public has every needful security in the present yearly licensing of Theatres.

We hope that you will support this attempt to remove a slight on our Profession. May we ask you to be so kind as to reply at once to:

J. M. Barrie
Leinster Corner
Lancaster Gate, W.

Yours Truly,
J. M. BARRIE
JOHN GALSWORTHY
GILBERT MURRAY

Gilbert Cannan, the campaign committee's secretary, was newly down from Cambridge and reading for the Bar. Like many other literary-minded young men, he was eager to become an author, and as this was a splendid chance to meet literary men, he threw himself into the campaign with zest.

Barrie wrote from Leinster Corner to Sylvia at Ramsgate on November 4th, 1907:

Dearest Jocelyn,
I am having a life of it over this censorship business. Receiving committees, telephones, telegrams, etc. all day and every day.

When I can I'm working hard at my play, which is dull, with occasional bright moments.

Madge seems to have had a happy time with you, but can't tell me how your indigestion is, which was what I sent her down for. Mary writes that she is to be back on Sunday. She seems to have influenza and grand rides daily[1] . . .

I would have sent the boys fireworks but the post office won't pass them.

I sit up for Madge every night till 11.45[2] and then we go to bed. At least write and tell me how you are. I want to know so much that I think you might do this.

Your
J.M.B.

Peter Davies: Though I have few letters from J.M.B. to S. from now on, or of hers to him, it is obvious that there must have been many. Taking it all round, I am not sorry they have mostly disappeared; except in the sense that her letters might have thrown light on her character and personality —but her letters to other people might have been of more value in that sense. I think her attitude to him was a special and peculiar one, not very representative of her true self. Indeed, on reflection, I doubt if he brought

1. Mary was at Black Lake Cottage.
2. Madge Murray had a part in *Peter Pan*.

out or even recognized (or wanted to) the true characteristics of anyone
he made much of; he was such a fantasy-weaver that they ended by either
playing up to him or clearing out.

When he was strongly attracted by people, he wanted at once to own
them and to be dominated by them, whichever their sex. The owning he
was often able to manage for a time to a greater or lesser degree, with the
help of his money, which made generosity an easy business for him (not
that the rich are usually generous), plus his wit and charm and the aura of
success and fame which surrounded him. The being dominated was more
difficult of attainment, as he was a pretty strong character in his own
strange way. There's no denying that, from A. Ll. D.'s death onwards, he
did increasingly 'own' S. Ll. D. and her boys after his fashion. And
S. Ll. D., a strong character herself, couldn't help dominating him. Later,
I think, he achieved something of the same peculiar equilibrium with
G. Ll. D., and much more so with M. Ll. D. . . .

The above is not a serious attempt to define the relationship between
S. Ll. D. and J.M.B. To do that would be beyond my powers and is
beyond the scope of this record. But these stray thoughts occurred to me
after reading the preceding letter, so I thought I might just as well put
them down, erroneous as they very likely are. I think, by the way, that
S. Ll. D.'s was a far from simple character.

The Campden Hill Square house was ready for occupation in
December, and Sylvia moved in early in the New Year. Jack returned
to Osborne, George to Eton, and Peter to Wilkinson's. The house
was in some respects more attractive than the two earlier homes in
Kensington Park Gardens, and Sylvia soon had it comfortably
furnished with their possessions from Berkhamsted. Peter Davies
says:

And very early in the proceedings J.M.B. affixed to the dining-room
ceiling, by means of a coin adroitly spun, the penny stamp with which he
used to hall-mark his acquaintances' houses, whether he effectually owned
them or not . . . To 23 C.H.S. came, besides Mary Hodgson, Minnie the
cook, maker of excellent lentil soups and rice and chocolate puddings,
and the pretty, buxom new house-parlourmaid, Amy, who stirred the
young Adam in some of us, more or less obscurely.

And here, I think, S. did succeed, gradually, in regaining something of
the zest for life. The boys were a fond amusement and distraction for her,
relatives came frequently, and the dog-like J.M.B., still living at Leinster
Corner and constantly in attendance.

*   *   *

In February, 1908, Barrie and Mary went to Flint Cottage on Box Hill for George Meredith's eightieth birthday. Meredith's mind was as sharp as ever, his affection for the 'young' author—Barrie was now forty-eight—undiminished. This affection also took in the author's wife, of whom Meredith had grown very fond: not only was she still pretty, but she showed her own liking for him without reserve. Did Meredith sometimes wonder what went on in the intimacy of Barrie's home when no one else was there? George Meredith possessed a degree of perception. Anyone with eyes to see could have perceived that an ardent nature like Mary Barrie's had a great capacity for love—but the one person who should have known this without any doubt did not appear to be much interested. Barrie's glance was cold, remote, when it met that of his wife.

He had begun a correspondence with yet another woman. If Mary knew anything about it she said nothing: she never asked questions. Many people wrote to him about his plays, or to ask advice about plays they wanted to write themselves. He replied to them, but was in the habit of politely cutting short any attempt to scrape acquaintance on the strength of a kindly letter. He made exceptions, however.

Millicent, Duchess of Sutherland, wrote to him in May, 1908, inviting him to a social function at her London house. She was a leading figure in Society, beautiful, intelligent, devoted to the arts and especially to the theatre. Barrie replied to the invitation:

Dear Duchess,
I shall come if I can summon up courage, if I am here, for I am going to Paris for a fortnight in June. It terrifies me to go anywhere, and when the moment comes I may go into hiding instead. I think it's about the 17th we go to Paris for *Peter Pan* is there. I want yourself not your guests.
Yours sincerely,
J. M. BARRIE.

The visit to Paris was with Frohman. Barrie wrote to Michael Davies from the Hotel d'Albe, Avenue des Champs-Elysées, on June 15th:

My dear Michael,
Paris is looking very excited today, and all the people think it was because there were races yesterday, but I know it is because tomorrow is your birthday. I wish I could be with you and your candles. You can look on

me as one of your candles, the one that burns badly—the greasy one, that is, bent in the middle, but still, hurray, I am Michael's candle. I wish I could see you putting on the redskin's clothes for the first time. Won't your mother be frightened. Nick will hide beneath the bed, and Peter will cry for the police.

Dear Michael, I am very fond of you, but don't tell anybody.

The End.

J. M. BARRIE.

Michael Davies, now eight, was going daily to the Norland Place School at the foot of Holland Park Avenue, and was already showing signs of his father's brilliance. Barrie's sentiments at the end of this letter were literally true; he had already singled out Michael as a favourite among the boys, while continuing to treat them all in his now customary whimsical manner.

The boys' summer holiday that year was spent at a small farmhouse in the New Forest—this time without Barrie. Sylvia, for once, was alone with her sons, who spent happy days butterfly-hunting with net and killing-bottle.

Barrie had two important dates that autumn. Captain Scott and Kathleen Bruce were married at Hampton Court Palace on September 2nd, and his play, *What Every Woman Knows*, had its first night on September 3rd. Gerald du Maurier played the hero, John Shand, and Hilda Trevelyan played Maggie, who grieved because she lacked charm, but who had—inevitably, being a Barrie heroine—lashings of the commodity. In America, Maude Adams opened in the play in Atlantic City, and went on a long tour before Frohman brought the production to New York. More money in the till for everyone concerned: many thousands of pounds for J. M. Barrie. Not that he noticed, particularly. Golding Bright was attending to the business side of the royalties, and Gilmour, like the good fellow he was, tackled the income tax fiends, and did mysterious sums with stocks and shares. Barrie was saved all those boring worries, and so had time for more interesting things.

Among those interesting things was the growing friendship with Her Grace of Sutherland. She wrote again, praising the play and admitting that she was thinking of doing some writing herself. Barrie replied from Leinster Corner on September 17th, 1908:

Dear Duchess,
I like you for writing me about the play—also for other reasons—and I

hope you will write something soon, as you enjoy writing, but if I were you I wouldn't bother writing, there is something else you are so good at, I won't say what it is, but it's 'What Every Man Knows.'

Yours sincerely,
J. M. BARRIE.

Barrie was constantly adding to his friends at this time. Marriott Watson, Quiller Couch and A. E. W. Mason were of the inner circle, but he had got to know another writer, Maurice Hewlett, who, with the others, often went down to Black Lake Cottage. In December Mary came up to London to join her husband for their annual visit to *Peter Pan*. They were joined in their box—a large one, again made out of two put together—by Sylvia Davies and her five boys, and, this year, by the good-looking Gilbert Cannan. He was now a barrister, but was thinking of leaving the Bar and writing full-time for the theatre. Barrie was encouraging, and Mary very friendly. It was clear that she and Mr Cannan got on exceedingly well together. The Davies boys were excited by more than Mr Barrie's *Peter Pan*. He had proposed a wonderful Christmas present for them—not less than a visit to Switzerland for winter sports. Before coming home for the holidays, George had written to his mother from Eton:

Dearest Mother,

I have asked my tutor about clothes for Switzerland. He said you have to have a knickerbocker change suit (a good warm one), sweaters and thick stockings. He also said puttees were jolly good things to have, to keep your legs warm (two pairs each).

From what he said about it it sounded topping fun to be in Switzerland. He said it's quite warm for part of the day. He said the most comfortable hotel to stay at was the 'Palace'. I wish he was going to be at St Moritz. It's the first year he hasn't been there for Christmas for some time. The journey will be pretty exciting, I expect. I expect to be ill going from Dover to Calais, or wherever you cross the Channel.

It will be glorious fun at St Moritz! I suppose there'll be tons of skating and tobogganing. My tutor said he used to 'ski' most of the time. I suppose that's rather an art, though.

Is Mrs Barrie coming? Perhaps she'll prefer to go Motor Touring or something else. We shall be a whacking party. It is kind of Uncle Jim to do it all.

I'm absolutely burning for the holidays—now more than ever! Eleven days more! I envy Jack with only four more days . . .

Peter Davies: Not St Moritz but the less fashionable Caux, above Montreux, was in fact selected for this exciting innovation in the way of Christmas holidays . . . probably it was a more suitable place for the oddly constituted party, consisting of J.M. and Mary Barrie, Gilbert Cannan, S. Ll. D. and the boys . . . The boys all enjoyed themselves hugely . . . I remember 'luge-ing' and ski-ing in a clumsy but exhilarating fashion; I remember a pair of very high yellowy-brown lacing boots of Mary B.'s which some-how impressed me.

Mary was in radiant spirits. She seemed ten years less than her forty-odd years, her looks enhanced by her unobtrusively good clothes, chosen to set off her still-slender figure. To the impression-able, romantic Gilbert Cannan, who at twenty-four had not met many sophisticated women, she was immensely attractive. And though he admired his host, the famous Mr Barrie, the young man could not help noticing that the playwright did not seem to appreci-ate his delightful wife, but persisted in devoting practically all his attention to Mrs Davies and her sons. It was an odd situation. Peter Llewelyn Davies remarks: 'It must have been a queer quartet of adults that conversed together after the boys had gone to bed.'

He goes on to relate an incident that happened at Caux:

One evening at dusk I was summoned to J.M.B.'s room, to find him sitting in a somehow dejected attitude, at the far end of the room, in the half light. As I entered he looked up, and, in a flat, lugubrious voice said: 'Peter, something dreadful has happened to my feet,' and glancing down I saw to my horror that his feet were bare and swollen to four or five times their natural size. For several seconds I was deceived, and have never since forgotten the terror that filled me, until I realized that the feet were artificial (bought at Hamley's), made of the waxed linen masks are made of, and that I had been most successfully hoaxed.

A macabre joke. Barrie could use his imagination to invent whim-sical, fey characters, but it had not the quality which comprehends the effect on a young boy of what might appear a terrifying phenom-enon, leaving a memory which, as Peter Davies says himself, remained with him through life.

Barrie was keeping up other friendships during the holiday. He wrote to Millicent, Duchess of Sutherland from Caux on 9th January, 1909:

My dear Milly,
How nice of you to send me the little RLS which has at last found me in

this snowy land. I value it immensely. The world here is given over to lugeing. I don't know if you have a luge, you have everything else. It's a little toboggan, and they glide down on it for ever and ever. And evidently man needs little here below except his little luge. Age annihilated. We are simply ants with luges. I say we, but by great good luck I hurt myself at once, and so I am debarred. We are returning in two or three days and I hope you are to be back and that I am to see you soon and explain you to yourself.

Yours always,

J. M. BARRIE.

Near the end of their stay at Caux, Sylvia became alarmingly unwell, suffering great pain close to the heart. A doctor who happened to be staying at the hotel, when approached, was unhelpful, on the grounds that he was on holiday. Barrie was extremely worried, but as they were to go home very soon, and Sylvia seemed better, no other steps were taken until they reached England. There is no record of what the diagnosis was, but Sylvia was never well from then onwards.

Back in London, life went on much as before. Peter Davies records 'a slow drift apart' of Sylvia and the Llewelyn Davies relations. Her father-in-law was eighty-three, and Margaret was his devoted companion. Arthur's brothers had their own families to occupy them, and Crompton, who was the boys' actual guardian, did much, in his tactful way, but would soon 'be caught up in his own all-absorbing marriage'. Peter Davies says:

There was in fact precious little any of them could do; and I haven't the least doubt that the curious position of J.M.B. was something that, however thankfully they may have recognized the value of it, they found rather hard to swallow. Be that as it may, this drawing apart, though inevitable, was a great misfortune from our point of view. Had it been possible to instil into us, in our impressionable years, more of the balanced, able, essentially sound Davies characteristics, we should have benefited accordingly.

Barrie was still busy with the censorship campaign, and was seeing quite a lot of John Galsworthy, whom he admired. In a letter to Millicent, Duchess of Sutherland, he described Galsworthy as

a queer fish, like the rest of us. So sincerely weighed down by the out-of-jointness of things socially . . . but outwardly a man-about-town, so neat, so correct—he would go to the stake for his opinions but he would go courteously raising his hat. The other day he was flung out of a hansom and went as gracefully as if he were leaving his card. That is him today but he has been all its opposites. I think he was once a cowboy, I have hopes he has been a pirate. He has been everywhere and has done most things and what turned him from one man into the other I don't know. He used to care for nothing but frivolity, shooting big game, and now so serious and could not put a pin into a butterfly.

Barrie's admiration for Galsworthy led to some very practical results. Galsworthy had written a fine play about a strike called *Strife*, which the Vedrenne-Barker management at the Court Theatre would have produced, but they were in financial difficulties. Barrie persuaded Frohman to put the play on for six matinées at the Duke of York's, with which the American impresario was closely connected. Granville Barker produced, and the dramatic critics were unanimous in their praise. Frohman moved the play to another theatre, but the public didn't support it and Frohman lost a great deal of money. He was not upset. He was so much under the spell of the little Scottish wizard that he would have done anything for him. There was a plan to get together a repertory of worthwhile plays, for which he offered the Duke of York's. They would have to wait, but with Barrie enthusiastic, and plays promised from Shaw, Galsworthy and Granville Barker, Frohman would remember the project.

The Censorship Committee had brought together many dramatists, and they decided to form a Dramatists' Club, with Arthur Wing Pinero as the first President. The campaign was gathering support, Gilbert Cannan still diligently acting as its secretary.

In April, Barrie travelled to Edinburgh to receive a second honorary degree, bestowed upon him by his old university. He wrote to Sylvia from the Royal Hotel on April 3rd:

Dearest Jocelyn,

I am now slowly recovering from the functions, which continued for about six solid hours. The gown turned out to be the gayest affair, all red and blue, and if Michael had met me in a wood he would have tried to net me as a Scarlet Emperor. We wandered the streets in this guise and I even walked half a mile in mine alone. Edinburgh was so full of birds of paradise that not a stone was thrown. But the five missed the chance of their lives in not encountering me in the streets arrayed in my glory. I feel strangely drab today in my old purple tie.

Edinburgh is looking at its best, which is I think the best in the world, for it must be about the most romantic city on the earth. But it strikes cold on me nowadays, for the familiar faces have long been gone and there are only buildings left. I am going on to Kirriemuir this afternoon and may go to see my oldest sister on Monday.

Your affec

J.M.B.

The 'oldest sister' was Mary, who had married Alec's assistant, John Galloway, and now lived in Aberdeen. Dr Ogilvy was dead; Alec, now retired, had inherited Strathview and lived there. His two sons, Charles and William, after doing well at Edinburgh University, were thinking about careers. Charles wanted to follow in his uncle's early footsteps and become a journalist, and Barrie had promised to give him introductions and what help he could. Lilian, the eldest girl, was a teacher and her three sisters were inevitably 'in the scholastic line'. Barrie warmly invited any of them to visit him, either at Leinster Corner or at Black Lake Cottage.

He could always rely on Mary to make week-end house-parties at Black Lake something of an event; she was a hostess of genius. She was also proving useful in another way: Gilbert Cannan had to deal with mounting correspondence about the censorship campaign, and Mary invited him to bring it down to the Cottage so that she could help him with it during the week. He went often; he found it quieter to work there than at Leinster Corner.

Early that summer, the Prime Minister offered knighthoods to three men of the theatre: Herbert Tree, Arthur Wing Pinero and James Matthew Barrie. Tree and Pinero accepted, and duly appeared in the Birthday Honours. J. M. Barrie gracefully declined. He gave no specific reason, only that he preferred to go on being Mister Barrie.

In June he accompanied Frohman to Berlin, where the impresario was seeing plays with the object of choosing them for production in England and America. Barrie had no personal stake in any of the plays; Frohman liked his company, and Barrie was fond of Frohman. On his return, Barrie wrote to Sylvia from Leinster Corner on June 17th:

Dearest Jocelyn,
I shall try to get to the school tomorrow at ½ past 4 and see Peter off. At three I am going to see about the Meredith letters and don't know how long it will take.

How I wish I were going down to see Michael and Nicholas. All the donkey boys and the fishermen and sailors see them, but I don't. I feel they are growing up without my looking on, when I grudge any blank day without them. I can't picture a summer day that does not have Michael skipping in front. That is summer to me. And all the five know me, as nobody else does. The bland indifference with which they accept my tantrums is the most engaging thing in the world to me. They are quite sure that despite appearances they are all right. To be able to help them and you, that is my dear ambition, to do the best I can always and always, and my greatest pride is that you let me do it. I wish I did it so much better. It is always such a glad thought to me to find you even a little finer woman that I had thought. I am so sorry about those pains in your head.

Your affectionate

J.M.B.

Peter Davies: George Meredith had died on May 18 and J.M.B. had been asked by Morley, one of the executors, to write the Biography, which eventually he declined.

This letter is the nearest thing to a pledge, or solemn undertaking to S. by J.M.B. which appears to have survived. I have been a little surprised, by the way, to find so little of the love-letter about any of his letters to her which remain. No doubt they are only a few of many that were written, but on the whole they do not give me such an impression of intimacy as might have been expected.

Were the headaches and ill-health to which allusion is made in this and the next letter foreshadowings, as yet unrecognized, of the doom which was to declare itself in the autumn of this year? It seems probable; though to some observers, this summer S. had seemed gayer and happier.

Barrie went to Black Lake Cottage at the end of June, and wrote to Sylvia on July 5th:

Dearest Jocelyn,
I hope you are feeling pretty well, but I don't believe it, and that saddens me. At all events I can trust to the others being lusty and am looking forward to your being here with George. I have not heard definitely yet when Miss Adams is to be in London, but I expect it will be Thursday so that I'll come up that day and come down with you on Friday. If so, my notion is to lunch with you on Thursday.

My temperature has been bobbing about, and I went to bed again on Saturday, but it seems better now . . . I read a good deal in Meredith's notebooks. He kept little notebooks just like mine . . . and entered in one

I found 'Woman will be the last thing civilized by man,' and 'Who rises from prayer a better man his prayer is answered.'

I do wish you were feeling stronger, and had not so many things to do. I'm very unhappy about it.

Yours,

J.M.B.

[Peter Davies's comments on this letter are given later, on page 179.]

Chapter 14

DIVORCE

On the last day of the run of *What Every Woman Knows*, July 28th, 1909, Barrie was at Black Lake Cottage, going over notes which might help him the following week, when he was due to give evidence before the official censorship committee which had been set up as a result of the campaign. Mary was in London, at her studio.

Barrie had an unexpected interruption. The gardener, Hunt, wished to speak to him. The man was in a considerable state of agitation, and at first found it difficult to say anything, but soon words poured out. Mrs Barrie had been criticizing his work, and he wasn't going to stand for it. She wasn't so perfect herself. He felt it his bounden duty to tell Mr Barrie what his wife Kate told him she'd seen in the house—and not for the first time, either. Mrs Barrie and Mr Cannan were carrying on.

Barrie was stupefied. He could not believe such a thing possible. At the same time, he knew that the man would never have dared to make such an accusation without some cause. He could not bring himself to ask any questions, or to demand to see the gardener's wife. There was only one thing to do and he forced himself to do it. Putting away his papers, he got his hat, coat and stick, went to the station, and took the next train to London.

Mary arrived at Leinster Corner from her studio that afternoon to find her husband waiting for her. Nervous and almost trembling, he asked her to deny the monstrous charge. Mary told him it was true: she wished she had had the courage to tell him about it earlier. She wanted a divorce.

A divorce! That meant a scandal. He could not face it. He asked her to reconsider, but Mary repeated her demand. A divorce. Now that all had come into the open, something definite could be done. He must see Sir George Lewis. After an agonized hour of pleading,

Barrie asked her at least to go with him, so that they could all three talk it over, and Mary agreed. She was calm and confident; she knew what she wanted, and she intended to force her husband to take the necessary steps.

Sir George Lewis had been a fashionable solicitor too long to show surprise at the situation, but he tried to talk Mary round. She refused to listen. Would she compromise on a Bill of Separation? No. She and Cannan wanted to get married. Sir George delicately pointed out the disparity in their ages, and Mary laughed. What did age matter? She was just over forty and looked a good deal less. She loved Cannan and he loved her—that was what mattered.

James Barrie was desperate. Nothing had been said of his own long years of neglect of his wife: Mary chose not to speak of them. She simply repeated that she wanted a divorce. Barrie appealed to the solicitor to make a last effort; no matter what had happened, he would forgive her, and never speak of it again, 'if Mary will put away the thought of Cannan'. Mary ignored this. She had committed misconduct, and did not defend or excuse it. It would happen again. Nothing less than a divorce would do.

Mary Barrie was taking a step which, in the social climate of the time, was bound to ruin her reputation. She had, however, many friends, and the people who mattered would not ostracize her. Most of them had long known the state of affairs.

H. G. Wells wrote to her from 17, Church Row, Hampstead (no date).

My dear Mrs Barrie,
How are things going with you? I'm concerned by vague rumours that everything isn't well between Barrie & you. Can't someone do something? I don't like to think of you as getting poor and embittered & that's the turn the stories give things. My best respects to Cannan, too.

I've had rather a bad time. Amber & I are being forced never to see or write to each other. I suppose it's the same thing in the long run—except that I rather hanker after bolting—but it hurts horribly & leaves one the prey to all sorts of moods. Anyway we've brought a very jolly little daughter into the world.
Good wishes to you,
Yours ever,
H. G. WELLS.

Sir George Lewis continued to try to persuade Mary to change her mind and to beg her to see 'reason'—a scandal would devastate

Barrie and it was still not too late to withdraw, in spite of the gossip and the preliminary legal action. He prevailed on her to see him and Barrie once again. She wrote to Wells about this interview a week or so later: Wells had been down to visit her at Black Lake:

Dear Mr Wells,
Things are exactly where they were when you left. My overtures were rejected because I could not perjure myself by saying that not only would I give up G.C., but I must promise never to *think* of the past or long for it, but give myself up to loving J. and accepting his loving advances. He seems to have developed the most ardent passion for me now that he has lost me; that frightens me. I must go back to what I was, but to fight that, in the circumstances, is more than I can promise to do. Poor thing, he is distracted and I am dreadfully sorry; he says he knows I would be happier with G.C. and that we ought to marry, one moment, and the next clamours for me. Anyhow I am to have money and that will help things somewhat, but I have no fear for my happiness, none at all, and it all seems too good a thing to be true. You have been a dear friend, I shall never forget it. Don't mention a word, will you, to anyone.
Ever sincerely,
MARY BARRIE.

She does not appear to have talked about Sylvia or the Davieses to anyone; it is as if she was resolved not to complicate the issue in any way.

[There follow Peter Davies's comments on J.M.B.'s letter to Sylvia dated July 5th, 1909, p. 176.]

Peter Davies: If S. did take G. down to Black Lake Cottage for that week-end (which was doubtless the week-end of G's Lord's Leave from Eton), it must have been the last visit paid by any of the family to the scene of 'The Boy Castaways', and, with near-by Tilford, of so many happy memories. For it was at the end of this month—the 29th—that the Black Lake gardener opened J.M.B.'s eyes to what a good many other people had suspected for months past, so that he hurried back to Leinster Corner to confront Mary B. with the charge, which neither she nor Gilbert Cannan attempted to deny . . .

I really don't see how anyone conversant with the facts can possibly blame Mary B. or her twenty-years-younger lover. And I don't suppose they did, though the law naturally pilloried them as the guilty parties. It was a species of crucifixion, too, for the wretched J.M.B., however much he may have brought it on himself; one of the things that darkened his life from then on, however much it may have benefited him in the long run in various ways . . .

Had [Sylvia] seen it coming? I don't know. I don't know what the relations were between her and Mary Barrie, whether they loathed each other, were bored by each other, got on quite well together, tolerated each other, or what. That she must have had many thoughts about the whole affair, and about its possible effects on her own and our future, goes without saying . . .

Any situation involving J.M.B. was inevitably peculiar. That S. found him a comforter of infinite sympathy and tact, and a mighty convenient slave, and that she thankfully accepted his money as a gift from the gods to herself and her children—all that is clear enough. I think that she laughed at him a little, too, and was a little sorry for him, with all his success, as anyone who knew him well and liked him was more or less bound to be. I mean sorry for him in a general way, quite apart from the pity which his misery over the fact and machinery and publicity of divorce must have stirred in any generous breast. But whether she regarded the divorce as, ultimately, a simplification of the relation in which she stood to him, or the exact reverse, who can say?

The petition went forward; Mary was beyond pleas, beyond reason, beyond everything except her determination to make a new life for herself. The news soon spread round their mutual friends. Some of them did their best to forestall the worst of the scandalmongering before the publicity broke. The following letter was written to Charles Scribner, Barrie's publisher in America:

> *Woodside,*
> *Fleet,*
> *Hants.*
> *Nov. 9, 1909.*

My dear Scribner,
Your business letter of today touches on poor Barrie's trouble—I could not well refer to it in my reply—but I don't know what you may hear or have heard—& so, as I know both her and him well & have seen both lately & know the story well, I want to write to you so that you, as his true friend, as you are, may contradict false rumours on your side & save our friends from the tongue of the scandalmonger.

The whole truth is that Mrs B is a woman—with a woman's desires—which for many years she had controlled (& she had no children, which made it harder). Barrie is a son born to a mother—long after the rest of her family[1]—& as so often is the case—with genius but little virility.

Now—people are now saying that Mrs Barrie had many lovers. This is false—I am certain of it—I have good authority. There was no rumour of

1. This is a mistake; Barrie was only three years younger than his sister Isabella.

it till this divorce came as a surprise. She was, as it happens, overcome by this man for whom she has left Barrie. She loves the man, as a young woman loves a man—& still loves Barrie as a mother loves a helpless child.

Barrie urged her to return to him & give up the other—she, having at length after long battling against it, given in to the longing of her heart after a virile man, & no doubt the secret woman's longing for the birth of a child, would not.

That is the story & one may say with truth, that there is no sort of vice on her part & only the most generous behaviour. Nevertheless, it is deeply to be regretted & I hardly know how Barrie will fare—left to himself without some woman's care for him.

With my warm regards to Mrs Scribner and your daughter,

Yours very truly,

W. M. MEREDITH.

Other friends used their influence with the press to keep the newspaper reports toned down to the flattest level. They sent a private letter to the editors of the leading papers:

The divorce suit of Barrie v. Barrie & Cannan is down for hearing at the Michaelmas Term. The plaintiff in the suit was in early life a distinguished journalist. More recently his work in fiction and the drama has given pleasure of a high order to hundreds of thousands of readers and spectators wherever the English language is spoken. He is a man for whom the inevitable pain of these proceedings would be greatly increased by publicity. Therefore it is hoped the Press, as a mark of respect and gratitude to a writer of genius, will unite in abstaining from any mention of the case beyond the briefest report of the hearing. The suit is undefended, and, apart from the eminence of the plaintiff, raises no question of the slightest public interest.

The letter was signed by Lord Esher, George Alexander, William Archer, Edmund Gosse, Maurice Hewlett, Henry James, A. E. W. Mason, Arthur Pinero, Beerbohm Tree and H. G. Wells.

Barrie had another emotional worry at this time; there were ominous signs that Sylvia was ill and was probably going to get worse. Her fainting fits were coming more frequently, and there were symptoms which made her doctor insist on her seeing a specialist. He made a thorough examination, and confirmed what her own doctor had suspected—that she was suffering from cancer. The growth was near the heart and lungs, too close for operating, and it obstructed her breathing.

The name of the disease was not mentioned either to Sylvia or to her sons, but it soon became obvious to them that she was very ill. Barrie was not told the truth, either, only that she had something serious the matter with her. He was in a peculiar state, unable to work, unable to concentrate, and he was glad to accept an invitation from A. E. W. Mason to stay at the latter's flat in Stratton Street.

Sylvia's strength fluctuated; sometimes she could walk about without too much discomfort, at other times she spent most of the day lying on a sofa, resting. She gathered strength during the summer, and by August was well enough to take her sons for a holiday to Postbridge, in Devon.

Barrie wrote to her there from Stratton Street on August 12th, 1909:

Dear Jocelyn,
I hope you are all settled down comfortably now, and that there is a bracing feeling in the air despite the heat. In this weather the boys need not expect to get as many trout as the waters will all be small and clear but after all the sun is better than trout and they will find lots of other things to do. I sent some gut, etc. and some fly hooks. . . . I wrote to Madge the night the play ended, sending her some money for the other two . . . I don't know whether Madge has been told of things, but suppose so. It was just a grateful letter. I am still quite well and tomorrow will go down again with Mason to his Wotton House and come back here on Monday.

I may possibly go with him to Switzerland at end of month. I wouldn't climb, but could get some good walks with him. However, I've settled nothing. I went with him y'day to see the Test Match at the Oval.
Yours ever
J.M.B.

Peter Davies: This was written a fortnight after the storm had burst . . . If he remembered in his then state of mind to send one of his periodical allowance payments to his three nieces, one must certainly take off one's hat to him . . . Leinster Corner had become hateful to him, and he had been glad to take refuge in Alf Mason's flat, where . . . he would walk up and down, up and down all night in his heavy boots until the sound of it drove everyone within hearing almost as frantic as the miserable little figure itself . . .

Had S. and he met since the Black Lake gardener's revelation? One can't help noticing that for the first time she is 'Dear Jocelyn' and not 'Dearest,' and that he signs himself more conventionally than heretofore.

This may imply mere agitation, or a sort of acknowledgment of provocation offered in recent years to his wife, or a cautious hint from Sir George Lewis.

Barrie wrote again to Sylvia from Stratton Street on August 26th, telling her he was going off to Switzerland with Mason and would be staying at the Monte Rosa hotel at Zermatt. He mentioned in passing that 'Sir George thinks my case will come on early in October as the undefended cases come early,' went on to recommend books for the children to read, and said he had been to Leinster Corner to get warm things in case it was cold at Zermatt. There was one more personal note: 'It is always so painful to me to go to Leinster Corner now.'

His further letters were equally restrained, beginning 'My dear Jocelyn', and ending 'Yours ever, J.M.B.' Sylvia replied from Postbridge in the same terms, describing a holiday she had had at Zermatt in her young days, and telling him that Michael would be going to Wilkinson's with Peter the following month. Barrie wrote once more, this time giving a Chamonix hotel as his address:

The weather has been bright and sunny again . . . The great climber Whymper is here and we have long talks with him. He is now about 70, married lately to a girl of 22 and they have a baby. Mason's two guides are brothers and they have another eight brothers.

Your affec

J.M.B.

Barrie and Alfred Mason returned to the latter's flat in London early in October, and the undefended suit for divorce was heard on October 13th, before Mr Justice Bigham. The proceedings in court did not take long. Barrie answered the questions put to him as briefly as possible, but not always with complete accuracy, as can be deduced from Mary Barrie's next letter to H. G. Wells, who had sent her his latest book:

My dear Mr Wells,
How kind of you to send 'Ann Veronica'. I have read it 'at a gulp' and simply loved it. Thank you. The horror is over and I am living a lonely life down here. G and I are to be separated until we marry in April. We are playing the game for the look of the thing but it is very dull. I dig in my garden, weather permitting, and write letters. I was in Town the other day on business and saw one or two people, and they all said that you and your wife are to be separated. I took upon myself boldly to

contradict this and I hope I was right. Let me know your news, for I am full of sympathy for all of you. J. came out badly in court. 3 lies. First. Memo, it was the only time. 2nd. It is *my cottage*, lease is in my name and I bought it with my money. 3rd. It is seven years since we separated and that does not spell happiness until 18 months ago. This has damaged us a lot in the eyes of the public but with our friends, well, they all knew better.

My love to you both,

M A R Y B A R R I E .

Wells replied:

17 Church Row,
Hampstead.
(no date)

Dear Mrs Barrie,
Sillies you are! Go & live together & get Babies as soon as you can like two sensible people. One could think there was Magic in Marriage. Fancy you & your friends conspiring to glorify the Damned old Fetich. Also—and this is impertinence—I wouldn't marry if I were you unless you know you are going to have Babys [*sic*]. No earthly reason why you should for if so be you soon should disagree, it gives you both amazing powers of making Hell for one another. So take an old Sinner's advice & *tell* them you are married when the time comes, & don't marry unless there is a child to legitimate. I'll always say I know you are & declare I was a witness at the registry office if you want confirmation. This by the way, but affairs go on—tumultuously & with complications—but quite well on the whole. Too long a story to tell. Of course I don't leave Jane. Why should I? But as Shaw says, incorrect rumours are the best concealment in the world. Thanks for your valiant denials. Poor recluse! You have our warmest sympathy.

H.G.W.

Many of Mary's friends knew, and had long known, the basic cause of the break-up of a marriage which had been unhappy from the beginning. She now frankly told them what they had long suspected: that Barrie was impotent and the marriage had never been consummated. Her correspondence with H. G. Wells makes this abundantly clear; and many years later, when she was living in France, she confided a great deal of information about her life to Compton Mackenzie, one of the most sympathetic of men.

When her friends asked her why she had not left Barrie earlier, she had replied that after the shock of the honeymoon, she had hoped that her husband would take medical advice and that something could be done. But Barrie had always refused to discuss the matter, let alone do anything about it. In the end she had withdrawn into herself, and except for keeping up appearances before others, they had lived as strangers. Mary would have gone on trying to maintain some semblance of a normal marital relationship if Barrie had not indulged his extraordinary fantasies for the worship of beautiful women and their children. It was the continual harping on the wonder of motherhood that hurt most. But there were other things; his terrible silences, which sometimes went on for days at a time: the fact that he had for years shut her out from his companionship, ignoring her before their friends in such a way as to lacerate her pride.

It had been bad enough before, but when the Llewelyn Davies relationship developed the situation became intolerable; she had often wondered how long she could endure the strain of pretending before the world that all was well, when in fact she had been leading an unnatural and miserable existence. The coming of Gilbert Cannan into her life had transformed everything. Keeping up appearances no longer mattered: hurting Barrie did not matter: nothing mattered except the wonderful fact that the life of an attractive woman was not over, but would be beginning again—with someone to whom she had become precious. She would thrust the years with Barrie out of her mind, bury them.

She could never do that, however. The bitterness of those years was revealed, years later, in three books which she wrote: *Men and Dogs*, *The Happy Garden*, and *Happy Houses*. In these books a good deal of her past life slips out when she is ostensibly telling about her dogs, or the gardens she made, or the houses she transformed and furnished with taste. *Men and Dogs* is full of oblique references to her first marriage:

When the dogs loved me they did it without forethought or afterthought because they couldn't help it, but men didn't love me unless they wanted to, unless I fitted in with their idea of me . . . I only loved clever men, and clever men, it seems to me, are made up of reserves. It is out of their reserves they bring their clever things. You think they will one day open their reserves, and you will be the favoured one who was admitted to the cupboards where they kept their cleverness. But that is an illusion . . . I loved my dogs so passionately because they could never, never be clever in that way. They could never be complicated, as the men were complicated. Perhaps my love for the dogs, in the beginning, was a sort of

mother love. Porthos was a baby when I first saw him, a fat little round young thing . . .
It was at the time my first married life came to an end, and I was living alone at the cottage with Luath. He became dearer to me than ever. He was hardly ever away from me. He slept in my room, he ate with me, he walked with me, he talked with me. I busied myself with my beloved garden; he lay nearby watching. He knew something strange was happening, that things were not as they used to be.

She was offered another dog, to be a companion to Luath; he was a bobtail called Sammy:

A bobtail is more human because he shows what he feels, in very much the same way as a man. Being still in a natural state and not able to keep—like man—his emotions bottled up inside him, and having no tail to enable him to let off steam, he flings his arms round your neck . . .
I don't want a dog to be the least bit human. There are quite enough of us already. I prefer him to be absolutely and entirely doggy . . . Let humans keep to their own, inferior humanness, to their reserves, their clevernesses, but for goodness sake let us leave our dogs to express themselves in their own natural, spontaneous way.

In *The Happy Garden* she invents two characters called Jane and John, and as she takes Jane round her garden—a description of the one at Black Lake Cottage—she talks about gardening in general and marriage in particular:

House and garden should be one. They should give and take and strive always to be worthy of each other.
'Like marriage,' sighs Jane.
Exactly. And, as in marriage, there is neutral ground—the courtyards —where they can deposit their differences of upbringing and prejudice and properly admire each other's qualities, and make due allowances for each other's failings.
'Ah,' says Jane.
'Has John no qualities?' say I.
'Much worse!' she says. 'He thinks he has no failings.'

There are also a couple of young married people in *Happy Houses*. All through the book there are nostalgic glances at her own past. Robin, the husband, is a writer; he has a whole page in a weekly review to air his opinions and to review books and plays. He writes books, and knows celebrities. Living with him is not easy:

We grow up perpetually subscribing to other people's opinions, and the result is the dull, dead compromise of thought and feeling against which everybody, being imaginative, revolts successfully. Every individual wishes to have his or her life living and splendid; collectively our timidity forbids the fulfilment of that desire except to the very few who defy the collective compromise, and fight their way through the various tortures of neglect, insult, silence, which the rest of us mete out to them. Nature, it has been observed, says to each of us, 'Will you have your life living or dead?' Collective opinion answers that question in one way, individual desire answers it in another.

She often brings the word 'silence' into her books. She could never forget the appalling shut-out feeling Barrie's silences brought. But the sentence which remains in the mind is one which tells most about that tragic marriage: 'What wonderful children visit the dreams of a childless woman, and how little wonderful they are compared with a living child.'

*   *   *

Barrie had told his friends that he could never go back to Leinster Corner to live, and Sir George Lewis's wife, whose guest he had often been and who liked doing things for her friends, found a flat for him at 3, Adelphi Terrace House in Robert Street, behind the Strand. It was on the third floor and the sitting-room faced south. From the windows one had wide views over the Embankment Gardens and the river, and one could see as far as St Paul's in an easterly direction and the Houses of Parliament to the west.

Lady Lewis knew that Barrie was in no condition to enjoy fine views, but the black mood would wear itself out in time and the dynamo begin to turn again. She had the flat decorated, helped by E. V. Lucas's wife, Elizabeth, a charming woman, already as much a friend of Barrie's as was her talented husBand. Lady Lewis also engaged a manservant for the flat, a north-countryman called Harry Brown, a sterling character who quickly came to understand his temperamental employer. Brown and his wife, as cook, came to be the mainstays of Barrie's domestic life; they were never flustered or put out, and they never took advantage of his undoubtedly casual methods in financial matters. Lady Lewis had excellent judgment in choosing servants.

Barrie moved into the flat, bringing with him from Leinster Corner the few pieces of furniture which had associations for him from his early days, and sent the rest to be disposed of. He immediately began to fill up his days. Where his private life was concerned, he showed an expressionless face, and no one dared ask him questions. He concentrated on what had now become second nature to him—his public image. There were many invitations to private and public functions. He wrote to Sylvia from 3, Adelphi Terrace House on April 30th, 1910:

Dearest J,
Tonight is the Academy dinner, and you may conceive Brown and me hard at work inking my coat sleeves . . . I feel sure a philosopher could deduce all sorts of profundities from a study of an Academy dinner. In all the world there cannot be a much more solemnly dull festivity . . . No one would like it so well if it were less dull. The day the President makes a joke or the Japanese Ambassador smiles, it will begin to go down in public estimation . . . It is the rigid etiquette that we are so proud of; for the time being we all feel ourselves as important as the red-coated footmen at the Carlton. Once a year we feel we have calves. That must be it.

Peter Davies: Either the making absolute of his decree, or a first taste of the pleasures of bachelor life, or both, had apparently had an exhilarating effect on J.M.B. . . . Note the resumption of the 'Dearest Jocelyn' . . . it was no longer necessary to be circumspect now that the decree had been made absolute.

George was doing well at Eton, and enjoying every day to the full. He wrote regularly to his mother. On July 1st, 1910, telling her of a cricket match in which he would be playing, he said: 'I have written to ask Uncle Jim to fulfil his telephone promise and come down tomorrow.'

Peter Davies: From the family point of view, perhaps the most interesting thing in it is the use of the term Uncle Jim . . . symbolizing the intimacy which had so rapidly increased since 1907, until he was closer by far to us as well as directing our destinies, than any of our real uncles. Uncle Jim he remained to the end to those of us who survived, though for a short while after his elevation to the Baronetcy we knew him variously as Sir Jas, Sir Jazz and the Bart.

A few days later, Sylvia was writing to Barrie:

Dear J,
I shall not be able to get to Eton tomorrow after all, I am sorry to say . . . Will you do something for me? I want 1½ doz. white collars (George wears the shape) for Peter and 2 doz. white ties (also like George) as they are best bought at Eton. The shop is called New & Lingwood. Ask for

collars for tails and Peter will know what size and can try one on if wanted. He must bring them home with him . . .

I suppose George can't be let off camp for his delicate mother's sake.

Affec:

S.

Peter Davies: That S. should have contemplated going down to Eton herself shows that she was not at this time entirely inactive; but I think that all movement was now a serious effort to her, and that at frequent intervals she suffered great discomfort. J.M.B. is now clearly seen in the rôle of leading uncle, if not step-father; perhaps guardian angel best describes him. The purchase of collars and ties at this stage indicates that definite arrangements had been made, in case I failed for the scholarship, to go to Eton as an expensive Oppidan, necessarily of course on J.M.B.'s money. The saving in money which the scholarship would mean can only, it is clear, have been of secondary importance, though one may guess that the thought of some small reduction in the extent of her obligations to J.M.B. may not have been unwelcome. But I think what chiefly pleased S. was that it constituted a link, slender enough but recognizable, with the so much more substantial scholarship prowess of A. Ll. D.

[He got the scholarship.]

The summer holiday was spent that year at a house near the northern end of the Devon and Somerset border, near Exmoor, for the sake of the fishing. Sylvia was sure that she was strong enough to face the long journey and the discomfort of what was little more than an isolated farmhouse. Her doctor said that if she wished to go, she should not be denied. Nurse Loosemore, who had nursed her before and was now in regular attendance, said the doctor and Barrie between them were quite mad, and told Mary Hodgson to make herself and the boys scarce on the journey 'as *anything* might happen'. Apparently nobody had been down to the farm to see what comforts, if any, existed there, or how accessible it was. Everything had been done by correspondence.

Sylvia's own doctor, Dr Rendel, accompanied the party for the journey, which was as well, for it was an exhausting day for the sick woman: five hours of train from London followed by fifteen hilly miles in a car across Exmoor. Sylvia, Nurse Loosemore and the boys stayed in the farmhouse, while Barrie took rooms in the neighbouring village of Brendon. Jack Davies, now a cadet at Dartmouth, came down a day or two later.

Emma du Maurier travelled to Devon to see her daughter. Barrie and Peter met her with a hired car at Minehead, and Mrs du Maurier would have enjoyed the lovely scenery had she not been thinking all the time that it was terrible for Sylvia to be so far from good doctors. When she reached the farmhouse she found Sylvia depressed and restless; Dr Rendel had returned to London and the local doctor had been called in. He was deaf and asked silly questions, said Sylvia. Mrs du Maurier told Barrie to telegraph Dr Rendel, saying that it was essential they should have a good doctor at hand and could he suggest anyone.

Crompton Llewelyn Davies had also come, and found rooms at Brendon. He was, as ever, kind and helpful, taking the boys climbing to the top of Dunkery Beacon, ready to be of assistance wherever he was needed. On August 5th Dr Spicer arrived from London—Dr Rendel had acted quickly—and a room was got ready for him at the farmhouse. When Sylvia heard of this she wept, and said, 'I believe I am very ill.' Her mother tried to pacify her by saying she had thought it would be a good thing to have a doctor in the house, in case he was needed during the night. No one talked of the dread in their minds. Peter Davies writes:

From now onwards, while we fished and golfed and walked furiously, or made expeditions to Lynton and ate huge teas with bilberry jam and Devonshire cream, or on idle days watched the buzzards circling slowly, high above the valley of the Lynn—while, in fact, we went our boyish ways—S. weakened rapidly, and I think she never again left her room.

He also relates that Barrie brought down from London the star actress who had taken the lead in his plays in the United States, Maude Adams; she was on a visit to England and Barrie was determined that she should see and be seen by Sylvia and the boys, 'my boys'. Sylvia was too ill to do more than smile. Even that was an effort. Everything was an effort now.

She died on August 27th. The doctor, Nurse Loosemore, Emma du Maurier and Barrie were in the room; the boys were out. Peter Davies recalls that afternoon:

As I went in at the gate, it struck me that there was something peculiar in the aspect of the house: in every window the blinds had been drawn Somehow or other the dreadful significance of this sombre convention conveyed itself to my shocked understanding, as with heart in boots and unsteady knees I covered the remaining thirty or forty yards to the front door. There J.M.B. awaited me: a distraught figure, arms hanging limp, hair dishevelled, wild-eyed.

In what exact words he told me what I had no need to be told, I forget; but it was brokenly, despairingly, without any pretence of philosophy or resignation or stiff upper lip. He must have been sunk in depths far below all that, poor Jimmy. I think it was I that propelled him, as much as he me, into the room on the left of the little entrance hall, where we sat and blubbered together. Good cause for blubbering, too, for both of us: but I remember, and wish I didn't, sobbing out 'Mother! Mother!' at intervals during the sad and painful scene, and realizing, even as I did so, that this wasn't altogether natural in me—that, though half involuntary, it was also a half deliberate playing-up to the situation. I can forgive myself now, after thirty-five years, for this rather shameful bit of nervous reaction; the rest of it, the tears and misery and desolation, were genuine enough . . .

Jack Davies had a different reaction. He wrote to Peter many years later: 'I was taken into a room where [Barrie] was alone and he told me, which angered me even then, that Mother had promised to marry him and wore his ring. Even then I thought if it was true it must be because she knew she was dying.'

Michael and Nicholas were sent to stay with Mary Hodgson at her home; the other boys returned to London with the adults. Jack recalled 'a hideous journey, with the coffin in a van, covered in purple cloth', and Barrie at every stop doing sentry-go outside.

Sylvia had made a long and detailed will, in which she set down her wishes as to who should look after her sons:

I would like Mamma and J.M.B. and Guy and Crompton to be trustees and guardians to the boys . . . J.M.B. I know will do everything in his power to help our boys—to advise, to comfort, to sympathize in all their joys and sorrows. At present my Jack is going into the Navy—if he should grow to dislike it and if there is anything else, I know he [J.M.B.] would do all that was best. I want all the boys to treat him (and their uncles) with absolute confidence and straightforwardness and to talk to him about everything. I know he will understand always and be loving and patient . . .

I do not want my Michael to be pressed at all at work—he is at present not very strong but very keen and intelligent: great care must be taken not to overwork him. Mary understands and of course J.M.B. knows and will be careful and watch.

Peter Davies: Though it is nowhere explicitly stated, there is a clear enough underlying assumption that the principal part in the direction of her sons' destinies would be taken by J.M.B. He is named more often and more prominently than any of the other 'trustees and guardians'. On the other hand there is no suggestion that he was to have sole control, either financially—but perhaps the financial vagueness of the will suggests that this was taken for granted—or as guide, counsellor and friend.

In another note, Peter Davies remarks that he finds it grotesque that he should remember so little of his mother's funeral

and yet that one should clearly remember going with J.M.B. and G., presumably the morning after the funeral, to an old-fashioned, long-since-pulled-down shop in the Haymarket, called Little, to purchase exciting, slender 8-ft fly-rods, and fine casts and flies, with which to divert ourselves during the remainder of the holidays! For it had been decided, by those who took charge of our destinies, that G. and I should go back with J.M.B., not indeed to Ashton [Farm] itself, but to Oare, a mile or so higher up the little river, there to fish till Eton and Wilkinson's claimed us; while J. went his separate way to stay with Guy and Gwen du M. at Longmoor . . .

I dare say it worked well enough, and that the new rods helped, as no doubt J.M.B. with generous cunning knew that they would, to do the trick.

Chapter 15

'MY BOYS'

WHATEVER the legal position was of the five Davies brothers with regard to J. M. Barrie, there was no doubt whatever in his mind that they now belonged to him: they were 'my boys'. He had several meetings with the uncles and with Emma du Maurier—who had never cared much for him and who liked him no better now, in spite of his kindness and generosity.

Sylvia had left her little bit of money to her sons, and there was more in trust for them under the will of their grandfather, George du Maurier. Added together, the income was nowhere near enough for the standard of life which Sylvia had always wanted them to have, and which Barrie considered as a sacred trust. The Llewelyn Davies relations and the du Mauriers were helpless in the face of this kind of will-power. In any case, they were not in a position to make objections. They could not undertake, even between them, the nurture and education of five boys. This little Scotsman was able to do it— and nothing, they saw, was going to prevent his carrying out his determination to be the arbiter of their destinies.

They were an attractive family. George, now seventeen, was an Oppidan at Eton. Jack, rising sixteen, was nearly through Dartmouth. Peter, fourteen, was a Tug, a scholarship boy, at Eton. Michael, already Barrie's favourite, was ten, and bore a strong resemblance to his mother: he was gifted, sensitive and impressionable, with a great deal of charm. The youngest, Nicholas—Nico— was not quite seven, a cheerful little boy who had another year to go at Norland Place before joining Michael at Wilkinson's.

Barrie himself was fifty years old, and, to all intents and purposes, a bachelor. He kept on 23, Campden Hill Square and the staff for the boys, with Mary Hodgson in charge, and divided his time between the house and the Adelphi Terrace flat. But, as he told the boys, Campden Hill Square was his *home*—his home and their home. He

had become so much a part of their lives during the past years that
it should not have been difficult for them to accept the situation. The
Davies brothers, however, were not puppets; they were exceedingly
intelligent human beings, each with a marked individuality. They
accepted the 'guardianship' of this strange man because they had no
alternative. What they thought, they kept to themselves. George,
Jack and Peter had been fascinated by his gift for story-telling when
they were children but now they were boys, growing into young
men. They knew instinctively that he still thought of them as
children. He could be a delightful companion when he set out to be
so, but they were becoming acutely aware that he was entirely
different from anyone in their own circle of family and friends.
Without being able to analyse the relationship, they felt, deep down,
that they did not care to be *possessed* in this way.

To Barrie, everything was natural and straightforward. He
regarded himself as being *in loco parentis* to the boys. There was a
peculiar satisfaction for him that they should be at Eton. He had
been enthralled by the idea of the English public schools from an
early age, and had once written an article entitled 'Old Hyphen'
which was about these schools. Years later, he commented on this
article in *The Greenwood Hat*:

Old Hyphen and his young friends in an English public school were
wildfowl unknown to Anon in the days in which he wrote of them, but
they pop up frequently in the *St James's* in his first two years, and were a
standby when the larder was at its lowest. Greenwood could be got with
a schoolboy paper when he would not rise to another fly.

Again, during a speech he made at the Girls' High School at
Wallasey, where his niece, Lilian—Alec Barrie's daughter—was
headmistress, he said:

Your great public schools: I never feel myself a foreigner in England
except when trying to understand them. I have a great affection for one at
least of them. They will bewilder me to the end: I am like a dog looking
up wistfully at its owner, wondering what that noble face means, or if it
does have a meaning. To look at, these schools are the fairest things in
England. They draw from their sons a devotion that is deeper and more
lasting than almost any other love, and I well know that among their
masters are men than whom there are no finer in the country. Those
schools must be great, and yet I don't quite see how it comes about. Of
course they send yearly on their way a few good scholars and not so few
eminent in the games that we love in this land and are right in loving, bu

the other four-fifths or so, what do they get from their famous schools? The generals and other illustrious old boys answer that question triumphantly at the school festivities we have been speaking of, but leave the outsider still benighted. It is not scholarship—pooh—it is not even physical prowess, it is not an awakened soul or any exclusive manliness nor even a superior way of wearing waistcoats. They describe it briefly and unanswerably as a something, and perhaps wisely leave it at that, putting us in our place for ever, and satisfying the youth still at school who may have been worrying a little on the subject.

Barrie became a more dedicated Etonian than the most old-school-tie-conscious Old Etonian would ever have allowed himself to be. The Llewelyn Davies boys had to have the best, and Eton was the best public school. He looked upon his responsiiblity for sending them partly as a sacred trust to Jocelyn, and partly as a subconscious passion to be associated in some way with one of the most aristocratic of all English educational institutions. Barrie was never ashamed of Kirriemuir or of his family, but as the social limits of his life widened, he automatically raised his standards. He had not been born into the upper stratum of society, but by the grace of—well, by the power of his magic pen, he had got himself there. It gave him real happiness.

Snobbery? Barrie has often been called a snob because he 'loved a laird', but it was a natural and harmless form of snobbery in one who had been born in a weaver's cottage, and was now a famous man. He showed none of the false pride of the self-made man; he was always courteous, and his enormous correspondence is evidence of the thoughtfulness which he put into answering hundreds of unknown correspondents who wrote to him for advice, information —and, of course, money. There are a great many real snobs who would not have put pen to paper for unknown correspondents. And pen to paper it really was, for Barrie had no secretary and wrote everything in longhand.

*   *   *

Notebooks were being crammed with notes, as usual.

'Murder play (dinner first act)'. Odd sentences, key words, embryo plots. The dynamo was again working at high pressure in that remarkably fertile brain.

He spent most of the week at Adelphi Terrace House and the week-ends at Campden Hill Square. Mary Hodgson ran the house-

hold very efficiently, and Michael and Nicholas were always glad to
see him when he appeared. He had new stories to tell them every
time he came, and they were still young enough to like exciting
stories. They would be going to Eton when the time came, and
Barrie knew he would hate the house at week-ends, with no boys
rushing round or sitting on the hearthrug with upturned faces,
listening while he wove tale after tale for their delight.

He saw a great deal of his friends. E. V. Lucas introduced him to
a fresh circle, and he enjoyed their respect and admiration; there was
a 'distinct, profound and mystical satisfaction in being J. M. Barrie'.
His friendship with Captain Robert Falcon Scott had grown close
since their early meetings. When a son was born to Kathleen Scott
on September 14th, 1909, Captain Scott wrote to Barrie asking him
to be godfather. Barrie replied from Lausanne on September 23rd:

> Your letter had to follow me about, hence delay. I shall be delighted to
> be godfather to the boy and am very glad you asked me. May he be a
> great source of happiness to you both—or let me say, please, to all three
> of us. Also, I am very glad the expedition is to come off, and it will be a
> real pleasure to me to subscribe. If there's anything else I can do, be sure
> I will. When I am back in London I'll write to you and then let us have a
> talk about it.

Scott had published his plans for a British Antarctic Expedition
which would set off in the summer of 1910, and £10,000 was
collected from the public. The government made a grant of £20,000,
and further grants came from the governments of Australia, New
Zealand and South Africa. There was sufficient money to buy and
equip the *Terra Nova*, which was the strongest of the old Scottish
whalers. The *Terra Nova* left Cardiff in June, 1910, and arrived at
Lyttleton in New Zealand at the end of October. The epic of that
Antarctic journey and its outcome belongs to the world's roll of
heroic endeavour.

*   *   *

In 1911, Coronation year, London was full. A grand Shakespeare
Ball was to take place at the Albert Hall, in aid of the establishment
of a National Theatre, and Millicent, Duchess of Sutherland, wrote
asking Barrie to help her with ideas for a costume which would
outshine all others. Barrie promptly engaged the artist, Dion
Clayton Calthrop, a nephew of Dion Boucicault's, to design a

striking costume for her, incorporating his own ideas. He wrote to her on April 20th, 1911, asking a favour:

I wonder whether you would in the goodness of your heart set some factor in Sutherland searching for a house for me up there for August and September. I bring four boys with me; what they yearn for is to be remote from Man and plenty of burn trout fishing, of which they never tire from the rising to the setting of the sun. The rate would not so much matter but there should be space for about ten of us including maids. How delightful it would be to me if I were in calling distance of you. Just conceive me looking old and weary and then you appear round that clachan. Is it too good to be true?

I hear of you being in London occasionally after you've gone, but I never hear from you yourself, which certainly makes me sad, nor of that play which I hoped to know well by this time. Do come and be seen again and disregard those other people. They can't need you as much as I do, and even though they did, disregard them just the same. I want to see you in your Shakespeare gown. I want to design it so they may say I have built the true Shakespeare memorial. I want to write to William and tell him how you looked in it.

Yours,

J. M. BARRIE.

The Duchess suggested Scourie Lodge, on an inlet in Sutherland, and Barrie found it just as he hoped, remote from Man and with plenty of good fishing in lochs and burns for the Llewelyn Davies boys. Friends came and went, staying at a hotel not far away, but it was the holiday of the boys' dreams, out in the open air all the time, fishing.

Barrie talked to his friends about 'my boys' with the greatest pride. Jack was at sea, and letters came infrequently, but Barrie kept up a regular correspondence with George at Eton. George was in the full flush of his Eton career, in Pop[1] and the Twenty-two,[2] a known figure throughout the school, very well dressed, aware of his popularity. He had entered for the essay prize, which he won. Peter Davies says: 'That he should have won this particular prize, for which there was plenty of competition, is strong evidence of his intellectual capacity and all-round quality.'

1. The nickname given to the Eton Society, which consists of some twenty to twenty-five senior boys, usually elected for success in games or for being out-standingly popular.
2. The Eton name for the Second Eleven at cricket.

As was to be expected, Barrie was always greatly interested in any mention of cricket. He wrote on June 3rd, 1912:

My dear George,
Floreat Etona. I hope the weather is to be propitious . . . It is four years since the day when your mother and I were there and you made us stay on for the fireworks and were really just a small boy, impaling yourself by the waterside on railings. I did not then know even that there was such a thing as Pop. It has swum into my ken like some celestial young lady.

It is sad that your bowling arm has not been doing the rest of you justice lately, but I am still ready to believe that any day it may retrieve itself, and I have a blessed confidence in your taking the thing in a right spirit shd hopes in the end be disappointed. You remember Rooseveldt's [*sic*] mother, 'She done her d—dest, angels could do no more' . . .

The great thing for me at all events is the feeling that if your father and mother were here on this 4th June they would be well pleased on the whole with their eldest born . . .

> *Your affec.*
> J.M.B.

On June 19th he was writing:

Nicholas having got a superb bow and arrows has nearly done for all the inhabitants of the Campden Hill district. He is now prepared to use them against any batsman who is not tied in a knot by your bowling. I found Michael surrounded by his presents when I got back from Eton. He has a grand salmon net from your granny, which in low water I shd say would do for scooping the fish out of the pools. I have seen a picture of Amhuinnsuidh. The house is nearer the sea than Scourie Lodge—just separated from it by a terrace which I take to be a tennis lawn.

Peter Davies: Amhuinnsuidh, a vast mansion on the isle of Harris, built in what Osbert Lancaster might describe as Stockbrokers' Scotch Baronial style, was taken by J.M.B. for the summer holidays of that year. The cost must have been fabulous. The fishing was to match . . . I was just at the stage when poor J.M.B. had to give me, on the banks of a burn, a small talking-to for indulging at Eton in what my tutor euphemistically termed water-closet talk. He very nearly penetrated my juvenile defences by telling me it had always been his view that a man without some element of coarseness in his nature was not a whole man, which must have disconcerted me, coming from him . . .

The earlier part of the letter affords a passing glimpse of the strange household at 23 Campden Hill Square, between which and his flat in the Adelphi J.M.B. at this period divided his time. Michael and Nico, both now at Wilkinson's, were the permanent residents; the other three of us returned to the fold from time to time; the presiding genius of the place was Mary Hodgson, faithful to her trust, though inevitably disapproving of so much of the nouveau regime . . .

Crompton concerned himself closely with our affairs both as friend and lawyer, from the death of A. Ll. D. to that of S. Ll. D. He was the most emotional of men, and indeed there must have been something about that house to wring the withers of any but the least sensitive . . .

*   *   *

Early in 1913, Kathleen Scott set out for New Zealand, via the United States, to meet her husband on his return from the Antarctic. On February 12th, the *Terra Nova* with part of the Expedition reached Lyttelton with the news that the Polar party led by Captain Scott had been found in their snowbound tent, dead, some months before.

In London, the news struck everyone like a national disaster. Barrie was prostrated. This mood of black despair lasted until he learned that Captain Scott had written several letters before his death in the snowbound tent, and that one of these letters was addressed to him, to J. M. Barrie. He was exalted. Here is the letter

[Captain Scott's lack of punctuation, and his way of sometimes putting a dash instead of a full point, have been copied. Other dashes are indicated in the normal positions.]

My Dear Barrie,

We are pegging out in a very comfortless spot Hoping this letter may be found & sent to you I write a word of farewell— It hurt me grievously when you partially withdrew your friendship or seemed to do—I want to tell you that I never gave you cause— If you thought or heard ill of me it was unjust— Calumny is ever to the fore. My attitude towards you and everyone connected with you was always one of respect and admiration— Under these circumstances I want you to think well of me and of my end and more practically I want you to help my widow and my boy/your Godson. We are showing that Englishmen can still die with a bold spirit fighting it out to the end. It will be known that we have accomplished our object in reaching the Pole and that we have done everything possible even to sacrificing ourselves in order to save sick companions— I think this makes an example for Englishmen of the future and that the country ought to help those who are left behind to mourn us— I leave my poor girl and your Godson. Wilson leaves a widow & Edgar Evans also a widow in humble circumstances. Do what you can to get their claims recognised.

Goodbye—I am not at all afraid of the end but sad to miss many a simple pleasure which I had planned for the future on our long marches— I may not have proved a great explorer, but we have done the greatest march ever made and come very near to great success.

Goodbye my dear friend
Yours ever
R. Scott

We are in a desperate state feet frozen etc. no fuel and a long way from food but it would do your heart good to be in our tent, to hear our songs and the cheery conversation as to what we will do when we get to Hut Point.

Later We are very near the end but have not and will not lose our good cheer we have had four days of storm in our tent and now have no food or fuel— We did intend to finish ourselves when things proved like this but we have decided to die naturally in the track

(see over)

as a dying man my dear friend be good to my wife & child— Give the boy a chance in life if the State won't do it—He ought to have good stuff in him—and give my memory back the friendship which you [? inspired] I never met a man in my life whom I admired and loved more than you but I never could show you how much your friendship meant to me— you had much to give and I nothing.

[The letter was written in pencil on four leaves torn from Captain Scott's notebook and was posted to Kathleen Scott from Australia by those who found Scott's body.]

What went wrong between them? What dart of ill intent entered Barrie's heart and stayed there, rankling, before the explorer went off on his last journey? Years later Barrie dropped hints which indicated that there was something he bitterly regretted, but he never told what it was. Neither did he ever publish or quote the full text of Captain Scott's letter: there were always those personal passages in the first and last paragraphs missing.

He wrote to Kathleen Scott from Adelphi Terrace House on April 11th, 1913:

Dear Lady Scott,
I have been hoping all the time that there was some such letter for me from your husband, and the joy with which I receive it is more than the pain. I am very proud of the wishes expressed in it, and I hope in time you will be able to say you were glad it was written. I know a hundred things he would like me to do for Peter, and I want, out of love for his father,

to do them well. And I want to be such a friend to you as he wished. I should have wanted to do that had there been no such letter, and more. I feel I have a right to ask you to give me the chance. I am longing to hear when I may see you.

Let me sign myself most affectionately,

from

J. M. BARRIE.

She asked him to help her frame a statement as to how the Polar party met their end. Barrie replied:

Dear Kathleen,
Something short and simple as this is what I think might follow the message to the public. 'Wilson and Burrows died first, and Captain Scott enclosed them in their sleeping bags. At some unknown time thereafter, he removed the fur coat from his shoulders, unbared his shirt and seated himself against the centre pole with his head flung back and his eyes wide open, awaited death. We know this because it was thus these three were found when the search-party looked into the tent six months afterwards.' What do you think? Some of the wording may not be quite right, but the brevity is.

Yours,

J.M.B.

Barrie was now to come into the public eye in a new light. A few years before, he had tactfully refused a knighthood, but this year, 1913, his name appeared in the Birthday Honours. He had accepted a baronetcy; he was now Sir James Barrie, Bart. The Davies boys thought this funny, though in a queer kind of way they were proud of him, too. The younger boys called him Uncle Jim: to the older ones he had always been Mr Barrie. They tried 'Sir Jas' but Barrie did not like this, so Uncle Jim he became to them, too.

Charles Frohman was over for the summer, and he, naturally, was bubbling with enthusiasm at his little friend's elevation to a title. Frohman was as kind and friendly as ever, but he was no longer the powerful theatrical magnate he had once been. He had been very ill the previous year, and the number of his productions had fallen off. This year would be even more of a gamble, but he was still full of plans, and the affection between the two men was as strong as ever.

Barrie had written several short plays, and his notebooks were scrawled with ideas, but he had no major play in mind. He did not, however, stop writing. Letters to his friends came from his pen in a never-ending flow. He kept up a regular correspondence with

Charles Turley Smith, who lived in Cornwall. Turley, as he was called by his friends, stayed with Barrie when he came to London, and they always had a session at the 'dambrod'—draughts were almost as much a passion with them both as cricket, about which they wrote to each other endlessly. Barrie once said in a letter to this friend: 'I have so many letters to write that it comes to my not writing the ones I want to write,' but he often managed to get a letter off to Turley, who sent him spring flowers directly they appeared. On May 10th, 1913, Barrie wrote to him: 'Many thanks for the bluebells and a squeeze of the hand for every one you plucked. Still more for the affection that made you know how sad I would be about Michael gone to school.'

And later, in reply to Turley's letter of congratulations on his Honour: '!!! This is my reply to you about the baronetcy, and I rather flatter myself that you are grinding your teeth because you did not think of such a good way of referring thereto yourself.

'Nicholas was good on the subject. I had told him the night before to look in the papers next morning for surprising news, and he was up betimes and searched the cricket columns from end to end.'

Michael Davies had left Wilkinson's and had entered Hugh Macnaghten's house at Eton. The wrench had been greater than it had been with the other boys; a special relationship had grown up between Michael and Barrie.

They seemed to understand each other more completely than had been the case with the other boys. Michael possessed the Llewelyn Davies good looks, but his personality was unusual, too. He had the temperament of a sensitive writer; talent was there, and sensibility and awareness. Barrie had grown to love him dearly, and the boy had always given him a son's affection. They wrote to each other every day from the very beginning of Michael's time at Eton.

On November 18th, 1913, Barrie was writing to George, who had left Eton and was now at Cambridge:

My dear George,
Yes, it was all very sad, and I knew how you were feeling it. Many things besides this will remind you of the last days at Ashton . . . Your mother did not want your minds to dwell on sadness even for a moment when you were younger . . . She did not wish her funeral day to be made long and wearisome for you . . . It can only be afterwards that a boy realizes the unselfishness of a mother's love. It is a pain as well as a glory to him. Of course there is much you can do for her still. And one thing is to work

well at Cambridge, for the future so depends on it, and you can guess how she thought of your future.

Peter Davies: I don't know what circumstances gave rise to this letter. Possibly there had been some discussion about wills and things, as George was now in his twenty-first year.

It is an admirable letter, as indeed all J.M.B.'s to George are. Yet, might it not be argued, without impropriety, that it requires no very great unselfishness to be anxious to spare one's children the dreary and to them incomprehensible ordeal of one's funeral? . . .

I know very little indeed of George's time at Cambridge, which only lasted a couple of years . . . He turned from a boy into a young man, and must have spread his wings a little in the vacations. I don't think he was precocious, and I am sure there were very few dark or difficult places in his character. He was exceptionally attractive to both sexes, but not spoilt. He had a devoted and in many ways invaluable mentor in J.M.B., but the way cannot have been altogether easy for him, as the first of the family to grow up against so peculiar a background.

*   *   *

A Mansion House Fund, subscribed by the public, provided an income for the dependants of the men who had lost their lives in the Antarctic Expedition. Kathleen Scott would not at first accept anything from the Fund, as she was confident of being able to earn her living. She was persuaded in the end to accept a certain amount for her son's education, in case she died; and after the other dependants were adequately looked after, she suggested that the balance of the Fund should go to found the Scott Polar Institute at Cambridge.

Barrie went to her house in Buckingham Palace Road on several occasions to see her and his godson. On May 9th, 1914, Kathleen Scott received a letter which must have made her smile:

The News Editor of the *Daily Chronicle* presents his compliments to Lady Scott and would be obliged if she would affirm or deny a report which has been forwarded to the News Editor this afternoon, that she was married to Sir J. M. Barrie six weeks ago. The News Editor hesitates to trouble Lady Scott in this matter, but on account of the many rumours which have been in circulation lately, begs to suggest to her ladyship that an official statement from her, in regard to the matter, would be of service.

There is no record that Kathleen Scott showed this letter to Barrie, but it is probable that she dealt with the enquiry succinctly and with finality.

Barrie went north in July. Alec had died on 16th July at Strathview. Another grave in the cemetery at Kirriemuir. What were Jamie's thoughts as he walked behind the coffin with the chief mourners, Alec's widow, two sons and four daughters? It is difficult to guess, for Barrie could lacerate himself over romantic images, imagined obligations, yet remain strangely untouched when the obligations were real. He owed a great deal to the patient, generous Alec, who had given him his chance in life and had never withheld praise or encouragement. Barrie would always be ready to help Alec's widow and children: he would repay those early school fees and university charges with interest, over and over again.

But had he, deep down, shown his brother how grateful he had been? He would ask himself that question more than once. Meanwhile, a famous son of Kirriemuir had come to the funeral of his respected elder brother, who, after thirty-six years as one of His Majesty's Inspectors of Schools, had gone to his long rest. And if the phrase 'he died full of years and honour' applied to anyone, it applied to Alexander Ogilvy Barrie.

George went to Italy in the Long Vacation of 1914 with two Eton-Cambridge friends, Micky Lawrence and David Heaton. Barrie wrote to him at Fortezza, Aulla, Massa Carrara, on June 29th, 1914:

My dear George,
It seems to be a little heaven below, and your first introduction to Italy something you won't forget. London is very close just now, and when evening comes I envy your roof garden and the fireflies. I have seen them but not in their glory as you are getting them. Italy I only know in the north where I walked for a bit a hundred years agone. I hope you got a fish that first night you went out to try for them . . . I went to Winchester the first day of the match to be with Michael, as Peter had other fish to fry. Both sides batted well but on a good wicket very weak on bowling.

Peter sends me orders to take him to the opera at Long Leave.
                                        Your affte
                                              J.M.B.

He wrote again on July 13th:

My dear George,
Peter and I set out on Saturday to wire you the result of the Eton & Harrow match and forgot about it in the stress of going to the opera.

Both nights of Long Leave did he drag me to the opera. Neither he nor Michael patronized the match, and, again, as on a former occasion you remember, we were at the White City thinking all was up with Eton, while the XI were gloriously turning defeat into victory. Another piece of news just arrived tonight is that Michael who went in for the College Scholarship exam came out seventh. He will stay on at Macnaghten's, but I am glad he went in and some other boy can be made happy with the scholarship . . .

Very near your birthday now!

Your affcte

J.M.B.

Peter Davies: No doubt it was naughty of me, as J.M.B.'s faintly caustic phrase implies, to steer clear of the Winchester match, to say nothing of Lord's. All the same, his (only semi-) humorous references to my callow enthusiasm for the opera—to which, nevertheless, he gallantly accompanied me—are a reminder that, being himself totally unmusical, he not only did not encourage such leanings, but in one way and another could not help discouraging them. The operas were Khovantchina and (I think) Boris Godounov, with Chaliapin singing; and one had also at the time a calf-love for the Russian ballet, then an exciting novelty, and that was still more emphatically frowned on and ridiculed. He may have been right; but I felt obscurely then, and feel strongly now, that a little more encouragement in the artistic way would have been very good for us all; would have filled a real need in our sprouting natures. The fact is that music and painting and poetry, and the part they may be supposed to play in making a civilized being, had a curiously small place in J.M.B.'s view of things. I think it was of far more interest to him that George and I and all of us should excel in games and fishing, as well as of course being thoroughly good *mens sana in corpore sano* specimens, than that we should acquire any real culture in Matthew Arnold's sense of the word.

The lighter side of life was thoroughly catered for, and for that I am duly and deeply grateful. 'Hullo Ragtime' and its successors, with which J.M.B. was so oddly and closely connected, was one of our major preoccupations and delights, and what we didn't know about revue was scarcely worth knowing . . . And if one had to discover the 'Sentimental Journey' (in a little volume with A. Ll. D. on the fly-leaf) and Shelley (ditto) for oneself, one was guided with much wise criticism down the paths of Kipling and Stevenson and Thackeray and Meredith, to say nothing of Phillips Oppenheim and O. Henry. And of course there was the intimate connection with his own plays.

* * *

At the declaration of war in August, 1914, George, Michael and Nicholas were with Barrie at Auch, in Argyllshire, beginning their summer holiday. Jack had already been mobilized as a sub-lieutenant in the Navy. Peter was in London for the O.T.C. camp, but he went up by the night train to Scotland, taking with him a letter addressed to George which he had picked up at Campden Hill Square. The letter proved to be a circular communication from the Adjutant of the Cambridge O.T.C., pointing out that it was the duty of all undergraduates to offer their services to the country forthwith.

Peter and George travelled back to London in a carriage full of reservists rejoining the colours. Next day they went to Cambridge. Within a few weeks they were in the army as junior officers. On November 15th, Barrie was writing to George at Sheerness:

Very glad to get your letter and to hear there is some chance of your getting a couple of nights soon. I shall be your humble servant for the occasion. It is very strange to me to read of your being at your musketry practice, for it seems to me but the other day your mother was taking bows and arrows out of your hands and pressing on me the danger of giving you penny pistols.

He wrote again on November 30th:

My dear George,
I was very gratified by your writing to me for your mother's birthday. I would rather have you do so than any one alive; you can understand how I yearn to have you sitting with me now and at all times. What you don't know in the least is the help you have been to me, and have become more and far more as these few years have passed. There is nothing I would not confide in you or trust to you . . .
I've done 'Der Tag', my war play, and will get you a copy. It's also possible I'll turn the Barker revue into a shorter thing for Gaby. Jack wires he may get up tomorrow tho' whether only for the day he doesn't say.
Your loving
J.M.B.

Peter Davies: A clear indication of the very deep and strong bonds which united J.M.B. and G. Ll. D.

Barrie's war play *Der Tag*, produced at the Coliseum on December 21st, 1914, was his comment on the war. W. A. Darlington said: 'It had some of the faults inherent in all art that is made to serve a political purpose, but it put into dignified language the cause for which the Allies were fighting . . .' And again:

Gaby Deslys, a French music-hall performer with good looks but no conspicuous talent except for the wearing of clothes which contrived to be at the same time voluminous and scanty, was a favourite with London audiences. Barrie had conceived a great admiration for her and wrote a revue, called *Rosy Rapture or the Pride of the Beauty Chorus* specially designed for her. Frohman put it on at the Duke of York's on March 22nd, 1915, and it failed completely. It was a curious trait in Barrie's character that he could never bring himself to admit that he had no ability for devising this kind of entertainment.

George went to France. He wrote to Barrie on January 3rd, 1915:

Dear Uncle Jim,
I have got some spare time now that is not occupied with sleeping, and I'll try to see how much news I can give you. The fear of death doesn't enter so much as I expected, the hardships are the things that count, and one gets very soon into the way of taking them as they come . . . Don't you get worried about me, I take every precaution I can and shall do very well. It is an amazing show, and I am unable to look forward more than two or three hours. Also don't get anxious about letters. I'll send them whenever there's a chance, but there are less chances than I expected.
Your affec. GEORGE.

Barrie was writing to him on the same day, giving him news of the other boys. Jack was on a large destroyer, Peter was doing signals at Chatham. He had taken Michael and Nicholas to the play, *David Copperfield*, 'and every time Owen Nares came on as David there were loud gasps of Oh how sweet. Almost too sweet, I shd have thought. The make-up of the other characters was very good, but the inside of them not so special.'

George wrote from Flanders on January 18th:

Dear Uncle Jim,
My last entrance into the trenches was stopped by sickness, and I stayed in bed in my billet . . . Health is of enormous importance here. We are resting again now, so I shall be all right. The Burberry and boots have come here and are fine. As to the ski boots, I don't know what I should do without them. I put little slippers inside them and keep as warm as possible.

Barrie wrote by return from Brighton, where he was staying with E. V. Lucas and his family. He wrote:

Chills are all fever of a kind, and I so earnestly hope time is given you to shake it off properly. Such weather conditions must be the grimmest of combatants . . . Wherever you are I hope you see near your bed the flowers I want to place there in a nice vase, and the illustrated papers and a new work by Compton Mackenzie which I read aloud to you! I shall be so anxious till I get another line from you.

Your loving

J.M.B.

Peter Davies: I think this letter well illustrates—taken in conjunction with others which have gone before—the peculiar and characteristic form which J.M.B.'s affection for George and Michael took: a dash of the paternal, a lot of maternal, and much, too, of the lover—at this stage Sylvia's lover still imperfectly merged into the lover of her son. To criticize would be easy; yet I don't think it did, or would have done, George any harm.

George wrote as often as he could, knowing how Barrie worried about him. Barrie, as always, replied by return. He told George that he was sending a Thermos flask and some eatables from Fortnum and Mason, and gave news of some of his own doings:

We haven't done any rehearsing for the burlesque yet, as Gaby's recovery from an operation on her vocal cords has been slower than was expected. She has gone to the South of France to recuperate, and probably will rehearse in a week or two. Mr Lucas is busy with the songs. There's one the husband sings in English and she in French. He is a Tommy.

HE: Of all the girls that I do love
    There's one who lives near Calais,
    She is the darling of my heart
SHE: And she is now his Ally

The hamper went off from Fortnum and Mason's with a tongue, ham, turkey and other eatables. Barrie wrote:

I am always at Nico about writing to you, and he is always deciding to do it tomorrow, with the results known to you. He seems to have got to a stage when letter-writing assumes the appearance of a Frankenstein to him.

He went on to give an opinion about the conduct of the war:

It is not expected that the 'German blockade' of these shores will mean much trouble, but of course occasional merchant ships will be sunk. I'm curious to know what America will do if it is as good as its threats. It has some ships, of course, and an army so small that I came to the conclusion after my talk with Roosevelt that it consisted of him and his four sons. It would stop their sending supplies to Germany at all events. Italy would be of more practical help.

Peter Davies: J.M.B.'s views as to the blockade which so nearly won the war for the Germans were probably those which prevailed in well-informed quarters in 1915. The joke about Roosevelt harks back to [the] visit paid to America by J.M.B. at the beginning of the war, which had the blessing of the British Government and was designed to bring America in on our side, but which for various reasons fell rather flat.

Nico who did, in fact, write to George—probably after some pushing—was now eleven years old. Michael, aged fourteen, wrote to George from Eton on March 3rd, 1915:

Dear George,
As I am at the moment afflicted with a belly ache and staying out, I seize the chance to write this news letter. Leave is past, last week-end I found Peter at 23, having got leave from Friday to Sunday evening, and Uncle Jim rehearsing plays with a bad cold. I went to the Coliseum, which was not at its best. However, that was made up for by the fact that we had the Royal Box, which I had not been in before . . . I had a letter from Jack this morning, in which he says he has done over 3000 miles in the last twelve days, which seems rather a lot.

George wrote to Barrie to say that the Fortnum and Mason box had arrived, or, rather, boxes and boxes:

We are a grateful party of officers and shall be in clover for the six days' rest that is coming. It is good of you. I shall probably ask for more in a fortnight or three weeks. This time I ask you for a new novel. I ask for the devil of a lot, but everything I get here is worth thirty times what it was in the piping times of peace.

Barrie wrote from Adelphi Terrace House on February 28th, 1915:

My dear George,
Your letter dated 20th Feb arrived yesterday and made me happy for the moment at all events. I had hardly finished reading and re-reading it (quite as if I was a young lady) when there arrives, unexpected, a gent of the name of Peter. He had managed at last to get two days' leave by bearding his colonel, and in he walked, larger than ever . . . By good luck it has also been Eton Long Leave so Michael was back also, and we have made something of a show at meals. I have just seen Peter off again, and one of my quaint memories will be of his sitting on the Duke of York's stage chatting to Mlle Gaby. Heavens, what a worker she is! I have never

known man or woman on the stage with such a capacity for work and always so gracious to everybody that they are all at her feet. Life, sir, is odd, as you have been seeing these last two months, but it is even odder than that. Such a queer comedy of tears and grimness and the inexplicable —as your du Maurier blood will make you understand sooner than most. It will teach you that the nice people are the nastiest and the nastiest the nicest, and on the whole leave you smiling.

A few things to note from your last. For one thing I enclose four pounds in French money, and for another it is always a blessed thing for me when you want something. So if you don't want, go on inventing . . . The one great thing for me is when we are all together again.

Loving

J.M.B.

Peter Davies: Some truly wonderful stuff in this letter, which only J.M.B. could have written.

On March 11th, 1915, Barrie had to write a letter to George which he knew would sadden the young soldier:

My dear George,
I don't know when news from quite near you may reach you—perhaps later than we get it—but we have just heard that your uncle Guy has been killed. He was a soldier by profession, and had reached a time of life when the best things have to come to one if they are to come at all, and he had no children, which is the best reason for caring to live on after the sun has set, and these are things to remember now . . . There was always something pathetic about him to me. He had lots of stern stuff in him, & yet always the mournful smile of one who could pretend that life was gay but knew it wasn't. One of the most attractive personalities I have ever known.

Of course I don't need this to bring home to me the danger you are always in more or less, but I do seem to be sadder today than ever, and more and more wishing you were a girl of 21 instead of a boy, so that I could say the things to you that are now always in my heart . . . I have lost all sense I ever had of war being glorious, it is just unspeakably monstrous to me now.

Loving,

J.M.B.

Peter Davies: Surely no soldier in France or Flanders ever had more moving words from home than those in this tragic, desperately apprehensive letter . . . Plenty of people, no doubt, were thinking and writing much the same sort of thing, but not in such perfection.

Its poignancy is dreadfully enhanced, too, by the realization that whatever of pathetic there may have been in Guy du M.—and I don't doubt there was a good deal (I think, by the way, he was almost as closely bound to his mother as J.M.B. to Margaret Ogilvy)—far, far the most pathetic figure in all the world was the poor little genius who wrote those words, and afterwards, no doubt, walked up and down, up and down his lonely room, smoking pipe after pipe, thinking his dire thoughts.

Barrie received the following letter from George, which had been written on March 14th, 1915:

Dear Uncle Jim,
I have just got your letter about Uncle Guy. You say it hasn't made you think any more about the danger I am in. But I know it has. Do try not to let it. I take every care of myself that can decently be taken. And if I am going to stop a bullet, why should it be with a vital place? . . .

It is very bad about Uncle Guy. I wonder how he was killed. As he was a colonel, I imagine his battalion was doing an attack. Poor Aunt Gwen. This war is a dreadful show.

The ground is drying up fast now, and the weather far better . . . There have already been doings in various parts of the line, & I would rather be George Davies than Sir John French just now. He must have got some hard decisions in front of him. Well, let's hope for a good change in the next month.

Meanwhile, dear Uncle Jim, you must carry on with your job of keeping up your courage. I will write every time I come out of action. We go up to the trenches in a few days again.

Your affect
GEORGE.

Peter Davies: In J.M.B.'s handwriting, at the foot of this pencilled letter, are the words: 'This is the last letter, and was written a few hours before his death. I knew he was killed before I got it.'

George's death took place in the very early morning of March 15. . . . The effect on J.M.B. was dire indeed. Oh, miserable Jimmy. Famous, rich, loved by a vast public, but at what a frightful private cost. Shaken to the core—whatever dark fancies may have lurked at the back of his queer fond mind—by the death of A. Ll. D., tortured a year or two later by the ordeal of his own divorce, then so soon afterwards prostrated, ravaged and utterly undone when Sylvia pursued Arthur to the grave; and after only four-and-a-half years, George: George whom he had loved with such a deep, strange, complicated, increasing love, and who as he knew well would have been such a pillar to him to lean on in the difficult job of guiding the destinies of Sylvia and Arthur Llewelyn Davies's boys —'my boys'.

For his brothers, George's death was, with no exaggeration, a bad
business . . . He had so much that was really good without being in the
least goody-goody, and was such fun, and so tolerant; and blood and
background and memories are a mighty strong bond; and how few, after
all, are those in all one's life with whom one can be completely at ease.
That he had a fair share of the celebrated du Maurier charm or temperament is certain; there was a good leavening of sound, sterling Davies in
him, too . . . I think he had that simplicity that J.M.B. saw in A. Ll. D.,
and which, though I only partly understand it, I dimly perceive to be the
best of all characteristics. In fact I think he had in him a very great deal
of the best & finest qualities of both Arthur & Sylvia . . .

This much is certain, that when he died, some essential virtue went out
of us as a family. The combination of George, who as eldest brother
exercised a sort of constitutional, tacitly accepted authority over us, who
was of our blood, and on whom still lingered more than a little of our own
good family tradition, with the infinitely generous, fanciful, solicitous,
hopelessly unauthoritative J.M.B., was a good one, and would have kept
us together as a unit of some worth; as it was, circumstances were too
much for J.M.B., left solitary, as well as for us, and we became gradually,
but much sooner than would or should have been the case, individuals
with little of the invaluable, cohesive strength of the united family.

[He goes on to describe two visits which he made, in the autumn of
1917 and in June, 1945, to George's grave, on which there were
roses and pansies growing. He ends:]

Then I walked away through St Eloi, about a mile off, as likely as not
past the place where George was sitting when he 'stopped a bullet with
a vital place', and so back to Ypres along the Messines road, feeling bloody
miserable . . . To make an end of this penultimate chapter, the epitaph
which a poet wrote for George and his kind seems as appropriate as
anything I know of:

Here dead lie we because we did not choose
To live and shame the land from which we sprung;
Life, to be sure, is not so much to lose,
But young men think it is, and we were young.

[These are the last letters with Notes in Peter Llewelyn Davies's
collection of Papers. He died before he was able to complete the
compilation, as he had intended.]

Chapter 16

INTERIM

BARRIE had long been friendly with Auberon Herbert, now Lord Lucas, a Liberal politician who had lost a leg in the Boer War while acting as correspondent for *The Times*, and who did not allow this disability to interfere with his leading a very full and active life. Barrie had got to know him and his sister, Nan Herbert, through Millicent, Duchess of Sutherland, and there had been mutual liking between them from the first.

Lord Lucas had turned his family home in Bedfordshire, Wrest Park, into a hospital, and his sister had taken charge. Miss Herbert was an accomplished, energetic woman with a talent for organization, and the hospital was very well run. At one point it was made into a convalescent home, but was turned back into a hospital as casualties increased. Barrie gave Miss Herbert substantial cheques for comforts for the patients, and he often went to Wrest Park himself, talking to the men and to the staff with a friendliness and lack of pomposity which made him very popular. With George's death still a heavy sorrow, he was able to forget himself as he walked in the grounds and stopped every now and again to speak to a blue-clad figure lying back in a chair.

There came yet another sorrow. Charles Frohman had written to say that he intended to come to London for his annual visit, as usual. He pooh-poohed the notion of danger from submarines. He always dined with Barrie at the Savoy on the evening of his arrival, and this year was to be no exception, war or no war.

Barrie, remembering the many times they had dined and talked, enjoying each other's company without any reserve, looked forward eagerly to his friend's arrival. Frohman was travelling in the luxury liner *Lusitania*, which normally carried first-class passengers in spacious comfort across the Atlantic. On this voyage it was crowded with extra lifeboats, and travelled slowly, off the regular course, under special orders. The ship was nearing the Irish coast in the early hours of May 7th when disaster struck. She was torpedoed and sunk, and Charles Frohman was not among the few hundred survivors who got away in the lifeboats.

Frohman's death was not only a grief to Barrie but a blow to his professional life. Would he ever again find a manager to take the same theatrical risks with his plays as Frohman had consistently done throughout their long association? Frohman had never been afraid of risks; if he believed in a play he backed his fancy. There were few English managers who would be prepared to do that if a play happened to be out-of-the-way. And Barrie thought of *Peter Pan*.

It was the personal loss that hurt most, however. There were few men with whom Barrie could relax so easily and completely; the expansive, affectionate American had had a knack of bringing out the best in him. It took years to build up such a friendship. Barrie felt that another little piece of his inner self had been chipped away.

Occupation, constant occupation, was a shield against the black dog of depression. Barrie looked for more war-work to occupy him. He had heard stories of the mothers with children who had been found wandering in the war-damaged towns of northern France, and he consulted Elizabeth Lucas about the most practical way of doing something for them. Mrs Lucas occasionally acted as secretary for him when his correspondence became overwhelming; at least, she brought a typewriter and replied to some of the letters, mainly from strangers asking for money or for his patronage, or for contributions to anthologies, or prefaces to their own works. Barrie could never bring himself to throw these letters into the fire; he himself answered his friends' letters, but a sense of responsibility nagged at him when the other mound grew too high. Mrs Lucas came and typed when she had time, but now Barrie wanted her to assist him in more important work. He wondered whether it would be possible to make some kind of unofficial home for refugee mothers and children.

Elizabeth at once threw herself into the scheme and she and her husband went over to France. There, with the help of a Quaker organization, she was able to rent a partially damaged château at Bettancourt, near Révigny, not far from Rheims. Red tape was cut, the château cleared of debris and cleaned, and the first refugees were collected and brought to Bettancourt. Barrie bore the entire expenses of the place, and did what he could to interest his friends in it. Charles Turley Smith became an orderly, and various girls in their circle went to the château to do what they could under Elizabeth's supervision. She worked unceasingly, smoothing out snags with the authorities—who said it was not officially recorded as a refugee home—getting supplies, caring for the frightened children, some of whom had been wounded or were sick.

Bettancourt was an unspectacular and unpublicized venture, and Barrie continued to finance it and to send out hampers of food until the château was finally evacuated. In the holocaust in France, where thousands were being killed every day, Barrie and Elizabeth Lucas must have saved the lives of at least a hundred children in that remote house.

Life in London went on at all levels. There were soldiers coming and going at the railway stations, people doing war-work, people giving parties in spite of limited food, full restaurants, full theatres. Most of the audiences were men in uniform and their defiantly smart companions, and the popular shows ran for months.

Barrie was alone in his flat that Christmas. Jack Davies had come home on leave, but he had many friends of his own as well as his brothers to visit, and Barrie saw little of him. Brown and his wife had been given the Christmas holiday and had gone. Barrie could have had Christmas dinner at a restaurant, but he preferred to cook a meal for himself in the small kitchen leading off the living-room, and he spent the evening quietly. He was working on a new play, which was to turn into *A Kiss for Cinderella*, and he wrote steadily, immersing himself, as he generally did, in what he was doing.

When the play was finished a few weeks later, he gave it to Gerald du Maurier to read. Du Maurier had gone into management with Frank Curzon, and though he insisted on several changes in the play, finding it too sentimental, he agreed to produce it and take the leading part, the Policeman. Hilda Trevelyan, who had established herself in the public mind as the perfect Wendy—in fact, the perfect Barrie heroine—played the Cinderella rôle. If the play was not quite the mixture-as-before, it was a foolproof recipe in the best Barrie vein of charm and whimsy.

Barrie's life still revolved round the young Davieses. Peter came to London on a military course and later went off to France with his regiment. He was nineteen, tall and thin, very self-contained; he had always been that, and Barrie was often a little uneasy with him now that he was grown up. Perhaps it was because Peter did not respond so readily to Barrie's kind of humour as the others had done. Like Jack, he too had many friends of his own: they were a different generation. Very different. They had left the sunlit world of early youth and accepted traditions behind them, and were plunged into an unimaginable chaos of violence and death. In retrospect, Barrie's early struggles seemed puny to him when he thought of what these young men were going through.

Michael and Nicholas were, mercifully, still at school. Barrie took them to Wales for Easter, to stay with friends of his, the 'Welsh Lewises', to distinguish them from Sir George Lewis and his wife. Hugh Lewis was a Welsh landowner whose son was a godson of George Meredith—sufficient for a friendship with this hero-worshipper. In any case, Wales was a change from Scotland, and as there was plenty of fishing and other sport, the boys liked going to the Lewises.

In September, 1916, news came that fire had seriously damaged Wrest Park. Miss Herbert and her brother saw that it would not be possible to have the ruined part rebuilt and again in use for a considerable time, and Lord Lucas sold the place as it stood and went back to the Flying Corps, which he had joined some time before. In spite of having only one leg, he managed to persuade his superiors that he was fit for active service, and some time later he was reported killed after a flight over the enemy lines. He was just forty.

Barrie was again haunted by the spectre of death that autumn, for his two nephews, Alec's sons Charles and William, were both killed in action. Their mother came to Adelphi Terrace at Barrie's urging, and he put everything aside in order to be with her most of the time. He had never lost his power to be able to imagine himself in the place of the afflicted and desolate, and it must have been some help to the bereaved mother to be able to lay bare her grief to this kind and sympathetic brother-in-law.

The château at Bettancourt was now finally closed; there were voluntary organizations and the Red Cross working for refugees in France, and Elizabeth Lucas had at last come home, after wearing herself out running the place, often with inadequate assistance. Barrie had done what he could both for Wrest Park and for Bettancourt, and now there was plenty in his private life to occupy him. An old play of his, *The Professor's Love Story*, had been revived with H. B. Irving, Henry Irving's son, as Professor Goodwillie, an

ironical twist of fate, for Irving had turned down the play twenty
years before because he did not like the leading part.

Barrie's thoughts were often with Michael Davies, who had been
to a Public Schools camp that summer and, like his contemporaries,
was wondering if the war would end before he left school. Michael
was now sixteen, and in another two years he would be of calling-up
age. Barrie hated this fact mentioned. He preferred to dwell on the
good news that the massive attacks in France had been held, and
there was now hope that the Allies would roll back the tide. Two
years was a long time; he would not allow his mind to take in the
thought that Michael might have to join the ranks of the doomed
one day.

Nicholas had gone to Eton, and the long Llewelyn Davies
connection with Wilkinson's had ended. Now Barrie had two boys
at the great public school. He wrote to them every day, first to one
and then to the other, and he expected them both to write to him
with equal regularity, telling him all they had been doing. Nicholas,
the extrovert, reported all his sports activities and anything else that
came into his head; Nico had settled down quickly and took to life
at Eton with immense enjoyment. Michael, quiet and imaginative,
had not always been happy at the school, and had only lately come
to accept the value of this kind of community. He wrote of the books
he had been reading, and sometimes expressed tentative opinions of
what was going on in the world, as he understood events through
the newspapers. He was obviously an unusual boy.

Barrie's relations with Peter did not get any easier. Peter had been
in action in France, and had been invalided home. He had been in a
military hospital in south London, and was now living quietly at
Campden Hill Square. He sometimes came to the flat, but Barrie
never seemed to get any closer to him. Peter's silences were sometimes as long as his own.

Barrie had no major work on hand, but he could not stop himself
writing; he kept up an enormous correspondence with his friends.
In a letter to Millicent, Duchess of Sutherland, dated January 12th,
1917, he said:

I either work a deal too much or not at all, and of late I have been slinging
off Heaven knows how many short plays. Mostly of no account, but one
... I rather fancy. About the war. All the four ladies in it being charladies
... it might amuse you, as it is meant to make the Society ladies who play
for charities toss their little manes.

This play was to grow into one of his most popular pieces, *The Old Lady Shows Her Medals.*

Slinging off short plays, however, did not make up for the lack of ideas which could be worked into longer, important plays, and he was beginning to fret at the absence of inspiration. There had never been any shortage of substantial ideas and themes in the past. The past? He wondered if it was better to look back or to shut the door firmly on all that had gone before. In another letter to the Duchess there is a revealing sentence: 'Do you remember . . . how bleak it would all be if there was nothing to remember, and yet how often one flies from memory.'

*   *   *

Mary Barrie, now Mary Cannan, had not been fortunate in her second marriage; the happiness she had so longed for had eluded her. Early in 1917 Barrie heard that Mary, who had married Gilbert Cannan after the divorce decree had been made absolute, was alone. She and Cannan had parted within two or three years. Mary was in straitened circumstances; in wartime there was no market for the decorative enamel work which had been her hobby and had then become a lucrative occupation. Her savings, including the money Barrie had given her, were gone. She had had to sell Black Lake Cottage, and she was now working in a hospital depôt, rolling bandages and packing medical supplies.

Barrie followed up the first rumours he had heard about his former wife and got an intermediary to go and see her and ask her to meet him so that he could give her some financial assistance. Mary held back through pride; she did not want the painful experience of facing him. Barrie wrote to her on March 15th, 1917:

My dear Mary,
It would be silly of us not to meet, and indeed I wanted to go to you all yesterday. I thought perhaps you would rather come here, and of course whichever you prefer, but that is your only option as I mean to see you whether the idea scares you or not. Painful in a way the first time but surely it need not be so afterwards. How about coming here on Wednesday to lunch at 1.30. If you are feeling well enough I wish you were doing war work. There must be posts you are so practically fitted for. We could have some talk about that. All personal troubles outside the war seem so small nowadays. But just one thing I should like to say, because no one else can know it so well as I, that never in this world would a young

literary man have started with better chances than Mr Cannan when he had you at the helm.

Yours affectionately,

J.M.B.

There is no record of this meeting, but Mary was not in a position to refuse such a generous offer. Barrie made arrangements for an allowance to be paid to her, and she later lived abroad, mostly in France. That Mary was very much in his mind is shown in a letter which Barrie wrote to Kathleen Scott on April 2nd, 1917:

My dear Kathleen,
I shall always esteem you the more for the generous impulse that made you send them to me. I always held that he had many fine qualities, and I hope they will yet bring him to port. Tomorrow the boys get back and I shall be away most of the month with them, but I hope you will be able to have a reunion with Peter [her son] before the holidays are over.
[There is a note in the margin of this letter, written by Lady Scott: 'He had talked about Gilbert Cannan, and I had told him that he had been a lad of high ideals. I said I would look out some letters which would show that.']

Barrie was keeping in close touch with Lady Scott. Because of the personal letter addressed to him by Captain Scott, he had the idea that the explorer had intended him to become the legal guardian of young Peter Scott. There was someone else, however, who had a greater claim. Peter Scott writes in his autobiography, *The Eye of the Wind:*

When my mother set off on the abortive journey to meet my father in New Zealand on his expected return from the South Pole, I was left in charge of Sydney Holland, Viscount Knutsford, and was looked after by the younger of his two daughters, Rachel, now Lady Malise Graham. Lord Knutsford was known as the Prince of Beggars; he was a pioneer in the art of raising large sums of money for charity. Hospitals were his special interest and the London Hospital in particular. He was known to me as Uncle Sydney and I went frequently to stay with him for holidays or whenever my mother was travelling abroad. He lived at Kneesworth Hall just outside Royston where he had installed an organ and kept ornamental pheasants and ducks and fished for trout, with which he had stocked a small lake.
He also played the clarinet and kept very tame bullfinches and Labradors (which he trained to land the trout), and I adored him. For the whole

period of my boyhood, he and his serene wife, known to me as Lady Mary, and his two daughters, made a happy place for many of my holidays.

Lady Mary was now dead, but with one of his daughters at home, Lord Knutsford had no hesitation in offering to become Peter Scott's guardian. Kathleen Scott wrote to Barrie and told him this. Barrie replied on October 18th, 1917:

My dear Kathleen,
The only change in Lord Knutsford's advice that I should like you to make is to substitute my name for his. If you have sufficient faith in me, it is my earnest wish that you should do so, or if you prefer it, at least please associate me with him in it. He can't love Peter more than I do, but he has the advantage of having the daughter, while I have no woman to work with me and fall back upon should my end come before long. Experience teaches me that the one drawback in my tending my boys is that I have no female influence for them. The loss to them is very great, and I must tell you this bluntly, as I think it only increases as the boy grows into a man. Of course the chances are great that you will live for scores of years after I am gone. I should love to be the chosen man and consider it a mighty honour.

He wrote from Adelphi Terrace House on October 24th, 1917:

My dear Kathleen,
Lord Knutsford is quite right in saying that you and you alone must decide. Nevertheless it is plain to me that you would like some advice, so here goes, it is very much from my heart. If it were just between him and me, I would beg you to risk making it me, but it would not be wise to make it either of us without further arrangements in case of our death, and if he is the man, the arrangement is already made, because of the daughter, while I have no one. This is so important to Peter, that I think I was quite outweighed, but I would like you to say in your Will, or whatever the paper is, that it would be a pleasure to you to think that I was [illegible] you as an uncle to Peter to whom he could turn whenever he wanted. I should try to be a good uncle to him.
Always yours sincerely,
J. M. BARRIE.

Lord Knutsford wrote to Kathleen Scott from Kneesworth Hall, Royston, Herts., at about the same time:

Dear Lady Scott,
You must do what you think best for Peter. I have no 'feelings' about the matter. If you think on the whole that Sir J.B. will be better, by all means

put his name for mine. Really, really, it is for you to decide and not me, and you know him well and me and R [Rachel] well, but you know him better than you know me. If you were to die tomorrow, before something had been drawn up, I would pack up Peter and adopt him under Rachel, and he would live as my son, but it would complicate matters if Sir J.B. were of equal power over Peter, and were to say 'he must come to me.' Sir J.B. has a family, you told me, whom he already generously looks after. I have none, and R is single, and if she marries, her husband will have to take Peter as part of the bargain. You may show this to Sir J.B. if you like. I quite recognize that he was your husband's dear friend, and that I was not, and I will very gladly be associated with him if allowed my own way in bringing up Peter, which is rather like the man who said to his wife, 'My dear, do not let us quarrel about what to call our baby. You may call him what you like so long as you call him Henry.' Just do your best, what you think best today for Peter, keep a power of altering it. Now do not you and he think that I am fighting to obtain Peter. I will accept whatever you like with cordial agreement and no hard feelings of any sort.

Yours sincerely,

KNUTSFORD.

P.S. What sort of life do you want for Peter. Could Sir J.B. or my family the better give this? R will be quite well off when I go to heaven, and can live in the country.

In the event, Kathleen Scott did not choose Barrie as her son's legal guardian, but he remained their close friend, and often dined at Lady Scott's house. It was she who first introduced him to a remarkable soldier, Bernard Freyberg, who was a New Zealander though he had been born in Richmond, Surrey. Freyberg had been taken by his parents to New Zealand as a child, and had been educated at Wellington College there, afterwards taking up dentistry. Military training in the Territorials had turned his thoughts to professional soldiering, and he became so keen on his new profession that he said, not once but several times; 'If I find myself falling in love with a girl in this town, I won't stop running till I get on the train, for I know there'll be a war soon and I'll die of a broken heart if I can't go.'

Freyberg became one of the best known soldiers in the 1914–18 war, winning the Victoria Cross and becoming covered with wounds as well as glory. He was incredibly brave. His biographer says: 'A man of humility and gentleness of thought, he will always belittle his own deeds of gallantry. Attribute great courage, tenacity and bravery to him and he will quietly reply that he has always been fortunate enough to command the finest troops in the world.'[1]

With Barrie, it was a case of instant hero-worship all over again, as it had been with Scott, years before. The tall, magnificently built soldier and the five-foot-two-inch high dramatist with the large head and deceptively simple manner became friends straight away, and remained so for the rest of Barrie's life.

The young Peter Scott met many famous men in his mother's drawing-room. Of Barrie he says: 'There is no doubt that Barrie knew all about how to get on with children. Although there were often long silences, I cannot ever remember feeling shy in his company.'

Barrie wrote to Peter Scott from 23, Campden Hill Square on December 22nd, 1917:

My dear Scott,
I am sitting here smoking tobacco out of your pouch. It is a lovely pouch, and I watch people in case they try to steal it. Who steals my money steals trash, but if anyone tries to steal my pouch he had better look out.

I am hoping to see you soon. I am with my boys, and they are as rowdy as ever. My love to your mother and to you.
          I am, my dear Scott,
                              your humble servant
                                             BARRIE.

He spent his time between his two homes as the spirit moved him.

                                   Adelphi Terrace House,
                                   April 9th, 1918.
My dear Peter,
Your mother thinks I do not write clearly, but I expect this is jealousy. It is funny to think of your being at a French school, parlez-vooing with the big guns firing and bells ringing and hooters hooting. What a lot you will have to tell us when we meet again. Michael and Nicholas are here just now, and tomorrow we are going to Wales for 10 days. Michael won the competition at Eton for flinging the cricket ball farthest. Peter[2] is where the fighting is heaviest, near Amiens. I think Brown [his servant] will have to go and be a fighter now as he is under 50. It will be queer if I am the only person left in London, and have to cook the food, and kill the cow and drive the bus.

1. *General Lord Freyberg V.C.* Peter Singleton-Gates.
2. Peter Davies had gone back on active service.

It will be rather difficult for me to be engine driver and guard at the same time, and also take the tickets and sweep the streets and sell balloons at the corner, and hold up my hands like a policeman to stop the traffic every time a taxi comes along. Then I shall also have to be the person sitting inside the taxi, at the same time I am sitting outside driving it, and if I run over anybody it will have to be myself, and I will have to take my own number, and carry myself on a stretcher to the hospital, and I will need to be at both ends of the stretcher at once. Also I will have to hurry on in front of the stretcher so as to be doorkeeper when the stretcher arrives, and how can I be the doorkeeper when I have to be the doctor, and how can I be the doctor when I have to be the nurse? You see, I am going to have a very busy time, and I expect that a letter from you would cheer me up. I will have to be the postman who delivers it.

Your loving

BARRIE.

He enjoyed writing letters like this to Peter Scott, just as he had enjoyed writing nonsense letters to the Llewelyn Davies boys, years ago. And now they were no longer boys, except Nico. Michael was nearly eighteen, and might soon be a soldier. The thought was pressing insistently on his mind, no matter how hard he tried to push it away. It was woven like a black thread into his everyday life. Nearly eighteen. No longer a boy.

Michael himself spoke of it openly; he wanted to go into the Scots Guards, where several of his friends were already serving. Getting a commission in this regiment took some time, and he was put on a waiting list. Meanwhile, he would return to Eton after the summer holiday and await events. Barrie took him and Nicholas to Glengarry, in Inverness-shire, but they found it a lonely land. Glengarry was deserted: they had the hotel to themselves. 'Michael feels the dreariness and sadness of it, too,' Barrie wrote to Elizabeth Lucas. 'We flounder about my lochs and streams with an effort.'

This place, he thought, was worlds away from the Marne but in a sense it had the mark of war on it, too, for the Highlands were denuded of their young men. How much longer was this terrible war going on? There was a sharp edge of anxiety in his soul when he looked at the two boys as they walked beside him, carrying fishing rods, in this silent place. Would this be their last holiday together?

He was glad when the time came for them to return to London, away from the empty moors and hills.

Chapter 17

THE SECRETARY

LADY CYNTHIA ASQUITH was anxious to earn some money. It was, in fact, becoming a necessity, and Lady Cynthia had come to the pass when she must do something positive about it, as her bills were piling up and her current income, including her husband's army pay, was nowhere near enough to meet the expenses of living.

She had heard that film acting was very well paid. A devotee of the cinema, Lady Cynthia had come to the conclusion that beauty, rather than talent, was the passport to screen fame. She herself was very beautiful, and she had long taken this pleasant fact for granted, for she had been openly admired since the day she came out of the schoolroom. Her wide-set eyes, abundant auburn hair and dazzling perfection of feature singled her out in any society gathering, and she wondered if the time had not come to make some capital out of her looks. She had already taken steps. A young officer she knew had introduced her to a film agent, who had, in turn, sent her down to a place called Catford for what he called a film test. It had been a mortifying experience; she had been treated like anyone else by the 'operator', had been made, over and over again, to express horror, distress, love, hate, and other emotions, all without the benefit of a cue—and there was no bonus for the infliction of a kiss. The electric light was terribly bright and everyone was shouting in a foreign language.

Still, the photographs of her taken during these trying hours had turned out to be good, and she was sure that she would get an offer from film magnates when these were shown round. It would be an awful life, having to be at the studio from half past ten in the morning till six o'clock at night, and it would be impossible to fit in all her other engagements, but needs must when the devil drove. The usual fee, she understood, was seven pounds a week, but she would stick out for ten, in face of all the inconvenience.

That the daughter-in-law of a recent Prime Minister, herself the daughter of a peer, should seek to earn money in such a glaring public medium was unusual, but Cynthia Asquith was an unusual woman. She was, in 1917, thirty years of age, and the mother of two sons. She had been married for seven years to Herbert Asquith, called 'Beb' by his friends, the surviving son of the ex-Prime Minister, whose eldest son, Raymond, had been killed in the war. Mr Asquith had not approved of Beb marrying into the family of a High Tory. And Cynthia's father, the eleventh Earl of Wemyss, had been furiously angry that a daughter of his should marry the son of a precious Liberal who had wanted to abolish the House of Lords. He did not give her a dowry. (Her two sisters got five thousand pounds each when they married.)

Beb Asquith was entirely different from his father. Handsome, gentle, talented, he had, under parental pressure, read for the Bar when he left Oxford, but he was not cut out for the law. His instincts were all for a literary life; he wanted to write poetry and novels, and it was this side of him that first attracted the lovely Lady Cynthia Charteris, for she, too, was devoted to literature, and hoped to do some writing herself one day. After practising at the Bar for four years without notable success, Beb Asquith joined the army on the outbreak of war, and was now a gunner in France. Apart from an allowance from his father and his pay, Beb had no private income, and marriage to a dowerless girl with expensive tastes brought acute financial difficulties at times.

There were other difficulties. Cynthia had never made a secret of the fact that she enjoyed admiration, and intended to continue going out with her men friends: she possessed a kind of magnetic vitality which drew them to her. She was genuinely in love with Beb—she would not have braved the Earl's storms and married him if she had not been—but she said gaily that she adored 'dewdrops', her phrase for extravagant compliments, and she could 'keep men in order' when there looked to be a danger of their overstepping the mark. Beb was sure of her loyalty to him, but it was not easy for him to watch her responding to the ardent attentions of other men at parties and balls.

Women found her fascinating, though in a different way. Cynthia was always interesting to be with, she exchanged gossip but never made mischief, she was an amusing and highly intelligent luncheon and dinner guest. Above all, she was sympathetic when people were in trouble; her friends knew that in a crisis she would be the first to spend time and energy trying to help in their distress. Money she could not spend on them, for money was a perpetual problem.

Money, in fact, had always been a problem in her life, from her earliest recollections of listening to conversations at home. The apparently rich Earl of Wemyss had his financial troubles. Most of them were brought on by his passion for gambling on the Stock Exchange; he was an inveterate gambler. He was often hard-pressed to find money enough to run his three houses: Stanway, near Cheltenham in Gloucestershire, Gosford, their Scottish home in East Lothian, and their London house, a large, shabby, corner mansion in Cadogan Square which Cynthia once described as being built of 'inflamed red brick in the period of most elaborate ugliness'.

The Countess of Wemyss had an insouciant attitude to money. She was extremely hospitable and liked entertaining her friends and relations, especially during her summer sojourn at Stanway, where she usually managed to add a number of recent acquaintances to the house-party. Hospitality costs money, and overflowing hospitality on the scale which Lady Wemyss loved costs a great deal of money. Whether the Earl's frequent irritated cries for economy were based on an actual or relative state of his exchequer is a matter for conjecture, but Cynthia had never known a time when money was not 'tight' in her parents' household, and when letting Cadogan Square for the London season had not considerably helped the family finances.

Cynthia herself made extra money, after Beb joined the army, by letting her house in Sussex Place whenever she could, and embarking on an existence which she called 'cuckooing', staying with her family or with understanding friends. A children's nurse, Nannie Faulkner, accompanied her to look after her son Michael, aged three. The elder son, John, had unhappily turned out to be mentally retarded; it had taken Cynthia several years to accept the heartrending fact that he was not as other children, and that she must get used to the knowledge that he would never be able to lead a normal life. He was now six, a gentle, biddable child, and was looked after in the country by a governess who had been able to teach him to read, and to interest him in the life of the woods and fields.

Cynthia had for some time been doing war-work as a voluntary nurse in a London hospital, and would have continued with this if she had been able to afford it. No film offers had been made.

Voluntary nursing, being unpaid, was no help with rising prices, and something had to be done.

* * *

Cynthia Asquith had met Sir James Barrie in April, 1916, when she had been a fellow-guest at a dinner-party given by Lady Violet Bonham Carter. She sat next to him, and found it a sad humiliation. She wrote:

He destroyed my nerve for ages, so great a bore did he convince me of being. I could *not* make him smile, and, instead of telling him about my children, I found we were discussing the cinema at unjustifiable length. I was even reduced to commenting on objects on the table—luckily there were some red bananas.

This uncomfortable introduction did not prevent her from writing to Barrie the following year; she had heard that one of his plays was about to be made into a film, and she asked to be considered for a part. No reply came to this letter, so she was astonished when a friend, the Countess of Lytton, rang her up in August, 1917, and offered her the part of Margaret in a new play of Barrie's, *Dear Brutus*, apparently at the instigation of the author, who was a friend of Lady Lytton's. Cynthia wrote in her diary: 'She said it would be lucrative. Perhaps it is my duty to my children and my creditors to accept, but I refused.'

Stage work required professional acting, and she had no intention of making a fool of herself. She met Barrie again the following June, when she dined with Pamela Lytton, but she talked most of the time to the McEvoys. Ambrose McEvoy, a fashionable painter of beautiful women, was painting her portrait, and she enjoyed the sittings because he 'squeaked out dewdrops'. Augustus John also wanted to paint her: a massive, 'very masculine man'. Cynthia knew that she did not go unnoticed in Society.

On June 23rd she went to the Berkeley Grill Room to dine with the Marchioness of Dufferin, whose new friend Barrie was the nucleus of the party. After dinner they all went round to Brenda Dufferin's mews house, where a mellow atmosphere was soon produced by the passing round of some fine old rum, a few bottles of which had been discovered in the cellars of Lady Dufferin's ancestral home. This time Cynthia saw a different Barrie. On her previous meetings with him she had not been able to find a crack in what seemed an impenetrable shell of sadness and preoccupation; the sunken eyes had looked through her. Tonight they were alive. He sat down beside her on a couch, and began talking in 'his little Scotch voice'. He did not refer to *Dear Brutus*, but made an oblique reference to her letter asking for a film part, which he had not answered. He could easily have put her into the film version of *The Admirable Crichton*, he said, but he didn't approve of her as a cinema actress. If she wished to earn some money, why not do some paid work which would be quite different, and would also be congenial? Why not come and help him as a kind of secretary? Not a typist, of course: he got all his manuscripts typed outside. Not the usual kind of secretary, either, one who prided herself on her efficiency—that was a word he disliked. She would be a very special kind of secretary. He got hundreds of letters, most of them from persons unknown, and she would have to deal with those. Apart from that—here Barrie was vague but charming.

'You would be a great help to me in many ways,' he said with his unexpected smile. 'You could do as little or as much as you liked. You could come every day, or twice a week, or whenever you wished.'

At first she hardly took him seriously but when she saw that he meant it she agreed to go to Adelphi Terrace to talk matters over. She went a few days later, and took the lift up to Barrie's flat. This was not the one he had first lived in; he had moved up to the top floor a year previously, to a larger flat which had been occupied by the artist Joseph Pennell, who had given it up. The living-room here had an even finer view from the windows than had the flat below. There was an enormous inglenook with seats, many bookcases, and, in a corner, a small kitchen. Cynthia Asquith's impression when she first entered the room was one of brown-ness; the walls seemed impregnated with wood smoke, and she noticed the great mound of silvery grey ashes on the large stone hearth, where logs were piled.

Barrie greeted her in a friendly manner and they sat down to tea, which the manservant brought in. Her host described what her duties would be, taking it for granted that she had accepted the job. As he had already told her, she would have to deal with a large correspondence, exercising her discretion as to what letters to answer and what to show him. She would also have to 'tease' him into taking his cheques to the bank, as he was apt to lose them in the welter of envelopes. He mentioned that Elizabeth Lucas had given him some secretarial help from time to time, and Cynthia wondered how long ago that had been, for he opened a chest full of papers which were in a state of confusion. There were no files, no attempt to fasten documents together; pages of manuscripts were mixed with pages from letters, and scattered among them were burst or empty rubber bands.

At length, very delicately, Barrie came to the matter of salary, indicating the mass of papers and miming them bundled into the rubber bands.

'The services of a woman who did that would be worth four or five hundred a year to me,' he said. 'You know, I'm away from London for the whole of the school holidays with my boys. At other times, too.'

Five hundred a year! Cynthia privately considered it preposterously good pay for somebody who had no real market value as a secretary; she knew no shorthand and could not type. And those long holidays! She had heard about the Llewelyn Davies boys—there were cricket caps on the wall, and she glimpsed schoolboy groups in framed photographs.

Barrie was watching her. She told him that she would let him know in a few days, and he said he hoped she would come, and saw her out to the lift. She wrote in her diary that night: 'It's a very soft job, and I think it would be too silly not to accept.'

The salary was not only handsome, but the fact that he would not want her to come every day but whenever she cared to fit in the time made her feel that it was too good to be true. A job from heaven. All the same, it would be as well to consult several of her friends before finally deciding; they might see snags which had escaped her. She wrote to Sir Walter Raleigh, whose judgment she greatly valued. Why not? he replied. Barrie was a genius, and it wasn't every day one was invited to work for a genius. He added: 'But take care you don't kill the golden goose by curbing his sentimentality. Not that it is really sentimentality. It's far more often —for he has a cruel side—satire that doesn't quite come off.'

Desmond MacCarthy, a close friend, had an acute flash of insight when he answered her letter. By then she had made her decision. He wrote:

I am so glad you have taken that situation . . . It seems to me . . . you like being adored—in that being no great exception. A Dulcinea is a necessity to Barrie. Sentiment is only irritating to an onlooker, and when it is combined with playfulness and real kindness and springs from a cold detached heart, it is a delicate tactful thing, delightful to receive. Barrie, as I read him, is part mother, part hero-worshipping maiden, part grandfather, and part pixie with no man in him at all. His genius is a coquettish thing, with just a drop of benevolent acid in it sometimes.

Beb came home on leave, so there was no question of her starting work immediately. Beb Asquith was not unduly impressed by her excitement over 'secretarying' for Barrie; he had never cared for Barrie's plays, and had almost disgraced himself when taken with a party to see *A Kiss For Cinderella* in April, 1916. Cynthia had written in her diary for that day:

Puffin [Anthony Asquith], Beb and I went to see the Barrie play. There I was awkwardly placed between dear little Puffin, who thought it all lovely and sweet, and Beb, who groaned with disgust at nearly every word. I tried hard to prevent Puffin's feelings being hurt. I remember so well how one hated the attitude of grown-ups when one was a child.

After a short but crowded leave, Beb returned to France again, and Cynthia went down the following day to see her son John, who lived with his governess at Eynsham in Kent. The boy was well, and she was surprised to find how easily he could read and put mechanical toys together; but there was always the grief of knowing that he would have to live separate from his family and be looked after alone. The governess was splendid, but costly. When she got home Cynthia sat down to 'do' her finances, and found that her current bills, which she could not pay, came to £300. She was thankful that she had miraculously fallen into a well-paid job.

On Wednesday, July 24th, she began work with Barrie. He had told her to come at about eleven o'clock, and she got there punctually, feeling nervous and uncertain of herself. What would he expect of her? She had heard all round that he had unaccountable moods and was capable of 'forgetting' promises made with every appearance of sincerity. How would he receive her?

She need not have worried. Barrie was pacing up and down the big room, pipe in mouth, but he was obviously expecting her, and was courtesy itself, sitting her down at a desk and pushing over a number of letters which had come by the morning's post. He gave her instructions on how to divide the letters into those he should see and those she must answer on her own initiative, then he said she had better have a pseudonym as his secretary. Cynthia, after a short pause, suggested Sylvia Straite, the name she had intended to use if she had gone into films, or Sylvia Greene.

'No, not Sylvia—any name but Sylvia,' said Barrie abruptly. 'Greene will do very well.'

It was decided that she should sign letters 'C. Greene', so as not to disclose her sex, and there the matter ended. She remained until the middle of the afternoon, lunching with her new employer and trying to sort out his correspondence, past and present. Barrie continued to be very friendly, but when she got home she could not help wondering about the sharp change in his voice when the name 'Sylvia' had been mentioned. Had it, by chance, been Mrs Davies's name? She had heard a great deal about that curious relationship. At dinner with a friend that evening she asked about the dead woman, and was told her name had indeed been Sylvia. Cynthia was horrified. What a damnable chance that she should have stumbled on that particular name. Had Barrie been dreadfully hurt?

She was never to know, for he did not mention the name again. Cynthia, as C. Greene, settled down in her capacity of 'special secretary'. She had to initiate her own methods. Though she had never done any office work she had a naturally orderly mind, and she wondered how Barrie could have worked in such a muddle. He opened the chest she had first seen, riffled about in it, took out some photographs, put them back, and had great difficulty in shutting the lid again.

Cynthia hoped they would come to some businesslike arrangement about hours; she did not want to leave this important matter vague. She asked if he could give her a rough idea of when she would be needed and how long she would be expected to work in a day.

'Oh, we can have the hours to suit you,' he said, leaving the matter as vague as before.

Cynthia decided to keep regular hours to begin with, at any rate. She went to Adelphi Terrace at eleven o'clock next morning, and found Michael Davies there—'his favourite ward and a most delightful Eton boy', she noted in her diary. Barrie looked supremely happy at having Michael there with him; the love he had for the boy was very apparent in his usually expressionless face. Even Barrie's rumbling voice sounded more buoyant as he and Michael talked, the boy swinging on the arm of a chair, Barrie sitting at his writing table and smoking.

The secretary tackled a new pile of letters. Today these included heart-rending appeals from actresses, begging for engagements in a play or for Mr Barrie's kind influence with managements; some of them enclosed photographs and cuttings of former triumphs. Cynthia began to have some inkling of what life in the professional theatre meant to those who clung to hope, asking for a chance to show what they could do in a Barrie part, which they were sure they could play 'with immense charm'. Pathetic letters, all to be answered by a polite but uncompromising C. Greene.

When she came the following morning she found Nicholas with Barrie. This boy, the youngest of the Davies boys, was quite different from his brother, more of the jolly schoolboy. Barrie was obviously fond of him, but it was a different kind of affection; there was less intensity about it, more of the tolerant uncle. They were talking of fishing and cricket and sports at Eton, and the atmosphere was very easy and pleasant.

Cynthia got a duster from the kitchen and attacked a pile of old papers in a cupboard, filling waste-paper baskets, hardly able to see what the papers were because of the thick dust which covered them all. The next day, she found another 'cave', full of hundreds of letters from Michael. When she asked Barrie what to do with them, he told her that not a single one of them was to be thrown away. She suggested getting boxes and arranging the letters in chronological order, which Barrie thought a good idea. Next day she brought along a very large box, which she had bought on the way. Barrie let her sort out Michael's letters, while he walked up and down, smoking hard. After lunch he gave her a large bundle of papers which turned out to be arrears of numberless American royalties; she had to add up the statements and turn the resulting dollar figures into pounds, shillings and pence, which bewildered her at first. It would have been comparatively easy if she had been alone and undisturbed, 'but the little man in the black alpaca jacket prowls up and down like a caged animal, and occasionally addresses a remark to me.'

By the end of the week Cynthia was very tired. Barrie's handwriting was difficult to read, almost illegible at times, and it was hard work copying out the addresses he wanted her to enter in a new notebook. He had evidently resolved to turn over a new leaf and to impress hidden capacities for tidiness upon this decorative secretary, who was turning out to be efficient as well, even though he had said that he disliked efficiency. On Friday he said cheerfully that he looked forward to seeing her on the morrow, but Cynthia made a significant entry in her diary for Saturday, September 7th: 'Stayed in bed mixing my intellectual drinks—Barrie and Maupassant . . . Bridge lesson. My first Barrie-shirking. I telephoned and write to excuse myself.'

She did not feel guilty. He had, after all, told her to arrange her own hours of work, and she would now take him literally at his word. She had been used to a full social life, he knew that, and she saw that with some re-arranging she need give none of it up.

Without explicitly discussing this with Barrie, she began the following week to carry out her resolution. Keeping her eye on the daily inflow of letters, she met friends for lunch or dinner, went away for week-ends and did not return until the following Tuesday. Barrie made no objection at all. He encouraged her to talk about her doings and her friends. His own friends came to the flat and she was immediately drawn into the conversations. Robert Lorraine, the actor, called one day and asked Barrie to write a play for him when he was demobilized from the Royal Air Force and would be free to return to the theatre. Barrie was non-committal: he had no play in mind at the moment and he was reluctant to discuss possible ideas. Cynthia was sure that there was no lack of them in that busy head, but he liked to go at his own pace.

No two days were alike. She came upon a bundle of uncashed cheques in a drawer which, in all, amounted to £1700: Barrie had not known they were there. Sometimes she did no work at all, beyond going through the post; if he felt like it he would sit on the edge of her desk and talk. He rarely discussed his manuscripts. When he was writing seriously he would post off the pages to Miss Dickens, an expert typist who had been doing his scripts for years. He was, as she had been warned, unpredictable. When he had a silent fit on it would last for hours; he would continue smoking and coughing and writing letters to his friends, paying no attention to her. She felt invisible on these occasions, and disliked the sensation. Then he would swing to the other extreme, walking up and down, interrupting her as she tried to think out tactful replies to insistent letters from strangers.

They found they had several friends in common, including

Bernard Freyberg and Charles Whibley, whom Barrie had not seen
for many years. Whibley was an admirer of Cynthia's, and she often
met him for dinner or a theatre. Now she brought him along to the
flat to renew the old friendship with Barrie. Whibley's prickly
characteristics had not lost their edge with the years. An extreme
conservative in politics, he detested the advance of what he called
'the new spirit', and seemed as prejudiced over a host of things as he
had been in the old days. His so-called patriotism antagonized a
great many people. Cynthia Asquith wrote:

One day, when he was in the worst kind of mood in which to find solace
in believing the very worst of the enemy, I remember his being infuriated
by a judicious mind's endeavour scrupulously to sift the evidence for
German atrocities. 'But I don't *want* the truth,' he fulminated, spluttering
with fury. 'I'm not looking for truth, I'm looking for hate, which for most
Englishmen is at the bottom of a far deeper well than truth.'

Barrie never talked politics himself, and when Whibley was in this
kind of cantankerous temper would turn the conversation. It was
easy to calm the other down by talking about Henley and their early
days in journalism, and the Allahakbarries, with whom Whibley had
played from time to time.

    With Beb Asquith back in France, Cynthia was free in the evenings,
and if she had no social engagement Barrie would often ask her to
stay and have supper with him, or go out to dinner. The employer-
secretary relationship was quickly changing to that of personal
friendship. Cynthia found herself studying him as a man, and he was
certainly a curious mixture. She wrote to Beb:

An extraordinary plural personality . . . For all that apparent haphazard-
ness there seems to be plenty of shrewdness, plenty of canniness. As for
the legend of his being himself the boy who wouldn't grow up, I see no
evidence whatever of this. On the contrary he strikes me as more than
old, in fact I doubt whether he ever *was* a boy. But then, for the matter of
that, Peter Pan isn't a boy, is he? He is a wish-fulfilment projection in
fable form of the kind of mother—Barrie's an expert at her—who doesn't
want her son to grow up.

Before long she realized, with some astonishment, that Barrie was
exceedingly lonely. He had many friends, but no one who could
really say they knew him intimately. He put on contradictory poses.
He would refuse—or get C. Greene to refuse for him—many
invitations to go out in the evening, yet he liked being with people.

More than anything else he liked a friend to ring up and say 'Can I come to dinner tonight?' He hated engagements far ahead: an invitation to dinner three weeks off could produce a nerve storm. But he was affronted if he did not receive official invitations which, by their very nature, had to be organized long in advance.

When, as he now did very often, he asked Cynthia to stay for an evening meal or go to the Savoy to dinner, she always tried to accept, sensing that he did not want to be alone that evening. He would talk to her about the plays he had already written, discussing them quite objectively. He was pleased when she remarked that her father-in-law, Herbert Asquith, had told her he thought *The Twelve Pound Look* the best short play ever written, and the first act of *Dear Brutus* the most ingenious. Barrie said he had had a difficult problem getting the characters into the wood in that play, but this act had been nothing compared with the third, which he wrote first because he knew it would be the most difficult.

Cynthia found Barrie's cough distressing to listen to, but already she knew better than to say anything about it. He was hardly ever without a pipe or cigar in his mouth, and she was sure his health must suffer as a result of his continuous smoking. She thought it was the cause of his frequent black moods, when he was 'grey ashes and devastatingly depressing'. He was often grey ashes during the autumn of 1918 because he could not get started on writing again. He had many ideas, but was unable to settle on one.

'Not long ago,' he told her, 'I wrote I don't know how many one-act plays. I was simply slinging them off—I believe I wrote six in one week, but scarcely any of them seemed worth keeping. If only I could exchange this spate for one engrossing idea.'

He could not, as he used to do, write plays and novels alternately. If a particular theme was right for a play it could not be right for a novel, and vice versa. For some time now his ideas had arranged themselves quite naturally into scenes and acts, and he thought in terms of dialogue, not narrative. But nothing of importance came, and he was miserable about it, fearing he was finished. He had always been extremely happy when he was 'at it', and when he went back in memory to his early days in Fleet Street and thought of his tremendous output of work, he feared he had now come to the end of his powers.

Cynthia would look at the little figure sitting on the couch in his favourite posture, one leg tucked under the other, pipe in hand.

How much of all this did he really believe himself, about being
'finished'? He was not yet sixty and his hair was still dark; he had
once said to her with a wry smile that he hoped people didn't think
he dyed it. When he was in good spirits he didn't look anywhere
near his age; when he was in one of his black moods he looked
twenty years older. He was certainly one of the oddest men she had
ever met.

*   *   *

The war was at last nearing its weary end, and Cynthia Asquith,
through one of her connections in high places, got Barrie an official
invitation to go to France as a guest of the American Army. He
jibbed at the prospect, but agreed to go when it was arranged that
his old friend Gilmour could accompany him. Gilmour had been in
the background of his life for many years now, and could always be
relied upon to 'understand' anything Barrie might say or do. He still
took charge of Barrie's income-tax and investments, without fee—
and quite often without thanks, for Barrie could be violently
argumentative about paying the tax due, even when it had been
agreed upon between Gilmour and the inland revenue men after
many tussles. But Gilmour was one of those large-hearted individuals
who looked upon friendship as accepting the friend, warts and all.

   Cynthia got Barrie off at last, glad to have a chance of clearing up
what seemed like acres of arrears without interruption. There was
still a small avalanche of tiresome letters to deal with every day; she
had grown a second skin where begging letters were concerned, and
seldom had to trouble Barrie over how to answer them. She wondered
if all authors were as conscientious as Barrie over this kind of
correspondence; and there were times when C. Greene had to
protect him from his own generosity.

   Barrie enjoyed his visit to France. The Americans treated him as a
Very Important Person and drove him round in an immense car to
see the remnants of the Front. The enemy were in retreat and the
end was not far off now. He went to Paris for the Armistice, where
he called on Lady Scott, who had been working there for some time.
They dined together at Ciro's, and later went out arm in arm to
watch the delirious crowds playing 'kiss-in-the-ring' on the Grands
Boulevards, mad, wild scenes, girls dressed as widows dancing with
the rest.

   The end of the war to Barrie meant, first and foremost, that

Michael Davies would not now be called up to fight. He had done well at Eton, Hugh Macnaghten writing in his final report that Michael was the most admirable boy he had ever had in his House. Michael wanted to travel on leaving school, but Macnaghten persuaded him that it would be better to go to Oxford first, and arrangements were made for him to enter Christ Church in January, 1919. Meanwhile Michael joined the Defence forces, and was for a short time on Wimbledon Common, a fully-fledged private in the London Scottish, 'with kilt expected daily', as Barrie proudly wrote to Elizabeth Lucas.

The Winters came to stay at Adelphi Terrace House. Maggie had developed into a self-important woman who was always careful to let new acquaintances know that she was a sister of the famous Sir James Barrie. She was anxious to 'keep up her music' while in London, and Jamie obligingly hired a piano for the period of her stay, and worked at his table while she was practising; noises of this kind did not disturb him, just as music itself did not touch him. William Winter was looking much older, but had not changed from the quiet, dependable man who had courted his dead brother's fiancée many years before, and had tried ever since to make up to her for not being a minister's wife. Their son, Willie, was a bit of a genius at chess, and liked to visit London as he wished to meet other masters of the game.

Barrie was a model brother, brother-in-law and uncle, and made his relatives very welcome—but they did not meet many of his friends. Perhaps he knew instinctively that Maggie would not mix with the kind of society in which he now moved. His clannish feeling for the ties of blood, however, was extremely strong, and when news came in December that his sister Mary had died in Aberdeen, he turned to Maggie with that family feeling reinforced. Still, when the Winters left, he was conscious of relief; they were part of an existence which was far, far away. Living for him meant his boys, and the literary and theatrical life of London, and his clubs, and dining-out at the big restaurants, and country-house parties. And, of course, his writing-table, next to Michael the most important of all.

Nico and Michael came to Adelphi Terrace House for the Christmas holidays, and, as always, Barrie missed them badly when they went off again, Nico to Eton and Michael for his first term at Christ Church. Barrie even missed Nico's gramophone, which had filled the flat with noise for hours at a time but which livened the place up. Whenever the boys went off, he began to look at the calendar every morning, thinking of the time they would be back again.

Peter Davies was demobilized from the army in February, 1919, and Barrie felt that it was a stranger who came home from the war. Peter's previous remoteness seemed somehow intensified. 'He had been through something more than a furnace, and what was left of him was for a long while little more than a ghost; a shattered remnant that even Barrie couldn't help,' wrote Denis Mackail in *The Story of J.M.B.*

There was a vast cleft between them, and Barrie could do nothing to bridge it. Both tried to establish some kind of relationship: Peter was only too well aware of what he owed to James Barrie. Both knew that it would be a matter of time; many soldiers who had survived the hell of the trenches found it difficult to adjust to a peacetime existence, and were bitter and disillusioned with those who had waved flags and shouted about glory from the security of home.

Jack Davies was now married. His wife had been Geraldine Gibb, the pretty daughter of a Scottish banker, and they had a flat in Edinburgh. Barrie had not been consulted about the engagement—which had upset him, as he had somehow taken it for granted that the boys would naturally want to talk over such an important step with him first. However, he met Gerrie and liked her and went to the wedding, and when Jack brought her to London to stay at the flat on one of his leaves from the ship, Barrie liked her even more. He wrote to Elizabeth Lucas: 'They went off today as devoted as ever and a complete world to themselves.'

Mrs Lucas was a good safety-valve; he could write anything to her. He was also fond of her daughter, Audrey, who had inherited her father's writing gift. Audrey was a contemporary of Michael's, and sometimes came to stay. Cynthia Asquith soon became friends with Elizabeth Lucas when she met her; she found her quick-minded, and, on occasion, delightfully ribald or ironic. Elizabeth, having been a great friend of Barrie's for many years, could supply Cynthia with many missing clues—to talk to her about Barrie was like meeting someone who had read the first volume of a book which she, Cynthia, had had to begin at the second volume. And as Elizabeth was devoted to him, Cynthia felt free to discuss him and his affairs without any sense of disloyalty or fear of misinterpretation.

It did not surprise either of them when Barrie took it for granted that she was now to be a hostess for him as well as a 'special' secretary. It gave him a naïve sense of pride and pleasure to ask his friends to luncheon parties with Lady Cynthia Asquith doing the honours at the other end of the table. There were menu problems. Mrs Brown was no longer in the kitchen as cook; she had developed a weak heart and had been compelled to retire from work. Brown remained, an invaluable factotum, but the doctor had said that Mrs Brown should really live in the country, and that would mean losing Brown one day, too. He was staying for the present, and Mrs Stanley had come as cook. Mrs Stanley was loyal and hard-working, but she had not the inspired touch which had made her predecessor a treasure. Mrs Stanley's efforts of roasts and nursery puddings were no more than adequate, and Barrie sometimes grumbled to Cynthia about their lack of variety. But he thought Mrs Stanley a nice soul and he hated to hurt her feelings. When he invited guests to luncheon or dinner he asked Cynthia to order in a meal from the Savoy.

Barrie liked expensive restaurants, one of his few personal extravagances. He was often to be seen at the Ritz, the Berkeley Grill or Claridge's. It was as if he never ceased to find satisfaction in the consciousness of being able to afford to go wherever he chose and to order what he fancied. He walked into these great restaurants, to be greeted by bowing head-waiters, and it was plain that he enjoyed every moment of his entrance, in spite of his phlegmatic expression.

He was more contented at this period of his life than he had been for a long time. Michael was safe at Oxford, enjoying himself as a young man should. True, there were moments when Barrie wished that Michael's ideas on what constituted enjoyment took safer forms. He wrote to Cynthia Asquith on July 6th, 1919: 'M got his two-seater, took only an hour's lesson & then went off in it thro' the streets alone. I then sat in it for two days so that we shd end together, as I think we nearly did . . .'

Barrie had no major work on hand, but he had an idea for a short play on a ballet theme, inspired by Lydia Lopokova, a Russian dancer who had been a success in America and now wanted a vehicle for a London appearance. Arrangements were already being discussed for putting it on at the Haymarket in the autumn, but before the play was half-finished, Barrie learned that Lopokova was no longer in London and was reported to be dancing in New York with the Diaghilev ballet. Barrie then turned his thoughts to another ballerina, Tamara Karsavina, who was connected by marriage to Kathleen Scott. Madame Karsavina relates what happened when Lady Scott brought Barrie to visit her:

'I have written a play for you,' he said, in his peculiar rasping voice, and then had a fit of coughing.

'I speak English with a Russian accent,' I warned him.

'Oh, can you speak at all?'

He then read the play. His strong Scottish accent, his cough, and to tell the truth, the play itself, rather confused me. I even thought, at times, that he was pulling my leg . . . When I studied the script, I understood the point of Barrie's remark, 'Can you speak at all?' I could not, according to the author, except with my toes . . . He used to say, 'Don't ask me what I meant. I don't know myself.' The theme of the play is that the Russian dancers are not like ordinary humans. They are called into being by a master-spirit and can only express themselves through their own medium . . .

I realized that my aim should be to strike a delicate balance between the sheer extravagance of the play and the deeper feeling underlying it. And to do this I needed music which would have poetic quality as well as rhythmical value . . . Arnold Bax was asked to write the music. I was awed at the task of choreographing my part within the weird framework of Barrie's play. But, as I listened to the music, the shape and curve, the rounds and angles of the movements sprang from the music itself . . . I had before everything to establish beyond question with my public that Karissima's[1] natural mode of progress was on her toes and her utterance that of a being in possession of a language surpassing human speech . . .

Barrie attended the rehearsals, and often called out from the stalls to delete or add some lines. A strange friendship grew between us. Strange, because he did not, or did not want to, see me a grown person, but as the Karissima he created, with a child's mind.

*   *   *

Beb Asquith had been demobilized, and was taking things quietly after four years of fighting. Friends had lent him and Cynthia a house at Thorpe, in Suffolk, and Cynthia divided her time between Thorpe and London. There was a chance of Beb's being taken on as literary adviser to a firm of publishers, and he wanted to get completely fit before settling down to an office job. He would not be

1. The leading part, the only non-speaking rôle. The play was produced at the Coliseum in the following spring.

Nina Boucicault, who created the part of Peter Pan.

Maude Adams, creator of the role of Peter Pan in America.

Charles Frohman, the American impresario.

returning to the Bar, much to his father's disappointment and annoyance. Beb intended to try to write seriously, now that there was a chance to begin again.

In April, 1919, on a day when Barrie was expecting Cynthia at the flat after a week-end at Thorpe, he received a letter from her instead. She would be staying on at Thorpe. She was not quite sure when she would be back. Would he send her some of the accumulated correspondence, or perhaps get an understudy for the time being?

Barrie was astounded, and also angry. A nice little bomb to send him on St George's Day, he wrote to her. Sending her packets of letters to answer was no good; he wanted *her* there. An understudy? He would probably drop her out of the window. He supposed he would have to tackle the accumulations of letters himself, if she really intended staying away. Cynthia Asquith did not reply to this reproachful epistle. He wrote to her again on May 7th: 'Pamela [Lytton] has been here and told me your guilty secret. No wonder you were afraid to put your cards on the table. Now I know why your eyes have fallen of late when they met my honest gaze . . .'

No doubt if Cynthia had told him, as matter-of-factly as possible, that she was pregnant and that he would presently have to get a temporary secretary, there would have been no need for her eyes to fall. But Cynthia had shirked what she knew must be an uncomfortable scene. Barrie's concept of motherhood was that of a young lady bending over a ready-made infant in a cradle, with an angelic smile on its sleeping face. Cynthia was sure he would have been too shy and embarrassed to treat her news in a natural way.

As it was, when she went up to London the following week to collect some things from her house and called at the flat for letters to take back with her, neither of them mentioned the subject— though Cynthia noted in her diary that every time Barrie spoke to her he 'tactfully averted his gaze'. She had already asked the house-agents to let Sussex Place, and she told Barrie that she intended to stay at Thorpe for the time being. Again she mentioned the desir-ability of his getting a temporary secretary, but he told her that if he got overwhelmed he would call on Elizabeth Lucas to help. Mean-while, Lady Cynthia Asquith must go on considering herself Sir James Barrie's secretary, and he did not wish to discuss the matter further.

Cynthia returned to Thorpe, and Barrie wrote to her every few days, sometimes every day, telling her what he thought and felt, and his plans for the summer. On June 13th he wrote: 'The Oxford term ends in about a week and unyokes Michael, but he won't be here long if he can get off on a contemplated reading party. He will be 19 then (everything seems to be going wrong with me).'

He thus put into words what Cynthia had long suspected: he did not want his 'boys' to grow up. He had long dreaded the day when Michael would want to lead his own life, with his own friends. The holidays had always been the highlight of his year, taking Michael and Nico to Scotland or to Wales. Now Michael wanted to go on a reading party. Barrie knew well enough that it was usual for undergraduates to spend part of the long vacation studying together, but with Michael he wanted it to be different . . . He would have liked it to be the same as it had always been for the holidays. Illogical—but Cynthia did not expect logic from James Barrie where his deepest feelings were concerned.

She wrote asking him to come and stay at Thorpe. He replied on June 20th:

Dear Lady Cynthia,
I don't suppose I shall be able to get down. I want to come but I shd have done it before Michael got back. They shrink, these boys, from going anywhere, the death of their parents is really at the root of it, and down in my soul I know myself to be so poor a substitute that I try to make some sort of amends by hanging on here when there is any chance of my being a little use to them. Even in admitting this I am saying more to you than I do to most.
                                                    Yours,
                                                            J.M.B.

Did they really shrink, these boys, from going anywhere because of their private grief—after nine years? Or was Barrie's obsessive possessiveness, his almost pathological instinct to 'own' people, responsible for both his pathetic excuses and the facility with which he deceived himself? With this possessiveness went a crippling jealousy, especially where Michael was concerned. Years later one of Michael's friends, Roger Senhouse, recalled that he went to Adelphi Terrace House with Michael for a week-end, and Barrie did not address a word to him from first to last.

Michael was beginning to find this possessiveness a strain. He once told Elizabeth Lucas that he felt a kind of oppression, the weight, as it were, of so much love and the material benefits which were heaped upon him. This gave him a sense of responsibility towards

Barrie, also a fear that whatever he did in life would probably not fulfil expectations. Barrie's love was becoming a crushing burden. Michael was expected to spend at least part of every holiday at Adelphi Terrace, which meant that he had to refuse invitations to go and stay with Oxford friends. Uncle Jim was always pleasant over such things, but Michael hated hurting him. Bringing his friends to the flat for the holidays wasn't at all the same thing. Besides, one never knew what kind of mood Uncle Jim might be in at any particular time.

Chapter 18

BEREAVED

CYNTHIA ASQUITH was finding life very difficult. The long months of waiting for her third child to be born were tiring enough, but money troubles were coming upon her thick and fast, and she could see no way out. The Sussex Place house had been let for a time, and that had been a help, but 'cuckooing' in Cadogan Square after they had left the borrowed house at Thorpe had had its bad moments. She noted despondently in her diary: 'Mama heckled Beb about his profession, and he looked depressed and furtive.'

Lady Wemyss did not approve of her son-in-law leaving a lucrative profession like the Bar and attempting to make a living by writing poetry. She expressed herself forcefully to him on more than one occasion, asking how he intended to support his wife and children? Cynthia upheld her husband when he was attacked in this way. She thought him a wonderful poet; he came to her with everything he wrote, straight from the mint, knowing that she was an honest and sensitive critic. For her part she was aware that she was necessary to his self-confidence, and she hoped that her encouragement would enable him to go on and write something that would make his name. Success would follow.

Pleasant day-dreams, but they didn't help her at this moment; they were back at Sussex Place with money going out instead of rent coming in. She wrote in her diary: 'I am in a real panic about money. Beb & I tried to make out a budget at lunch. I calculate my income would last for about 2 months' housekeeping. What are we to do?'

She was glad of the regular monthly cheque she received from Barrie as salary, but wondered how long that would go on. Beb was already restive about her 'secretarying', and took it for granted that she would not go back after the baby was born. Cynthia was not willing to commit herself one way or the other. Barrie expected her to continue, and was paying her on that basis. She tried to make her

husband see reason, to understand in practical terms that they must
have some extra money to his allowance and not-very-large earnings
as literary adviser. She intended to write articles for the magazines,
and she also had ideas for an anthology, and for children's books.
Meanwhile, she must go on attending to any correspondence which
Barrie sent her. Beb had to be satisfied with this very unsatisfactory
state of things.

Barrie had taken Michael and Nicholas to Scotland for August,
commissioning a friend of Cynthia's, before his departure, to buy his
secretary 'a lovely present'. Cynthia, being consulted by the friend,
decided on a trousseau of silk nightgowns for her lying-in, risking
the danger that Beb would find this 'too intime' a gift; she thought
that luxury in nightgowns added more than anything else to one's
self-respect at such a time.

Cynthia's third son, Simon, was born later in August, happily
sound in wind and limb. She enjoyed the excitement when it was all
over, and after a convalescence returned to Sussex Place—and to the
nagging worries which for a time she had put firmly out of her mind.
The money situation had altered for the worse; there were accumulated debts, and some creditors were pressing. Her usually resilient
spirits seemed crushed by dread of the future, and there were
arguments with Beb about when she should return to Adelphi
Terrace, if at all. Barrie was back in London, and she wrote to him
when she was in a very low state of mind. Barrie replied with a very
long letter on October 1st, 1919, in which he said:

Dear Lady Cynthia,
I am so sorry that you are feeling depressed. Sounds very like it, tho' do
you write depressed when you are gay and gay when you are depressed
(the only really funny thing I ever wrote was when wondering whether I
shd not [illegible] for the jugular vein instead). I expect you have fallen
down like the bucket in the well after the extraordinary gallantry of
women when the time comes for them to go over the top. You didn't fail
there at any rate ... I enclose your £40 ... I am letting correspondence go
largely to blazes. It will be a blessing when you get back here ...

There was further 'trouble with Beb', as Cynthia noted in her diary,
but she made a great effort and returned to the flat. There she found
Barrie's papers in the greatest muddle. Elizabeth Lucas had come,
for a time, but she had had to give up some weeks earlier because of
her own private affairs. Barrie had pushed all the incoming letters
'into an Augean stables of drawers'. He had refused to get temporary

secretarial help after Elizabeth's departure, and was surprised at Cynthia's angry reaction when she saw the accumulation of work which faced her. She was ill with nerves, and it did not occur to Barrie that after the strain of child-bearing she did not feel equal to the physical task of reading and replying to hundreds of letters.

Barrie chose to have a fit of temperament. He said he was hurt at not being asked to be the new baby's godfather, 'so I begged him to be'. Cynthia wondered at times how long she could go on with this peculiar brand of secretarying. In any case, well paid as it was, she desperately needed something that was even better paid. Barrie had many connections with film moguls. When she went away the following week for a few days' rest, she wrote to him, explaining that she must earn some substantial money as quickly as possible, and asking him if he could use his influence to get her a part in a film. He replied on November 19th:

Dear Lady Cynthia,
I have no doubt something of the kind could be done . . . I think it all very plucky of you and don't doubt you would find some entertainment in it also, if you were physically fit for strenuous work. You are not at present, and not a finger would I raise in the matter till you are—that's flat.

I have a feeling that you worry about things unnecessarily. You have to take life as a comedy, tho' it is often a pretty bloody one. Fond and foolish mothers tend mistakenly to think they should be wealthy for the sake of their children, who will otherwise miss this that and the other. On the contrary, blessed are they who are poor (which doesn't mean that we mustn't get all that we can . . .) I enclose £72 for your tax, which Gilmour says you have to pay. You need have no scruples about this, as even he says the understanding in such a case as yours and mine would be that your screw is without deduction for income tax.

He wrote again on December 3rd, saying that the letters were piling high, and enclosing a cheque for her salary. Nothing was said about her returning. Cynthia had already told him that she went every Christmas to Stanway, her parents' house in Gloucestershire. Barrie spent Christmas at the flat. Michael and Nicholas had gone to Ramsgate with Mary Hodgson, and Peter was away with friends of his own.

Barrie was working again, setting out the plan of a play that was coming to the surface of his mind. The germ of the idea had come many years before, and appears in one of his 1905 notebooks as 'a sort of Rip Van Winkle'. In 1912, during the summer when he had rented Amhuinnsuidh in the Outer Hebrides, the idea had come back again. These islands are full of legends, primitive tales whispered round the fire in a crofter's cottage, tales mixed with traces of the pagan past to produce superstitious beliefs in faery lore and 'seekers' from the faery kingdom. There are many phrases in these tales which a writer would immediately pick up: 'The sea likes to be visited' is one of them. There are also stories of children stolen by the fairies and returned many years later without having grown up.

In another notebook, one for 1912, Barrie had jotted down 'The island that likes to be visited', and in the Dedication 'To the Five', in the published version of *Peter Pan*, he refers to North Harris as 'the place where we caught Mary Rose'. A related legend which he also used is about mother-ghosts who return to their former homes to see how their children have fared. Barrie writes in *The Little White Bird*, published in 1902: 'The only ghosts, I believe, who creep into this world, are dead young mothers, returning to see how their children fare. There is no other inducement great enough to bring the dead back.'

So the stage was set, at least in Barrie's mind, for the play that was to become *Mary Rose*. He turned the Highland legend into the story of a young mother who mysteriously disappears on an island in the Outer Hebrides, leaving her infant son behind. She returns to her own home twenty years later, unchanged in mind or appearance. Her son, now a grown man and a soldier, treats her tenderly, but he cannot feel any real connection with her, and the ghost returns whence she came.

Barrie made numerous notes for the play, but this was becoming physically difficult as he was seriously troubled by pain and discomfort in his right hand. A year or so before, a small lump had come up on his right forefinger, and though he continued to write as usual with pen or pencil, he was alarmed to find that he was slowing down, and sometimes could not go on at all. He had always been ambidextrous to a certain degree, and now he trained himself to write with his left hand. Cynthia encouraged him in this, knowing that he found it almost impossible to dictate to anyone.

The result was startling. His hitherto careless, scrawled handwriting became more legible, though it stayed small. Characteristically, he made the most of his disability by declaring that writing with

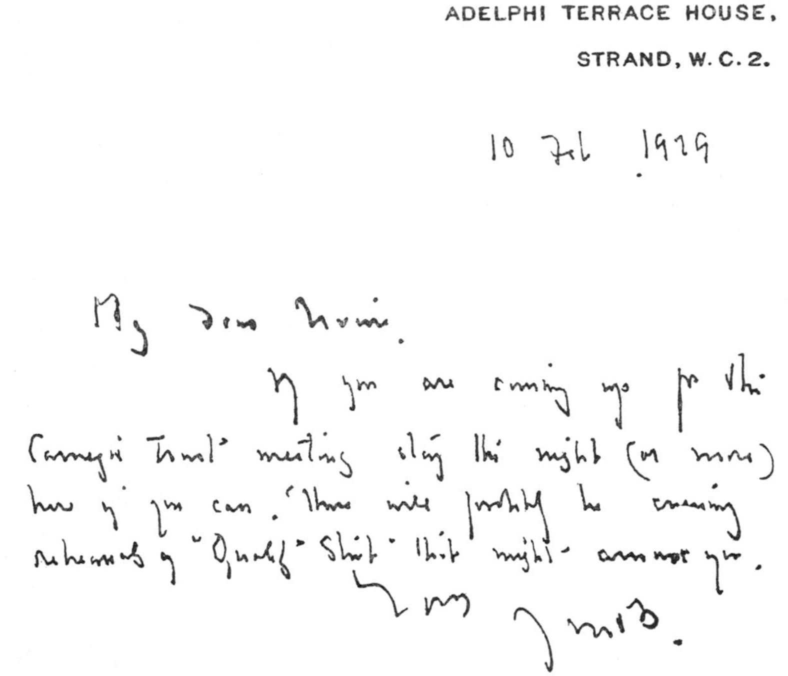

10 Feb 1919

[handwritten letter, largely illegible]

My dear Irene,

If you are coming up for the
Carnegie Trust meeting (say this might) (or more)
how if you can. There will probably be evening
rehearsals of "Quality Street" that might amuse you.

Yrs
J M B.

Right-hand: Barrie was naturally left-handed, but had been compelled to use his right at school. Stevenson once referred to 'the besotted ambiguity of my writing'.

both hands made him into two authors: work done with the left hand was more sinister than that written with the right hand.

As the year 1919 drew to an end, he felt recharged. The Highland fairy tale was developing, and he was also making some changes in *The Admirable Crichton*, which was being revived. Then there was a suspense thriller, a mystery murder play, which he had discussed with Michael. So far he had only been able to work out a first act, though he already had a tentative title, *Shall We Join the Ladies?* As it was Michael who had first suggested his writing a mystery murder play, Barrie was exceedingly anxious to make it a good one. The seeds of the idea had been in his mind for a long time—as with so many of his plays—and the device of an affable host inviting a number of people to dinner, knowing that each might be the murderer of his brother, appears many times in his notebooks, in scores of

To the Five,

Some disquieting confessions must be made in
printing at last the play of Peter Pan, among
them this, that I have no recollection of
ever having written it. Of that anon. What I
want to do just is to give Peter to the Five
without whom he never would have existed. I beg
you, my dear sirs, to accept this dedication with
your friend's love; and indeed as all the other
plays of mine that I care to print are being
bound up in this same volume I beg you, in

Left-hand: A few lines from the dedication 'To the Five' from *Peter Pan*.
Barrie wrote to Charles Whibley that his left-handed writing 'seems to
have a darker and more sinister outlook on life', and to Cynthia Asquith
he declared: 'Anything curious or uncomfortable about *Mary Rose* and
Shall We Join the Ladies? came from their being products of my left hand.'
He later wrote with either hand.

---

notes. Now he began to work on it in earnest, but he still could not
develop it beyond the first act. Would it be better to leave it as an
unsolved mystery? He would talk that over with Michael.

A recent honour had pleased him very much. He had been elected
Rector of St Andrews University. The Scottish universities each
have a Chancellor, and a Vice-Chancellor who is also Principal of the
university. These are by their nature permanent appointments until
their incumbents retire. There is also a Rector, an honorary officer;
he is elected by the matriculated students for a term of three years.
The new Rector gives a Rectorial Address but need not deliver it on
his election: he can give it at any time during his term of office.

Barrie had decided to defer his Rectorial speech until some future date. He had finished *Mary Rose* and rehearsals were already beginning, with the lovely young actress, Fay Compton, in the name part. The play opened at the Haymarket in April, 1920, and was a success from the beginning.

In August of that year, Barrie was lent a house on Eilean Shona, a little island at the entrance to Loch Moidart on the coast of Argyll. It was a windswept, hilly island with nothing on it but the big house and a few scattered hamlets. Barrie invited a house-party which included Elizabeth Lucas and her daughter, Audrey, and Michael and Nicholas brought some of their friends. With the lively spirits of the young people and the hubbub of talk and laughter, it promised to be an enjoyable holiday for Barrie, but within a few days he felt a new kind of apprehension. Michael was different. Outwardly he was the charming, attractive young man everybody admired, but Barrie knew every facet of that personality. At least, he thought he knew. Michael had changed. There were reserves that had not been there before. Barrie told himself that it was only a young man growing into manhood, but something deep within him whispered that it was more than that. Michael was ready to leave the 'family' life which Barrie had cherished for so many years of being substitute father to 'my boys'.

There was nothing very tangible to get hold of. Michael walked and climbed, went fishing with Nico and the others, was as companionable as ever. But he did not take advantage of opportunities to talk over the unfinished mystery play, as Barrie had expected and hoped: he seemed to have forgotten about it. There was a good deal of general conversation about art. Michael had once talked of studying painting in Paris, but Barrie had not encouraged him in that line—he knew nothing about painting and cared less. The others in the house-party discussed art at length, and Barrie felt out of it.

Michael began sketching, and presently had all the house-party as sitters. Barrie wrote to Cynthia, who was at Stanway: 'He is drawing such ink portraits of me that if I believed they did me justice I would throw myself from the highest peak. I have an uncomfortable feeling that his portraits of other persons are rather like them.'

Michael veered from one mood to another. Barrie watched him anxiously, and Michael knew he was being watched. He spent most of his time out-of-doors, climbing the hills, from which, he reported, all the western isles of Scotland lay at his feet. 'A good spying ground for discovering what really became of Mary Rose,' commented Barrie in his next letter to Cynthia.

He had got into the habit of writing her long letters when he was troubled in mind or spirit. More and more he felt out of things.

We are a very Etonian household and there is endless shop talked, during which I am expected to be merely a ladler out of food. If I speak to one he shudders politely and then edges away . . . Do my letters seem aged? I certainly feel so here. I have a conviction that they secretly think it indecent of me to play tennis . . . in their politeness they almost offer to hold me up when it is my turn to serve. By the way, what a polite game tennis is. The chief word in it seems to be 'Sorry' and admiration of each other's play crosses the net as frequently as the ball. I fancy this is all part of the 'something' you get at public schools and can't get anywhere else.

The tensions between him and Michael were beginning to tell on his nerves:

Michael has been drawing more sketches of me and they are more than enough. He has a diabolical aptitude for finding my worst attributes, so bad that I indignantly deny them, then I furtively examine myself in the privacy of my chamber, and, lo, there they are.

Michael was unexpectedly argumentative, too, at times. Often an opinion expressed or a remark passed about the news in the papers— which reached the island days late, in any case—would spark off a hot discussion out of proportion to the original subject. Barrie was glad to have Elizabeth Lucas there; she understood how disturbed he became and promised to do what she could to prevent controversial topics getting out of hand.

After she and Audrey had gone, Barrie grew suddenly tired of the holiday. Days of ceaseless rain had come after unbroken sunshine, and the young men were growing restless. Barrie wrote to Cynthia: 'Picturesque outlooks do not an Eden make, and I daresay I shall be thinking with Dr Johnson that the best road in Scotland is the way out of it.'

They were all glad to return to London. Nicholas went back to Eton; and Michael left for Oxford, with that sense of strain still between him and Barrie. Yet when Michael's letters came, they were affectionate and spontaneous. Barrie wrote to Elizabeth Lucas on October 17th, 1920, after a visit to Oxford:

It was nice of you to have that talk with Michael and I have no doubt that for the time at least it had a steadying effect. All sorts of things do set him 'furiously to think', and they seem to burn out like a piece of paper. He is at present I think working really well at Oxford and has at any rate spasms of happiness out of it, but one never knows of the morrow . . . He has the oddest way of alternating between extraordinary reserve and surprising intimacy. No medium. In his room at Oxford lately he suddenly unbosomed himself marvellously. One has to wait for these times, but they are worth while when they come.

*   *   *

Cynthia Asquith now added the labours of authorship to her already crowded life. She had sold articles to magazines for the past few months, and now she was making an anthology of verse and prose, in which a publisher was interested, and she had ideas for children's stories. It was all grist to the mill, and now that Beb was securely established in his job, she could safely rely on a regular salary coming in beside her own.

She found it more convenient to bicycle to Adelphi Terrace House than to go by public transport, and during the early part of 1921 she went there regularly, keeping up with the letters and helping Barrie to entertain. She had become 'special' in every sense; he now asked her advice on aspects of his social life. He knew 'everybody' in some circles, she knew 'everybody' in others. Being a friend and confidante, Barrie told her, was more important to him than any amount of secretarying.

He went to Sussex Place to see the children, and practised his child-magic on small Michael Asquith, now six, who responded to the sleight-of-hand tricks with gleeful laughter, and sat listening intently as Mr Barrie recounted wondrous tales. 'It still works,' Barrie told Cynthia, highly pleased. 'I was afraid perhaps my capacity in that line had dried up.'

He also wove his spell round Lady Wemyss, who was more than pleased to draw famous and interesting people into her orbit, and invited him to join her house-party at Stanway for Easter. Barrie accepted with equal pleasure. He had often written to Cynthia while she was staying at Stanway, and now he was to see it for himself.

Stanway House was the one place which Cynthia Asquith really loved. At one time the summer residence of the Abbots of Tewkes-bury, it had come into the hands of the Tracey family at the Dissolution of the monasteries. An eighteenth-century Tracey heiress married the eldest son of the fifth Earl of Wemyss, and Stanway had been their ancestral home from that time onwards. It was a house to stir the imagination, built of mellow Cotswold stone, with a beautiful Inigo Jones gatehouse and a magnificent tithe-barn. The gabled west front of the house had mullioned windows and a high oriel window; there were lawns to the south and east, stretching to a steep bank which rose to a wide grassy terrace. Beyond this was a hill crowned by a stone summerhouse called the Pyramid.

As the Earl of Wemyss never seemed to have enough money to keep the house in decorative repair, it had come to have what Cynthia described without regret as 'a restful shabbiness and gentle dilapidation'. She looked forward to showing it to Barrie. He travelled down from London with her and Beb, her father, and the Earl's brother, Evan Charteris. The Earl could be choleric on occasion, but Barrie's disarming manner brought out his good humour, and it was a pleasant journey. Beb said little. Tall and thin, with his poet's face and quiet manner, no one could tell what he was thinking. Cynthia was confident that he had accepted Barrie as being a permanent part of their lives: she had by now accepted it herself.

As she had expected, Stanway enchanted Barrie. He could hardly wait to walk out and survey the domain. There was the grandeur of the mansion itself, in its setting of lawns and terraces and age-old trees, with the village church and a cluster of cottages beyond. It was a cricketing village, Cynthia said, and they laughed together when she told him she had been mad on cricket from her girlhood and had once been ambitious to captain the first women's eleven against Australia. Another bond!

That evening she took him for a walk 'in the most lovely moonlight ever seen', and on the following day he went with her to the top of the Pyramid, where they sat in the summer-house while she pointed out the landmarks. Barrie took it all in with his writer's eye —and with a sense of personal possession, too. This was 'his' Cynthia's private world of happiness, and therefore it must be his, too. Before the day was out he was convinced that he had belonged to Stanway all his life.

He had the gift, when he chose to exercise it, of making people feel he had known them for years. Cynthia's sister, Mary, and Mary's husband, Tom Strickland, were in the house-party, and Barrie also met Irene, nicknamed 'Bibs', Cynthia's younger sister by fifteen years. By the time the other guests arrived, Barrie had taken on the colour of a Charteris kinsman, so thoroughly did he make himself at home. The house filled up, and Barrie was at the top of his form. His old skill at games came back when he was challenged to golf-croquet on the lawn, but his real triumph was on the special Stanway shuffleboard, played on the long refectory table in the great hall. Heavy metal discs had to be sent gliding along the table to come to rest between marked lines, and Barrie's accurate eye and determined practising soon had him expert at the game.

He was enjoying himself greatly. It was, somehow, a kind of fulfilment, getting to know Cynthia's relations, being accepted as one of themselves. He was proud of her beauty, and told her so. He encouraged her to be witty at dinner, and glowed with reflected glory when the tables rocked with laughter—there were several tables, Lady Wemyss preferring her guests to dine in small parties.

Barrie went out of his way to be charming to Beb, and did not seem to notice that Beb responded with a certain amount of stiffness and reserve. Cynthia noticed, however, and when they were alone begged Beb to 'understand'. Beb had no wish to misunderstand, but he was not sorry when the time came for him to go back to London, to his office. A house-party revolving almost entirely round a small, alien figure who somehow managed to be the centre of attention whenever there were a few people together—and who, incidentally, monopolized Cynthia as of right—did not encourage friendly feelings in the breast of Cynthia's husband.

* * *

Michael Davies and a friend had gone to Corfe Castle for Easter, staying at an inn and reading hard for their final schools. Barrie left Stanway in time to have a few days with Michael at Corfe, then returned with him to London. Nicholas had been to camp, as usual, and was now back at Adelphi Terrace, his gramophone giving forth music and his cheerful presence making the flat come alive. This was the best part of the holiday for Barrie, with his boys at home. Cynthia was still at Stanway, and he wrote to her every few days. He no longer addressed her as 'Dear Cynthia'. His tone had changed from bantering pleasantry to a loverlike familiarity which was quite different from anything he had ever written to a woman before:

Dearest Mulberry,
Do you know what that tree is? I might have guessed it because it was so unlike the others. However by their fruits ye shall know them, and it was by your fruits I first knew you were a mulberry . . .

In every letter he told her how much he missed her: 'It's sad my lassie is so far away tho' I know she is being a darling of a mother all the time . . .' He urged her to buy a dress at Reville's 'and send the bill to me'. He signed himself 'J.M.B. Your Servant', and in all the letters which followed, from then on, 'Master', or 'Loving Master'. He had dined with Bernard Freyberg, and told her that the best thing he could find on his return to the flat would be 'the sweetest girl in the world leaning forward with her soft face in her hands'. The extraordinary flow continued until she returned to London, and resumed her duties at the flat. She found masses of letters from correspondents awaiting her attention, but was no longer worried at the accumulations; they would have to wait their turn.

Barrie was going to rehearsals of *Shall We Join the Ladies?* which he was leaving as a one-act play. It was to be performed on May 26th as part of a triple bill to mark the opening of the Royal Academy of Dramatic Art's new theatre, the Vanbrugh, in Gower Street, and the starry cast for this occasion included Dion Boucicault, Fay Compton, Sybil Thorndike and Gerald du Maurier. Inspiration for the second and third acts had not come, and who killed Sam Smith's brother in *Shall We Join the Ladies?* remained, and remains, a mystery.

On May 9th, Barrie's sixty-first birthday, Cynthia dined with him at the Ritz, and two days later accompanied him on a visit to Thomas Hardy at Dorchester. It was an odd experience. Hardy and his wife were both 'owned' by an obstreperous dog who bit the guests and snatched food off the table. Hardy took them by motor-car to see the cottage where he was born, and Barrie climbed up two rotten ladders held together to see the actual room.

Back in London, Cynthia spent a day at the flat clearing up correspondence, and went down to Stanway, where her sister Bibs had just got engaged to the second Earl of Plymouth. Cynthia intended, on her return, to go off once more, this time to Margate with her two sons, Michael and Simon, and their nurse. Everything was fitting in nicely. Barrie let her make what arrangements she pleased, and Beb was being less difficult over her complicated, sectioned life.

The Margate sojourn settled, she went to the flat on May 19th to answer letters, lunched with Barrie and stayed until six o'clock. He was coughing a great deal, but was in excellent spirits, and talked about the forthcoming performance of *Shall We Join the Ladies?*. He hoped Michael would be able to come down from Oxford on the 26th for the performance. That evening, Cynthia dined with a friend, Joan Capel, and went to a theatre. After she had returned home and gone to bed, the telephone rang. It was Barrie, speaking in a voice she hardly recognized.

'I have had the most terrible news,' he said. 'Michael has been drowned at Oxford.'

Cynthia was appalled. She woke Beb, they dressed quickly, and he took her to the flat. Peter Davies and Gerald du Maurier were already there; Barrie had telephoned them first. Barrie was in a state of shock. He was like a man in a nightmare: she had never seen such a look on anyone's face. They tried, without success, to persuade him to go to bed, but in the end had to return home. Next morning Cynthia went early to Adelphi Terrace and found that Barrie had not slept at all. He had not gone to bed but had walked up and down the flat all night.

People appeared, the telephone rang incessantly, for news of the accident had appeared in the morning papers. Michael Davies and a great friend of his, Rupert Buxton, had gone for a bathe in Sandford Pool, and both had drowned. Cynthia remained at the flat all through that dreadful day. Nicholas came from Eton, silent and in great distress. Barrie was in his bedroom and stayed there, refusing to see anyone except Gilmour, to whom Cynthia had telephoned. Gilmour at once took over the arrangements for bringing Michael's body from Oxford to London, and seeing the appropriate people about the funeral. Cynthia telephoned Dr Shields, a personal friend as well as Barrie's medical man, asking him to come and give Barrie something to make him sleep that night. Shields arrived in the evening, and persuaded the stricken man to take some tablets and go to bed.

All Cynthia's finest qualities were brought out by the catastrophe which had befallen Barrie, for indeed it was a catastrophe. With his peculiar emotional make-up, having failed to achieve a normal home life and children of his own, he had long been in the grip of deeply seated frustrations, perhaps the strongest being frustrated fatherhood. The powerful urge of possessive affection was probably the chief compensation for what he had missed. With Sylvia Llewelyn Davies gone, this intense affection had been transferred to this

Lady Cynthia
Asquith.

Herbert Asquith,
'Beb'.

J. M. Barrie in his living-room at No. 3, Adelphi Terrace House.

particular son of hers, already a favourite from childhood. He had built ambitious hopes on Michael, just as if he had been his real father; but crashed ambitions were as nothing to the emotional trauma of bereavement.

Cynthia came to the flat every day and stayed late. She sent her children to Margate with their nurse, and herself remained with Barrie. She persuaded him to eat, to go to bed. She answered enquiries, parried friends and strangers who wanted to see and sympathize with him. Peter Llewelyn Davies, himself badly shaken by the tragedy, came and did what he could, but it was as if Barrie had vanished into a black, awful state of nothingness.

One cannot assuage grief when it claws at the vitals of one's being. Barrie's desolation was real and heart-rending to see. Once, when Cynthia was sitting with him, he began to talk about Michael. He said the boy had always had a fear of water which he had done his best to conquer. 'But he was never able to swim properly,' added Barrie. 'He went on trying. He went on trying.'

After consulting Beb, Cynthia decided that a quiet time by the sea might help Barrie; he and Nicholas could stay at a hotel and spend the time on the beach with her and the children. When the funeral was over, she took Barrie and Nicholas in a hired car to Margate, where she had booked rooms for them.

At first, Barrie suffered a strong reaction—his misery was so intense that she did not know what to do for him. Gradually the long, sunny days on the sands had a calming effect, and he began to play with the children, who climbed over him and made him run about. Simon Asquith was nearly two and his brother Michael was seven. They were as sunburnt as little red Indians, racing round in tearing spirits or riding along the edge of the sea on donkeys, oblivious of everything but their own small world. Nicholas, though so many years older, entered into their games with energy, and Cynthia noted in her diary: 'Nicholas is a great wag and entrances them.'

The unfinished thriller, *Shall We Join the Ladies?*, which was associated so closely with the dead young man in Barrie's mind, was performed at the opening of the Vanbrugh Theatre on May 26th. It caused a stir, and was praised by most of the critics. There was much speculation as to whether the author intended to finish it as a three-act play or leave it at the suspense point with which the first act ended. The question was always evaded by the author when asked, and it became a dramatic curiosity, but always highly effective when acted.[1]

Barrie did not go to the opening performance; he remained at the sea with Cynthia and the children. He was taking sleeping draughts because he could not sleep, and another reaction was setting in. On May 26th he did not even mention the play. They hired a car and drove to Broadstairs for an excursion. It rained, but after dinner the rain stopped and Cynthia and Barrie went for a walk along the sea-front.

'I walked all the way back with him without his seeing me,' she wrote in her diary that night.

1. When asked who really was the murderer, Barrie would reply, 'I wish I knew.'

Chapter 19

THE SQUIRE

BARRIE dreaded returning to London, but he knew he would have to pick up the threads of existence again. When he seemed to be better physically, Cynthia encouraged him to go back to the flat. They all returned to London by hired car at the end of the month, Barrie deeply dejected by the time they reached Adelphi Terrace House, Cynthia exhausted. When she later got to Sussex Place there were messages to say someone wanted to rent her house, and she knew she must follow that up immediately, for she had been spending a great deal of money and needed more.

There seemed to be thousands of letters to be coped with when she arrived at Adelphi Terrace House next day, and she did her best with them. Barrie was by turns apathetic and devastatingly miserable, but there were times when he could forget his grief. Gerrie, Jack's wife, had given birth to a son and Barrie at once took on the rôle of substitute grandfather on Jack's side. He went to see Gerrie at the nursing home with an armful of flowers, admired the baby and joked with the young mother.

It was harrowing later, when Michael's clothes and other belongings were sent to the flat, along with a box of letters which Barrie had written to him: they dated back to Michael's first half at Eton. Barrie took the letters and asked Cynthia to dispose of the other things. He turned to her to help him with all practical matters connected with the tragedy. She stayed to lunch with him nearly every day, and remained late if he wanted her. Beb had not complained for some time, but there was a scene on June 10th, when she told him that Barrie had suggested he should take them and the children to France in August. Beb said he had no wish to go, and he did not want Cynthia and the boys to go, either. There was a long argument which left Cynthia in tears, and she was still depressed the following day when she tried to tell Barrie of the decision. He apparently did not hear, merely indicating the letters on the desk which awaited C. Greene's attention.

She was still mournful as she started on the letters. She would have been glad of a free holiday after her ceaseless labours of the past few weeks, but she soon recovered her normal good temper, and the social round which was the breath of life to her did not slacken: luncheon parties with friends, tennis in Cadogan Square, polo at Ranelagh squired by an old admirer, visits to Kew with other admirers, theatres, bridge parties, dinner-parties, motor-car excursions with friends. There was hardly a day that was not full of engagements, once she had put in some time at the flat.

Early in July she again mentioned the suggested holiday in France to Beb, and there is a note in her diary: 'Crisis with Beb about the French plan.'

The crisis went on until the following day. Bibs was getting married, and most of the family were in town, shopping and making preparations for the wedding. Cynthia was busy all day, and that evening made yet another attempt to get Beb to see reason. He was obdurate. She had a sleepless night, and when she brought up the subject again in the morning, there was a real quarrel. The France plan must be abandoned, Beb said, and she wasn't to mention it again.

Cynthia was upset. Beb was being absurd. They could not possibly afford the kind of holiday which Barrie had suggested: they could hardly afford any holiday likely to cost a great deal of money. But when Beb took a stand it was difficult to move him from it. The day brightened a little when her mother called for her in a motor-car to accompany her on a further shopping morning for Bibs's wedding. The Countess of Wemyss liked to do things her own way, and insisted on buying the wine for the wedding reception herself; they drove about London an hour later with eight dozen bottles of champagne in the boot of the car. Her mother dropped her at Adelphi Terrace, and Cynthia had to face Barrie and tell him of Beb's decision.

Barrie was distressed. He had so looked forward to having them for this holiday! France was the place. Now he did not know what he was going to do—and there was Nicholas to consider. He did not think that he himself could enjoy *any* holiday, but it would have helped to have her and the children near him. Where did she and Beb intend to go?

To Stanway, Cynthia said, where they usually went; Beb would be able to get away from his office for about a fortnight, but she would stay longer. Perhaps it would be Scotland this year, as her mother talked of letting Stanway and opening their house in Scotland. In that case Cynthia and the children would go up to Gosford with them, but she preferred Stanway, darling Stanway.

Cynthia had a thought. Barrie usually rented a house in August. Why didn't *he* take Stanway this year—he had enjoyed his visit at Easter. There was plenty of cricket for Nicholas; the village played all the surrounding clubs. And Broadway was only five miles away, and he had many friends there. Barrie pounced on the idea. Cynthia would, of course, be hostess for him: they had many mutual friends. He grew animated as he talked and planned, and Cynthia was glad she had made the suggestion. Barrie and Nicholas would be helped over this difficult summer, she and the children would spend long, delicious weeks in the one house she really adored. Beb could hardly object for he loved Stanway too, and Mama had let the house.

* * *

The first house-party at Stanway in the August of 1921, with Barrie as host, was a mixed success. He had cast his net wide. Besides Nicholas, Jack and Gerrie Davies came, bringing their small son; then there were Charles Whibley with his caustic tongue and endearing personality, E. V. Lucas, Violet Bonham Carter, Professor Walter Raleigh, his wife and their daughter Philippa, Hugh Macnaghten and two Eton friends of Nico's. Charles Scrinber, Barrie's American publisher, was over in England so he and his wife came down for a night. The Winters were asked for a fortnight. Now that Maggie was the only sister he had left, Barrie felt a special responsibility towards her, and he liked William, her husband. He was not so sure about their son, Willie, who, though a chess genius, had a good many traits Barrie did not care for. Still, ties of blood were strong, and as Maggie had taken it for granted, when she heard the news about Stanway, that she would be asked, Barrie was glad to give them this holiday in the country.

Everything started well. Barrie, tenant of Stanway and therefore the temporary squire, would stand, as Cynthia wrote, 'contentedly gazing at the house, which, he said, varied like a living face; or he would wander into the tithe-barn and stare up at the great timber rafters of its roof.' He especially liked the oriel window with its

latticed panes, amber and deep green, which gave an illusion of
perpetual sunshine in the hall as the light filtered through. He was
later to describe this beautiful oriel in *Farewell, Miss Julie Logan*:
'The great bowed window . . . twenty-eight feet in height and more
than half as wide. All who come to look at it count its little lozens, as
we call the panes, which are to the number of two hundred and
sixteen.'

There was plenty to do. Cynthia took Barrie and Mr Winter to a
pond where they could fish, there was tennis, and, of course, cricket.
The village cricket matches provided unending interest; the pavilion
was a one-time third-class railway carriage which had been fitted up,
and everyone turned out to watch or play. Nicholas bowled well for
Stanway in a match against a Cheltenham eleven the day after his
arrival, and the children were soon batting and bowling among
themselves too, Barrie having given Cynthia's son Michael a
cricketing set. Barrie was in great form with them indoors, pleased
with their shrieks of delight when he threw stamp after stamp on to
the high ceiling. But his real passion was for the shuffleboard, for
which he practised when he was not doing anything else, and he
generally won.

His correspondence was sent down regularly from Adelphi
Terrace, and Cynthia, now C. Greene, spent part of the morning
with him in the old library, which he had taken as his private
sitting-room. He would then go fishing, or play tennis or croquet, or
go into the nursery, or call for partners on the lawn for golf-
croquet, or go for a walk—when he expected Cynthia to accompany
him, and would wait with barely concealed impatience if she
happened to be doing anything else. She found it tiring to fit
everything into the day. There was sufficient staff—with Barrie
paying all the bills she had been able to get extra help from the
village for the domestic running of the house. But she still had to do
the ordering and be on hand to deal with any crisis in the kitchen,
and to keep an eye on the number of guests every day. The de
Navarros came over from Broadway, there were frequent calls by
neighbours and local friends, and Barrie expected them all to stay
for a meal. Nurse Faulkner looked after Simon and Michael and any
children brought by the guests and callers, and Cynthia tried to
spend some time in the nursery every day, and to relax with her
sisters and other members of her own family.

No, it was not easy. She was hostess for Barrie, with all the social duties this rôle implied, and she had never before had to deal with such a mixed collection of people. 'The Winters are quite mute at meals,' she noted with exasperation in her diary. When Charles Scribner and his wife came, she had a stiff evening showing them round the house and grounds—Barrie leaving that to her as he was busy at the shuffleboard—and she realized that they had expected a much more formal gathering in an aristocratic English country house.

Barrie himself made difficulties. He was offended one evening because Jack and Gerrie started a game of cards after dinner without telling him, and was even more annoyed because he was beaten by Whibley and other challengers at shuffleboard later. Maggie Winter chose to blame all her beloved brother's irritation on Gerrie, with whom she had tried to get on terms of intimate friendship but had been kept at arm's-length by well-bred politeness. Maggie was resentful, and showed it. Cynthia wrote in her diary: 'Hysterical outburst from Mrs W. after dinner. She and I and Gerrie were sitting together and she suddenly bolted from the room dragging me with her and said she couldn't stay in the room with Gerrie, she found her so impossible. I talked to her in bedroom.'

The sense of strain and hostility in the house made Cynthia feel ill, and she spoke plainly about it to Barrie. He was surprised at her attack, and promised 'to turn over a new leaf as regards behaviour to Gerry'. This was more easily said than done. A few nights later Cynthia noted that Barrie's nerves regarding Jack's wife were getting worse and worse, and he was quite annoyed at finding Gerrie in Cynthia's room. Cynthia wrote later:

Now and again nervous distemper would discharge itself against some human target. A gust of resentment could make him temporarily un-reasonable—even unjust—in his diatribe against some real, or supposed, offender. But, distressing though that derangement might be, it was as superficial as the scum on the surface of a deep lake. Barrie's considered, as opposed to his hasty, judgment was always wise, kindly and remarkably just. It did not need much discernment to see that the way to treat Barrie's fits of resentment was to give his grievance its head—to agree that the offender's conduct was monstrous and join in the attack. Could you bring yourself to do this, Barrie would at once react and, veering round, defend the object of his own abuse . . . Remaining exasperatingly fairminded, I would feel compelled to reason with him, when at that moment, as any fool could see, rationality was the last thing he wanted. Nor did he ever care for argument for argument's sake. What he craved was sympathy. That could always lure him back to reasonableness.

By the middle of August Cynthia was noting: 'Barrie's guests very much on his nerves.' He used the old library as a bolt-hole whenever he was in one of his people-hating moods. But he could swing to the highest good spirits for an occasion. The Australian Test cricket team was at Cheltenham, and he at once invited them over for a Sunday. They came on August 21st, and it was a glorious occasion for the house-party and the children, and especially for Nicholas. Luncheon was laid on the long shuffleboard. Barrie, looking very small, sat beside the huge, amiable Armstrong, and Cynthia, to the envy of her son Michael, sat between Collins and Gregory. Collins told her that the rumour that the team only drank tea was unfounded.

The Australians gave a dazzling exhibition on the village cricket ground, later played cricket on the lawn with the children, and remained to an improvised dinner. The following day, some of the house-party went to Cheltenham to see them play, and Cynthia prepared for a quick dash to London to visit her son John, who now lived at Ealing with his governess.

It was, as always, a moment of heartbreak when she left him again, but there was nothing else to be done, and they *must* continue to afford the governess. She stayed at Cadogan Square, where Beb was living, as their own house was let for the summer. Beb returned to Stanway with her, and Cynthia would have been very happy, but the eternal money troubles were on them again. Beb's father had written reducing his allowance from £500 to £200 a year. This was a severe blow. Now Beb must see how necessary her 'secretarying' was!

Early in September Barrie reluctantly decided he must go back to London. He was expecting Bernard Freyberg to stay with him at the flat, and Nico had arranged to go to an Eton friend's home for a short visit. Cynthia got the cheques for the household expenses ready for him to sign, and went for a last walk with him in the woods. He was very depressed; he did not want to leave Stanway. Above all, he did not want to leave Cynthia; she was remaining with Beb for the latter's holiday. She knew it would be dull without Barrie, but she was exceedingly tired, and Beb was always easier when 'the little Scotchman' was miles away.

Barrie wrote to her immediately he got to the flat, saying he had been happier at Stanway than he could have been anywhere else:

As to you, how dear and lovely you have been all the time. Stanway is just another name for you . . . I could just have described you—not as being in Domesday Book as a fact but as a prediction. I could elaborate the idea as a story for Michael . . . I feel that you had a great deal too much to do looking after so many people and everlastingly so sweet and gracious . . . How many things I might have done to help you that I didn't do and how often I was irritable and depressed and selfish—it is as if I were trying to see whether I could break down the patience and sweetness and loveliness of mind that go to the making of Cynthia. I never succeeded and I hope I'll never try any more.

His London life was quickly resumed. E. V. Lucas entertained Charles Chaplin at the Garrick Club, and asked some of his friends to meet the comedian, then at the height of his fame. Chaplin wanted to meet Sir James Barrie, so of course the distinguished writer was asked, and—to his tremendous excitement—Nico was also included in the invitation. It was a wonderful evening, and Barrie took Chaplin back to the flat, where Gerald du Maurier joined them later. They talked until past two o'clock in the morning, and Barrie wrote all about it to Cynthia, saying that he wished he had been able to usher Charlie Chaplin into the nursery at Stanway, to teach Simon a new way of walking and how to fire a custard pudding at dear Nannie Faulkner's face when she mentioned bed.

* * *

Barrie had suffered from his cough and bronchial trouble for so many years that it had become an old familiar, but now he found he was catching colds very easily, and as he slept badly, even when he took some of Sir Douglas Shields's[1] draughts, he was often ill and depressed. He was too unwell to attend the rehearsals for *Peter Pan*, and shook off Cynthia's suggestions that he should go into Sir Douglas's nursing home in Park Lane and be properly looked after. What he needed, what he wanted . . . he did not really know what he needed or what he wanted. He was grey ashes.

Bernard Freyberg came to stay, and as he was suffering from old wounds which troubled him from time to time, Barrie immediately became well in order to help nurse him. If only Cynthia were there,

1. Dr Shields had been knighted.

too: 'You are all, or pretty nearly all, that is left to me. If it were not for you I don't see how I could go on, how life could have any flavour. So much am I your humble servant. I am that indeed . . .' He signed the letter 'Your loving Master (Servant)'.

Cynthia was well used by now to Barrie's form of 'dewdrops' and took them, as she had always taken extravagant compliments and expressions of homage, as a matter of course. What she was concerned about was getting him back on an even keel, so that he could begin working again; that was when he was at his happy best. She wrote him a long letter, saying that she herself was going to try to live a less hectic existence, to live 'more by rule'. Delicately she hinted that he would find that a help in his own life, and went on to suggest a course of massage for his chest ailment.

Barrie reacted vigorously. Live by rule! Massage! He scorned the idea of both, and went on to mention that there were heaps of letters and 'much confusion' awaiting her when she arrived. He was looking forward to having Beb with him, too. The Sussex Place house was still let, and Barrie had invited Cynthia and her husband to live at the flat for as long as they liked.

Beb had no alternative but to accept. He got to London a day or two before Cynthia, as he had to be back in his office, and found a room ready for him at Adelphi Terrace House. Barrie greeted him genially, but Beb was more than usually reserved. When Cynthia arrived, she quickly knew the reason: 'Poor Beb very distressed about his finances—having just received £50 instead of the £145 quarterly allowance from his father.'

Cynthia had obtained an advance from a publisher for a book about children, and had been commissioned to write a number of articles for magazines. But the money from these would not go far, and Beb was in low spirits. Poetry didn't pay; the only way to make extra money was to let their house. He disliked his wife's 'cuckooing' and especially disliked being without his own home for part of the year, with the children away at Stanway. Staying with his mother-in-law at Cadogan Square put him on edge, knowing as he did that she did not approve of his mode of life. Lady Wemyss could not always control her disapproval. Why could he not persevere and be a successful barrister as his father had been? Much as she disliked Herbert Asquith's politics, she privately admired his ability and tenacity: had he not climbed up to be Prime Minister? Beb could not keep Cynthia and the children in moderate comfort. When he was staying at her house Lady Wemyss was polite to her son-in-law but no more.

'Cuckooing' in Adelphi Terrace House brought a different kind of irritation. With only one sitting-room, he and Cynthia naturally made a trio with their host. Beb breakfasted early as he had to go to his office. Cynthia sat with him, or waited until Barrie was ready to appear. Her days were always full, but she fitted in her engagements to Barrie's needs now, not the other way round. When Beb got back in the evening, they dined *à trois*. If Barrie went to one of his clubs or dined out, Beb and Cynthia had an evening together by the fire, with Cynthia reading aloud—something she much enjoyed doing— or they would go out to a theatre or dine with friends themselves. But it was not home life. Beb wondered if they would ever get back to a normal home life again.

There were moments. Mrs Patrick Campbell came to dinner, and wore the three of them out by staying until past two o'clock in the morning. She read them her life story from a manuscript she had recently written, in which she had included a number of Bernard Shaw's letters to her, which Cynthia thought brilliant and adorable. Beb, however, with his legal training, pressed the actress to say whether she had Shaw's permission to publish the letters, and tried to make her understand the law of copyright. It was obvious Mrs Campbell thought she was a law unto herself: copyright, whatever that was, could go to the devil. She sat there, passionately talking, smoking three cigars in the process, and would not go until Beb brought her coat and got her a taxi.

Barrie could not stand late nights; he sometimes coughed incessantly, and again he caught cold after cold. Trouble soon began in his chest and throat, and it was at this period that he began to take the drug heroin. Cynthia and Beb were now back in their own home, the last tenant having gone, and Beb was relieved to be once again among his own possessions. Cynthia, however, was hardly ever there. Barrie seemed to be getting worse, and she called in a local doctor, Shields being away. The doctor advised having a nurse as Barrie was getting up in the night and walking about. Freyberg came. Barrie grew very difficult, and insisted on having his Will brought, and Freyberg, who was not at all well himself, tried to calm him down by saying he would soon be better.

As the insomnia was getting worse, the doctor prescribed heroin, but instead of surrendering to the impulse to sleep, Barrie 'sat up in bed in a state of ecstasy and inspiration', and insisted on smoking. Cynthia spent as much time as she could with him, soothing, cajoling him to eat and to relax so as to let the drug do its work. At last he gave in, and was soon asleep, only to wake up hours later in a state of the most terrible depression, a reaction from the heroin.

Freyberg and the nurse did not get on. The soldier had had much experience of dealing with nurses in hospitals, and he took a dislike to this one, disagreeing with the treatment the sick man was having. Barrie demanded heroin again, as it gave him 'such a blissful sensation', and the result was the same intense depression after he woke up. The doctor seemed to take no notice of this, and, to Cynthia's astonishment, allowed Barrie to get up. Peter Davies came to see him and stayed to lunch, and then helped Cynthia to persuade Barrie to go back to bed.

His illness went on for days, and Cynthia was there from morning till late evening. There was a scene with Beb one night; he wanted to know why, with Freyberg and the nurse and Brown and Mrs Stanley at the flat, she should have to be there all the time too, once she had dealt with the correspondence. Cynthia soothed him, saying that Barrie now depended on her to an enormous extent. She must be at hand most of the time, trying to convince the sick man that it was not worth taking heroin, no matter how blissful it made him feel, if the result was going to be constant depression. Barrie listened to her, said Cynthia, and it was her plain duty to do all she could for him. Beb was compelled to agree.

Barrie slowly recovered. Lady Wemyss asked him to come to Stanway for Christmas, and Cynthia was relieved that he was well enough to travel by December 22nd. He was obviously pleased that this was going to be a real family party, with the sons-in-law and the children and the close relations, and only himself as the outside guest. He did not in the least feel outside or a guest; he was completely at home the moment the car glided through the Inigo Jones gateway. In a sense, this was his country home. The fact that the Earl of Wemyss, the real squire, was there did not in the least take away from his sense of proprietorship, a sense left over from his summer's tenancy. He would, of course, take Stanway next year: that was already settled in his mind.

By Christmas Eve he was well enough to go for quite a long walk with Cynthia, and the next day he enjoyed charades with the children in the great hall. He played shuffleboard, determined to beat every-

one else—and succeeded most of the time. He won a draughts
tournament. He was himself again.

On December 27th, a letter came from London informing him
that it was proposed to give him the Order of Merit. When he told
Cynthia this news, she had to admit she did not know what the
Order of Merit was. As he had a 'slight gloater' over it, she gathered
it was something that pleased him very much, and from that
moment he was back to his old form. Nobody would have guessed
that he had just recovered from what had seemed a serious illness.
He was, as he had been in the summer, the life and soul of Stanway.

Chapter 20

RECTOR OF ST ANDREWS

In February, 1922, Barrie was invested with the Order of Merit at Buckingham Palace. He wore knee-breeches which, after consultation with Cynthia, he had made for him by a Savile Row tailor. He had not wanted to wear this 'fancy dress' at all, saying that he would look even smaller than he was in such truncated nether garments, but Cynthia prevailed upon him to obey sartorial protocol, and he gave way, though he thought it was absurd, and he was never likely to wear them again, in any case.

That over, his next anxiety was the preparation of his Rectorial address for St Andrews University. It was nearly three years since he had been elected Rector, his term of office was coming to an end, and he had to give the required speech. Cynthia, who was going for a short time to Stanway, left him at his writing-table, ready to begin his notes. She travelled to Gloucestershire with mixed feelings; her son John was staying at Stanway with his governess for a holiday. She longed to have her family growing up together, and after a few days she was writing to Barrie in a highly emotional state. A despairing sensation of aasebment, a feeling of guilt and inadequacy, came over her when she was with this afflicted boy, and she had no difficulty in dashing it all down on paper and sending it to Barrie, sure of his unfailing sympathy. He wrote every day, telling her that her guilty feelings were unjustified, that it was not surprising her sensitive soul was on edge, and she was the bravest person that he had ever met. He also enclosed a cheque in one letter 'for your Christmas frock' which she had bought some months before.

Cynthia returned to London in time to join Barrie, with Beb and Elizabeth Lucas, in a box at St Martin's Theatre, where Basil Dean had put on *Shall We Join the Ladies?* which was a curtain-raiser to John Galsworthy's *Loyalties*, a short three-act play. Barrie praised the performance of the curtain-raiser but said little more about it: the background of this dramatic fragment was still too painful to talk about. Elizabeth Lucas and Audrey stayed at the flat with him for a few days, he visited Lord and Lady Desborough at Taplow Court, he spent the night with Thomas Hardy at Max Gate. The days and weeks must be filled up, and Barrie had more invitations than he could accept.

The Rectorial Address was beginning to bother him. He had settled on a theme: Courage. A big theme, a magnificent theme, and he could not get down on paper what he wanted to say. To begin with, he could not make up his mind on what kind of courage he could talk about to a post-war audience of students, some of whom would have served in the war. Physical courage? Moral courage? It would be tricky. In one of his moments of insight, when he forced himself to hold up an undistorting mirror to the Jamie behind the image, Barrie knew that these young men and women of St Andrews would know if he made one false step.

He was, surprisingly, having trouble with his secretary. Cynthia Asquith had been staving off attacks of nerves, brought on by over-work and the unending round of social engagements she refused to curtail—she had long since forgotten her resolve to live by rule. And there was always the nagging money shortage. Beb was patient at present, and was trying hard to like Barrie, asking him to dine at his club, finding subjects of mutual interest to talk about when he himself dined at Adelphi Terrace. But when Barrie and Beb were alone together the chief subject seemed to be the fascinating, unique Cynthia; Barrie did not attempt to disguise his admiration for the other's wife, which he was sure must please Beb. It was a strange, naïve situation altogether, and Beb felt helpless.

The St Andrews Rectorial Address was not many weeks away; it was to be given at the University on May 3rd. Cynthia was still not well, and had a slight temperature, but she insisted on going to the flat every day. Barrie wrote steadily on foolscap sheets at his table; on her own desk, Cynthia saw a steadily growing pile of letters for C. Greene to answer. They suddenly angered her: she was tired of them! One day, after she had replied to what seemed to be thousands and thousands of 'sillies', she lunched with Barrie and unexpectedly broke down in tears, greatly upsetting him. As always when someone was in distress, Barrie soothed and comforted her, and sent her home in a taxi. She was not much better next day, but she returned to the flat and tried to make amends by working for hours without bothering him.

As Rector of St Andrews, Barrie had been entitled to submit names to be included in the list of honorary LL.D. degrees to be conferred by the University, including Thomas Hardy, Sidney Colvin, Robertson Nicoll, Bernard Freyberg, John Galsworthy, E. V. Lucas and Ellen Terry. The first draft of the Address was ready for Cynthia by the middle of April, and she copied it out in clear, large handwriting so that Barrie could read it without spectacles; she stayed up until after midnight and rose next morning at half past seven in order to get it finished, as she was lunching with Barrie at the Carlton. The manuscript was 8,000 words long, and he was surprised when she gave him the finished script at the table. It was a relief to go home to dinner and Beb that evening, without hours of writing in front of her.

The children were at Margate with Nannie Faulkner, and Cynthia and Beb went down to spend the week-end with them, Cynthia happy to be able to relax, the wearisome Address behind her, delivered. When she returned to London on Monday, and went to Adelphi Terrace in the afternoon, she was greeted by a harassed Barrie. He wanted a lot of alterations done to the script. She could cut out pieces and sew them or glue them to the new bits. He was going to rewrite it. He was going to rewrite part of it. He wasn't satisfied with it. He didn't imagine it could possibly interest anybody.

Cynthia took the various sections of foolscap which he gave her, and sat down to rewrite them as a coherent whole. It took her several hours, and when she at last handed the script to him he put it on his writing-table without comment. Three days later she dined with him at the Ritz, and he told her he had altered the Address again. She wondered how she could stretch twenty-four hours into twenty-five; she had just let her house and was packing away belongings, so every minute was precious. She copied out the rewritten parts next morning, did the letters, and rushed back to Sussex Place. Two days later she came to the flat to find yet more recopying to be done on the Address. She lost her temper, wept and scolded. This time there was no comfort and sympathy: Barrie required the script altered in several places, and it had to be done.

She could never remain angry with him for long. On May 1st she travelled to Edinburgh with him, Freyberg and E. V. Lucas also being in the party. Barrie and Ellen Terry were to stay with the

Principal at St Andrews, but Tuesday morning was spent with
Barrie showing them round Edinburgh, taking them to the haunts
of his student days, walking them up Calton Hill to see the views
towards the sea, directing them to admire this landmark and that.
In the afternoon they went on to St Andrews, to be received by Sir
James Irvine, the Principal of the University, and his delightful wife.
They began a friendship during that visit which was to endure;
Cynthia described Irvine as being 'as Scottish as peat', and his
outgoing friendliness at once attracted the visiting celebrity.

The ceremonies began unofficially after dinner with a students'
torchlight procession. Barrie was prepared to enjoy everything from
the start, but he was suddenly seized with doubts about his Rectorial
Address. He must look at it again. Cynthia did her best to get him to
leave it alone, but next morning he insisted on cutting paragraphs
and sentences out of it, in spite of the fact that copies had been
circulated to the Press.

The Volunteer Hall was packed for the main ceremony. Lord
Haig, the Chancellor of the University, was in charge of the proceedings, and even he could feel the tension in the crowded hall, with
all eyes focused on the short, motionless figure beside him on the
platform. Cynthia sat with Freyberg, hardly able to bear the suspense:
she knew what that white look on Barrie's face meant. It was the
look that preceded one of his long silences. He was clearly in no state
to face the massed, critical young audience.

To Barrie's super-sensitive antennae there was a tinge of hostility
in the air. He faced the concentrated gaze of a new generation, a new
breed, determined to take a new look at life after one of the bloodiest
wars in history. The traditional respect and reverence for age and
seniority had been swept away; these young men and women were
looking for something else. Well, he was ready for them. But he felt
every one of his sixty-two years upon him when Lord Haig presented
the Rector, and sat down. Barrie rose and took a step or two forward.
There was applause, then a silence. Cynthia froze where she sat.
The silence went on.

A student who was there that day says: 'We thought he wasn't
going to get started at all. He just didn't seem able to get a word out,
and I felt sorry for him. It was a silence I never want to go through
again.'

Barrie did, in fact, get started, but his voice was inaudible, and
this made matters worse. On the table beside him was a paper-knife,

and unconsciously he picked it up and began to play with it as he talked. Suddenly a voice rang out from the audience: 'Put it down, Jamie! You'll cut your throat!'

There was a roar of laughter, and silence again, but a different silence. Barrie put down the paper-knife, and now he was smiling. The image readjusted itself: he was himself again. Everyone could sense the change in him. He had not altered his position on the platform, but now his stance was firm, not uncertain. His voice came out strongly, and within seconds he had got them with him. He told them there was much he concealed from other people, but to them he intended to expose every cranny of his mind. He said his theme was Courage:

Courage, as you should use it in the great fight that seems to me to be coming between youth and their betters; by youth meaning, of course, you, and by your betters, us. I want you to take up this position: That youth have for too long left exclusively in our hands the decisions in national matters that are more vital to them than to us. Things about the next war, for instance, and why the last one ever had a beginning. I use the word fight because it must, I think, begin with a challenge; but the aim is the reverse of antagonism, it is partnership. I want you to hold that the time has arrived for youth to demand that partnership, and to demand it courageously. . . . Your betters had no share in the immediate cause of the war . . . but for fifty years or so we heeded not the rumblings of the distant drum . . . and when war did come we told youth, who had to get us out of it, tall tales of what it really is and of the clover beds to which it leads. We were not meaning to deceive, most of us were as honourable and as ignorant as the youth themselves; but that does not acquit us of failings such as stupidity and jealousy, the two black spots in human nature which, more than love of money, are at the root of all evil. If you prefer to leave things as they are we shall probably fail you again. Do not be too sure that we have learned our lesson, and are not at this very moment doddering down some brimstone path.

He told them of the two men inside his own nature, M'Connachie and James Barrie. He warned them about the M'Connachies in their own natures, adding, 'Unless you are constantly on the watch, you will find that he has slowly pushed you out of yourself and taken your place.' He told them about Freyberg winning the Victoria Cross. He talked about the nature of fame, and quoted Walter Scott and Henley and Johnson.

The Rectorial Address was nearing its end. Barrie fumbled in his pocket and brought out a letter, parts of which he said he would read to them. It was Captain Scott's last letter to him, written in the tent in the Antarctic where Scott met his end.

'The writing is in pencil, still quite clear, though towards the end some of the words trail away as into the great silence that was waiting for them,' said Barrie, and began to read from the letter.

Now came a pause. Without changing his tone, he said he was going to read them a sonnet, written by 'a lad that will never be old'. Only a few people in the hall could have known what it cost Barrie to say the lines which Michael Davies had once written at Eilean Shona during what was to be his last summer holiday:

Throned on a cliff serene Man saw the sun
hold a red torch above the farthest seas,
and the fierce island pinnacles put on
in his defence their sombre panoplies;
Foremost the white mists eddied, trailed and spun
like seekers, emulous to clasp his knees,
till all the beauty of the scene seemed one,
led by the secret whispers of the breeze.

The sun's torch suddenly flashed upon his face
and died; and he sat content in subject night
and dreamed of an old dead foe that had sought and found him;
a beast stirred boldly in his resting place;
And the cold came; Man rose to his master-height,
shivered, and turned away; but the mists were round him.

The whole speech was a magnificent set-piece, and how much was art and how much sincerity was, Cynthia thought, neither here nor there. What she was sure of was that none of the young men and women in the Volunteer Hall at St Andrews that day would forget it.

*   *   *

Barrie was exhausted. There were banquets, speeches, a quick visit to Dundee and more speeches, dinners, yet more speeches. He might feel beaten to the ground with tiredness but he did not spare himself. When his public made demands he was as punctilious as any professional actor—the show must go on. What it cost him in nervous strain only Cynthia Asquith and Freyberg knew. It all came to an end at last, and they were on the train to London. Barrie was grey ashes; he hardly spoke, but lay back against the cushions in the railway carriage with his eyes closed.

Behind the exhaustion, however, was a feeling of exhilaration, of satisfaction. He could hold an audience. It gave him a wonderful sense of power. He later admitted to Cynthia Asquith that he found a unique fulfilment in facing an audience and making them listen to him. He had given many speeches in the last few years, and enjoyed keeping his face poker-straight while making his audience laugh. Now, with the triumphant success of the Rectorial Address, he intended to develop this gift.

From that time on he began to perfect his technique. Timing must be right. Pauses must not be too long. He learned when to turn on the humour and when to seek the fugitive tear; when to banter, when to flatter. His voice with its Scottish burr had a touch of hoarseness, due to his smoking; this was an asset. His speeches became carefully spontaneous, but there were times when some of his listeners might wonder whether they were listening to real reminiscence or fiction. Cynthia Asquith, who listened to many of his 'performances' wrote:

He tended to wander in some entrancing borderland between fantasy and fact. For him the frontier between these two realms was never very clearly marked . . . He never invented or even embroidered deliberately to deceive, but the art of weaving fantasy with fact, always natural with him—the art which made his fortune—had come to be his master as well as his servant . . . But, though he told of many things that had happened to him, of what he really thought, of what he really was, he gave scarcely a clue.

Perhaps it was Elizabeth Lucas who came nearest to following such clues as there were to the man who hid behind the image. He wrote to her on May 18th, 1922:

Do you know that this day a year ago Michael was alive and as well as any of us and that next day he was dead. That is really why I am writing to you today. I feel that he is at Oxford today in his rooms and that tomorrow he is going out to be drowned, and doesn't know it. I spoke about courage as you know at St Andrews, but it does seem to me often as if there was something rather monstrous in my still being here. Peter is coming tomorrow to stay the night and will be everything that is kind.

Peter Davies had grown closer to Barrie since his brother's death, and often came to the flat, especially during the holidays, when Nico was there. He was still as lean and withdrawn-looking as ever, but there was unwonted gentleness in his new relationship with the older man. He must have guessed at the terrible loneliness which was like a dark background to the kaleidoscopic pattern of Barrie's life. The fact that he had never been as near to Barrie as George or Michael did not matter: Barrie found this renewed friendship with Peter precious, and he mentions him a great deal in his letters to Cynthia.

Michael was hardly ever out of Barrie's mind; the rawness of grief had not abated. Yet in a queer, inexplicable way, the genuine pain was becoming entwined with the diabolical instinct of the creative writer to use every experience as material for his work. He could write this in a notebook:

I dreamt that he came back to me, not knowing that he was drowned, and that I kept this knowledge from him. We went on for another year in the old way, till the fatal 19th approached again, and he became very sad, not knowing why, and I feared what was to happen but never let on, and as the day drew on he understood more and thought I didn't. Gradually each knew the other knew, but still we didn't speak of it, and when the day came, I had devised schemes to make it impossible for him to leave me, yet doubted they could help, and he rose in the night and put on the old clothes and came to look at me, as he thought, asleep. I tried to prevent him going, but he had to go and I knew it, but he said he thought it would be harder if I didn't let him go alone. But I went with him holding his hand, and he liked it, and when we came to the place, that pool, he said 'goodbye' to me and went into it and sank, just as before. At this point I think I never lost the feeling that he had walked cheerily into my room as if another year had again begun for us.

The above was all the dream and the notes to follow came out of thinking about it, all except this, that I learned from the moment of his return I must never let him know that anything had happened to him, that this, so to speak, was vital to his life. All must go on as if he had merely returned from some ordinary outing. If I wrote about this I should picture the old life going on as previously. So [illegible] as before that often for a length of time I cease to have uneasiness. I have no idea until the fatal day is approaching that he will again be taken from me then. I give details of our time together during the extra year lived quite ordinarily though strangely close to each other. I do some things that I wanted before until then I had not done. Fears of spoiling him and fight not to do it, how in agony I had to let him go away sometimes, to live ordinary life of youth. It is not necessary to make him nearly 21, he would be younger if I like, perhaps sinister hostile powers like clouds in Monsieur [illegible] fairytale. His gallant fear of water which he confides to me in the entire year, how this affects me, he might write from school of fears of water when learning to swim, so this vague shadow haunts the story. It might be called 'Water' (or 'The Silent Pool') or 'The 19th'.

Mary Hodgson coming back? He can't get past the fatal date. Our real letters in it? In some strange way his tastes, dispositions we [illegible]. He seems to know vaguely some new, strange things and to have forgotten other things. Fatal night arriving to me tight-pressed lips says: 'Going to bathe, must go, must.' In dream did he return like one so much older, or just as he left me, or a year younger? In last case it would mean he can't get past a certain age as well as an entire day. If the other comes it is [illegible] trying to take in guarded by others, he is in much agony of mind that I know to let him out goes to pool. To go with him on the fatal day is as sad as Charles Lamb 'crossing fields' with his sister, taking her to asylum, his hand on my shoulder. Must be clear that there is nothing sinister about it. I make him become an accomplished swimmer to help fight this fatal day (day better than night?). When he reappears it is as suddenly as from the next room, and in a matter of fact way he never knows he has been away. Effect on my own life. Give up ordinary work. He chides me for laziness. His joy of living greater than ever, something of childhood comes back. It is as if, long after writing P. Pan, its true meaning came back to me, desperate attempt to grow up but can't. Enquiring back I find he had always had difficulty to pass the 19th [illegible] once lost and by this pool of water comes back or build high wall, yet he is found drowned in it. We try going away, far away, and a similar pool is there, terrible when he vaguely knows it is, must be, a dreadful day for him. A love affair? How would I hint it, saying, 'I think you will go again.'

There does not seem to be any evidence that Barrie ever worked up this marvellous set of notes, torn out of himself, into a book.

*   *   *

Barrie rented Stanway again for six weeks during the summer of 1922. His domestic life at Adelphi Terrace had been changed by the departure of the faithful Brown, whose wife was still ailing. Brown bought a small farm in the country, and was as sad to part from his employer as Barrie was to lose him. He was succeeded by Frank Thurston, an extraordinary character, a trained butler who had a professorial *alter ego*; he knew some Latin and Greek, and could understand French and Spanish. Barrie liked having an oddity as a manservant, and was fond of drawing out his butler's erudition in front of guests. This eccentric was an entirely trustworthy and loyal servant, and he stayed with Barrie to the end of the latter's life. He accompanied his employer to Stanway, and the house-party that year had the benefit of his skilled and sophisticated ministrations.

Besides Cynthia and her family and Nico, the Winters came again, and also Alec Barrie's widow and her eldest daughter, Lilian, a humorous, sensible woman whom Cynthia liked, in contrast to her mother, 'a stout woman who talked all day of one of her other daughters who had married a canon'. Charles Whibley was there again, and this year Bernard Freyberg brought a wife—he had married Barbara MacLaren two months before.

Cynthia, again hostess for Barrie, found the party even more of a mixture than the previous year, and she had to keep her temper continually in check when Maggie gave herself airs, remarking on occasion that people did not realize what respect was due to Sir James. In particular she objected to those who familiarly called him Jimmy.

On August 9th a police-sergeant arrived from Winchcombe to inform Sir James that Queen Mary was staying in the neighbourhood and wished to come over to see Stanway on the following Monday. This, even Maggie Winter conceded, was something that the daughter of an earl could deal with. Cynthia had a hectic time making arrangements for flowers, flags and bunting to be placed in appropriate places, and was in an acutely nervous state by Monday. The Royal day passed without hitch, however. Queen Mary and a party of twelve arrived in the afternoon, the house-party were presented in the flower-filled drawing-room, the tithe-barn was inspected, the village, assembled on the Green, did their curtsy, the party came back to tea, and Cynthia was glad to see them go. Beb, who had been very quiet ever since he came down with her from London, looked very ill, and as soon as the last car went off she telephoned the local doctor, as Beb was due to return to London the following week. The doctor examined Beb, said that he must take great care and there was to be no smoking or alcohol. Cynthia would have liked to go back with her husband, but it was out of the question: Barrie depended on her for everything.

She sublimated her private anxieties and annoyance in constant activity. The following day she wrote an article for a magazine before lunch, played tennis, played with the children, went to a funeral, drove to Apperley with Nicholas and some of the others for tea and tennis, brought friends back to dinner, played shuffleboard,

'and then groped up to the Pyramid in dark with Barrie' to see the
lights in the surrounding countryside. The next morning she wrote
another article, and had an equally full day, but on the Saturday
there was a bad evening. Barrie did not like cards, and she and
many of the house-party were fond of bridge. 'Barrie annoyed by
card-playing, I caught his nerves and we both got into a bad state.'

Quarrels did not last long, but they were becoming frequent.
There would be good days, when they played tennis and cricket and
walked and had indoor games. Then, without warning, Barrie's
prickles would shoot out. His dislike of Jack's wife had not abated,
and he objected to Cynthia being friends with Gerrie, whom she
liked. Items in her diary tell of many a sudden flare-up: 'Walk with
Barrie after tea. Row with him over talk about Jack and Gerrie.'
Some of the guests departed, and others came. Cynthia was expected
to see to the social observances, over which Barrie was very strict,
so that she noted irritably: 'I hate doing chaperone.'

There was cricket every day, and Nicholas was in his element,
playing in the matches and having an uproarious time with several
of his Etonian friends, whom Barrie had invited. Nico was now
eighteen and had left Eton; he was an upstanding young man with a
tremendous sense of humour, and, Cynthia thought, a blessedly
uncomplicated outlook on life. He was going up to New College,
Oxford, in the autumn, and now Barrie would have no more personal
connection with Eton. But, Cynthia was sure, he would always think
of himself as being an honorary Old Etonian through his 'boys'.

Barrie had been preparing *Dear Brutus* for publication, and he took
it with him back to London, where casting conferences would soon
be held for the December production of *Peter Pan*. Cynthia remained
at Stanway. Beb came down again and though she felt exhausted, she
was happy to be alone with him and the children. Beb was a good
deal better. He was writing a novel, the beginning of which he read
to her on their first evening together. Cynthia herself had started
another book about children, and several articles had been commissioned by newspapers and magazines. Perhaps, between them,
they could make a little money . . .

It was so peaceful that neither of them wanted to return to
London. They did not discuss it, but Cynthia and her husband now
knew, with a kind of fatalistic resignation, that the privacy of their
marriage had been shattered. James Barrie had come right into their
lives and had no intention of leaving them again. They must, he

said, regard Adelphi Terrace as their second home every time they let Sussex Place. Their summers would be spent at Stanway with him. Already he adored their two sons, he told them.

Neither Cynthia nor Beb had foreseen such a situation. They had somehow allowed it to develop, and there was no going back.

Chapter 21

THE LAST YEARS I

IN a prescient assessment of Barrie's character, made in the note to a letter (see page 167), Peter Davies said he thought Barrie needed to own and be owned by the object of his affections. It is difficult to guess how much real affection he had for Lady Cynthia Asquith. He wrote her hundreds of letters all through the years she was his secretary, most of them to Stanway and other houses where she was staying, but many of them from Adelphi Terrace House when she was actually at Sussex Place and he would be seeing her within a day or two.

After the first few months, during which he addressed her formally, the letters became what from any other pen would be regarded as love letters. They now began 'Dearest Cynthia', 'Dearest Cyncie', 'Darling Girl', 'Precious Lass', with variations; most of them addressed her by the nickname which he invented and alone used, 'Dearest Mulberry', and nearly all are signed in the manner of letters already quoted, 'Loving Master'. The one thing all these letters lack is any trace of warmth. They are full of praise and admiration for her beauty and courage and patience, they are brimful and slopping over with sympathy for her various troubles. The luscious phrases roll out in letter after letter, until they become predictable and somehow mechanical. One has no sense of intimacy whatever. Were they, like Shaw's letters to Mrs Patrick Campbell and Ellen Terry, exercises in romantic prose that would later be used in plays? But Barrie wrote no major work during the later years. It is more likely that it was his pathological compulsion to *write* that brought these fantastic outpourings, together with a deep psychological need to have someone closely attached to him now that the years were running out: someone who would need him as much as he needed her, and who would therefore never leave him.

He was no fool. He recognized that Cynthia loved money and

luxury and was eternally worried by the fact that she and Beb could not always find enough even for the necessities of life. He knew she depended on her 'salary', a payment that was often tactfully augmented by handsome cheques on her birthday and at Christmas, and on other special occasions. But he also knew that she had a genuine sense of responsibility towards him, that when he was ill she would always be there, or drop what she was doing and come to him. She made no pretence of being 'in love' with him in the accepted sense of the word: he would have been alarmed if she had been. She had grown fond of him in a kind of way, though he was also quite aware that he angered and irritated her many times, and she could turn on him in fury. He once wrote to her:

Dearest Mulberry,
I do assure you I don't think it's unreasonable of you to be hurt by my doddering ways. I think it's wonderful beyond words that you have endured me and them so long . . . I am grieved beyond words that I didn't write to you about your not liking to be well [*sic*] for some time & terribly worried . . . I am apparently shut up in myself now to such an extent that I can't express it. It is because age has come upon me I consider rather suddenly. I go on loving you just the same.

*　　*　　*

Age had little to do with Barrie's thoughts or actions. He was as unpredictable to himself as he was to others; he allowed moods to overwhelm and encase him until the strange M'Connachie who had him temporarily in thrall suffered James Barrie to be released again.

He was the summer squire of Stanway for nine years, and the lists of his guests for the house-parties read like scores of items out of *Who's Who*. The Winters took it as a matter of course that they should come. Their chess-playing son Willie was an uncomfortable misfit, but Barrie noticed nothing. They were his relatives, almost the last he had, and he would do his duty by them as long as it was necessary.

Cynthia, though hostess for Barrie, invited a number of her own friends, and of course they immediately became Barrie's friends. She suffered intermittent bouts of ill-health, and soon discovered that when she was really ill, Barrie rapidly recovered from his current ailment and became solicitous at once. At Stanway they were constantly together, taking long walks on most days, playing with her children. Barrie attached Simon to himself with his usual skill, telling him stories of animals and pirates until the little boy shouted with delight and asked for more.

Jack and Gerrie Davies came to the house-parties every year; Barrie had long made his peace with Gerrie, especially as she was now a mother twice over, a baby daughter having joined her son Timothy. In 1924, at Stanway, marriage again threatened a close relationship which he had persuaded himself was unbreakable: Nicholas, still an undergraduate at Oxford, had fallen in love with a charming girl, Mary James, a daughter of Lord Northbourne. Barrie consulted Cynthia, saying he was worried because Nico had no prospects and did not appear to be interested in any particular profession. Cynthia was annoyingly on the side of the young people; she believed strongly in love matches.

Peter had at last decided on an avocation: he wanted to become a publisher. This was something Barrie knew about, and he had the right contacts. Again he talked to Cynthia, and after many discussions Peter went to a publisher's in Edinburgh to learn about book production and typography, did a stint with Barrie's old publishers, Hodder and Stoughton, and finished with his own imprint of Peter Davies.

Barrie kept in touch with his godson, Peter Scott, whose mother had re-married and was now Lady Hilton Young. Peter had gone to Oundle School, and was growing up. Everybody grew up, in time . . .

Except *Peter Pan*. The Christmas season in London and America would have been unthinkable without that famous annual. And when, one day, Barrie suddenly decided to give the perpetual rights in *Peter Pan* to the Great Ormond Street Hospital for Sick Children, the spectacular gesture took the headlines, and Barrie almost regretted the handsome gift because of the stream of begging letters which flowed into the flat as a result.

Barrie was as generous with his time as with his money. He had always been interested in the welfare of other writers, and ready to support any association which would give them the status which he felt was their due. He had been a member of the Incorporated Society of Authors, Playwrights and Composers (since re-named the Society of Authors) since 1891, and in March, 1928, he accepted an invitation to become their President, in succession to Thomas Hardy. This was a high honour. The Society had been founded in 1884, the first President had been Alfred Lord Tennyson and the second

George Meredith. Most of the leading men of letters were members, and the Society was influential enough to have obtained notable victories in the matter of authors' rights, copyright and other literary matters.

Being a President meant making speeches. He had made many in the past, but since the Rectorial Address at St Andrews he had changed his style. He was now more professional. He spent many hours preparing his first speech as President of the Society; Cynthia Asquith found him, day after day, writing and re-writing what he told her was for a very important occasion. But he took as many pains preparing his 'few words' when he presented the local cricket club at Stanway with a pavilion to replace the old railway coach as he did for a large assembly at Eton when he talked on *Captain Hook at Eton*. He rehearsed as carefully for a speech at the Girls' High School at Wallasey as when he faced a very different audience at the ceremony installing him as Chancellor of Edinburgh University.

He enjoyed making speeches more than ever. Each was an occasion: almost like preparing a manuscript for publication, or rehearsing the act of a play—with himself as principal performer.

Nico married Mary James, and got a job in the City with a firm of bill-brokers. No more would his gramophone be heard in the flat, or summer holidays be built around him: from now on he would be living his own life. Barrie liked Mary, and was glad because Nico was so obviously happy, but Cynthia found him looking at the school-groups on the wall, and she listened patiently when he spoke of the past and 'my boys'.

One day she came to Adelphi Terrace House to find him sitting at his desk, completely immersed. aBrrie was writing. He had been unwell for days, complaining of his cough and his chest and various pains; now she noted in her diary: 'Barrie still writing hard and wonderfully rejuvenated.' She dined with him two days later, and he told her he had begun another book. He read her the first four chapters. It had 'some exquisite writing', but she hoped it would not get too eerie. During the next two weeks he was like an erupting volcano, and when she reminded him that he had a speech to prepare for the forthcoming Literary Fund Dinner he had a nerve storm; he had not forgotten, he said, and had begun to rough out the speech, but it was giving him a lot of bother and he could not get on with his own writing.

On April 5th Barrie went to Brighton to stay at the Royal Albion, where he knew he could work in peace in the private sitting-room they always gave him. He was still in a frenzy of work when he later returned to London, but stopped on May 10th, to celebrate his birthday, which had been the day before, by taking Cynthia to dinner at the Ritz. He was seventy, and it was the tenth anniversary dinner they had had together. The giving-of-presents rôle was reversed this year: 'He gave me a lovely birthday present—£500.'

He was in excellent spirits, and remained in a state of elation all the time he was working on the new book. Lady Wemyss invited him to Stanway for Christmas. He came back early, and decided to go to Brighton again, as he worked better there. Cynthia and Beb and the children must come, too. Cynthia told Beb of the invitation, and Beb turned obstinate. She wrote in her diary: 'Great crise with Beb about our going to Brighton for week-end with Barrie. He didn't want to leave his house just after returning. Very tiring.'

Beb persisted in his refusal to go, but Cynthia was defiant and went off with her son, Simon. She also took a woman friend, 'who I had got as chaperone'. Beb arrived at Brighton the following day. He probably realized it was no use arguing: Cynthia put Barrie first in everything.

Barrie finished his novel, which he called *Farewell, Miss Julie Logan*. It was a love story and ghost story combined, told in the first person by a minister living in a lonely glen, near a great baronial mansion. Barrie's thoughts had been much on Scotland of late years, and the setting for this book was the Glen Prosen of his youth. It was not really a book; it had come out at twenty thousand words, a quarter of the length of an ordinary novel. He refused to make it longer or to change it in any way; as no publisher would take it, he would offer it to *The Times* for a Christmas supplement.

There were complications. *The Times* editor was not sure about this length for a supplement: it was too long. In the end he accepted it, but it made no great stir, and Cynthia could see that Barrie was disappointed and chagrined at its cool reception.

Now there was further cause for emotional disturbance. Peter Davies had got engaged to one of Lord Ruthven's beautiful twin daughters and intended to get married. Barrie again turned to Cynthia. Was this quite wise? But she could see no possible objection. Peter was established as a publisher, and the girl was as pretty as a picture. In any case, it was Peter's life. Barrie was mulish. He probably thought he should have been consulted first. He was in a peculiar mood; he was still upset by the poor reception *Miss Julie Logan* had received, and was beginning to dread the possibility that he no longer had a public for anything new from his pen. Then there was this bother about Peter . . .

Cynthia noted in her diary that she went to Adelphi Terrace House and found 'B. low about Peter's marriage.' He had become reconciled to the idea a fortnight later, for she wrote: 'Lunched with B. and went house hunting with him for Peter Davies. Spent quite an hour in a charming house in Chester Terrace . . . B. practically decided to take it.' The diary does not give any clue as to Peter's reaction to this.

On May 9th, 1931, she celebrated Barrie's seventy-first birthday with him, this time at the flat. He read one of his very early plays, *Ibsen's Ghost*, to her, gave her a bound copy with notes on the play in his handwriting—and a cheque for £500. Again, in November of that year, she records that she went to the flat, 'paid thousands of bills, etc. . . . received present of £500!'

*   *   *

Barrie was very ill in the spring of 1933, at the end of a visit to Stanway. It was the usual trouble, bronchial congestion, and his insomnia brought on attacks of nervous irritability. Cynthia got a nurse from London, whom Barrie disliked on sight. He demanded heroin to make him sleep. The nurse was quite unable to deal with the situation, and when Barrie again asked for heroin, 'tried religious persuasion!' Cynthia wrote.

Sir Douglas Shields motored down from London, and thought that it would do no harm and might have a sedative effect if the sick man was given small doses of heroin. The drug had the opposite effect: Cynthia noted that Barrie became very talkative and 'broached subject of my writing his life!' He dozed during the day and was very difficult when he woke up: 'From dark hints I guessed he was suffering from distressing and universal complaint.' Shields had to return to London, and a local doctor, in whom Cynthia had faith, decided that a small 'opening up' operation given with a whiff of gas might alleviate the pain in the chest. This had the desired effect, and though Barrie was confused and depressed for the next few days, he seemed to have found relief from the congestion.

Cynthia had arranged to go for a Mediterranean cruise with Beb, and she wondered if Barrie would be well enough to enable her to

get away without worrying. He had disliked the idea of her leaving
him from the moment the cruise had been suggested, and said that
he was not really at all well. The doctor told Cynthia that the patient
was 'playing up'. Barrie asked for more heroin, which was reluctantly
given, and the result was the usual one—intense depression after the
first exhilaration. Cynthia wrote in her diary on April 29th: 'Reduced
me to hysteria in morning which did some good. Tried to convince
him mental confusion caused by heroin and he agreed to try without
today. Pain obviously much better. Village nurse in and out for dres-
sings—otherwise I was in attendance. His furies of depression poi-
sonous beyond belief. Felt completely vampired.'

He pretended to think that Cynthia was sure he was dying, and
when he saw that she was really distressed, he began to recover—
'Marvellously better—really quite himself for an hour. Intense relief
—the anxieties and Beb champing about Cruise has been absolute
nightmare.'

Another nurse had come down from London, and she and
Cynthia took Barrie up to Shields's nursing home in Park Lane in an
ambulance. Once installed there, with Sir Douglas in attendance,
Barrie was in excellent spirits, but when Cynthia visited him next day
he was as wan and wretched as ever. Impulsively she suggested
giving up the cruise, and to her horror he concurred. She decided to
forget this, and went on with her preparations.

On May 3rd, when she visited Barrie, there was another change
in him. Peter Davies's wife was due to give birth to a child: 'Found
B. in a fever about Peter as though it was he who was having the
baby. Nurse said he was quite all right until I came.' Cynthia was
almost desperate. She knew how angry Beb would be if they did not
go on the cruise, which they had long planned, yet if Barrie were
really ill . . . She rang up Elizabeth Lucas and they had a long talk
about Barrie's illnesses, his psychology, and attitude towards the
cruise. Elizabeth pointed out that Barrie was in the best possible
hands at the nursing home in Park Lane, and this situation would
always arise if he had the slightest excuse for preventing Cynthia
from going anywhere without him.

Cynthia and Beb departed for their cruise, and Barrie, visited by
his friends and with an experienced staff in charge, recovered from
his illness and was soon looking forward to Cynthia's letters.

*   *   *

Barrie went to Scotland for the summer of 1933. He took Balnaboth House, in Glen Prosen, for a month; it was a white-walled house near the river, with gardens stretching into the glen, a few miles from Kirriemuir. He invited a house-party of friends from London. He had few relations to ask; the Winters must come, of course, and nieces, if they could get away. There was a bazaar-opening at Kirriemuir, beset by reporters and photographers, and some familiar faces in the crowd, aged as they were. James Robb! He and his daughter came to luncheon at Balnaboth, and recalled days spent fishing or scrambling over the hills. Cynthia found Miss Robb hard going; she looked like a tallow candle and stayed five hours, while Cynthia's back ached and she wished them gone. James Robb had brought Barrie a present of an Angus canary, which Barrie promptly christened Robb; but he, too, must have found the visit hard going for Cynthia records that he went to his room for a rest during the afternoon.

Barrie was in one of his worst moods during the first week of that holiday. Cynthia had brought a suitcase packed with letters which C. Greene had to deal with without troubling him. Barrie had declared Balnaboth open house, and old friends and neighbours from Kirriemuir called continually, until he grumbled to Cynthia that everyone interrupted him at dinner. She blamed it on his 'overdoing the affable', and they quarrelled. Cynthia wrote in her diary that Barrie had become vitality-sapping, and there is an entry: 'Rapprochement after silent estrangement. He complained that I didn't "admire him any more!" '

There was a climax to the summer. The Duke and Duchess of York were staying at Glamis Castle, and they brought the two Princesses to tea at Balnaboth, giving Simon Asquith, whose fourteenth birthday it was, a great thrill. Cynthia noted the occasion in her diary with an acid touch for what she considered to be malaprop behaviour on Barrie's part: 'Very gay tea, with crackers and cake. Duke very nice and easy and the children enchanting. Barrie's court manners very queer. He kept sweeping in front of the Duke . . . We played darts, and went into the garden, and all ate raspberries.'

The following day they went to Glamis, where Princess Margaret was having a party for her own birthday, her third. Barrie sat next to her at tea and the old magic worked, for she was heard to declare later: 'I know that man. He is my greatest friend and I am *his* greatest friend.'

On his way south, Barrie went to stay with Sir James and Lady
Irvine at St Andrews, and they thought he seemed in the best of
health and the most scintillating spirits. With his recurring bouts of
illness, there were times when Barrie was sure he would never feel
well again—but now, he said, seventy-three was no great age. He
would surprise everybody yet!

Chapter 22

THE LAST YEARS 2

In January, 1934, Peter Scott took Barrie to see a play called *Escape Me Never* by Margaret Kennedy. Peter Scott, now twenty-four years old, had trained as an artist, and he was also an expert yachtsman and a born naturalist. Barrie had always kept in touch with him, and lately he had seen more of his godson, for Peter Scott had been coming to the flat to paint the playwright against the background of the huge fireplace in the big room at the Adelphi.

The star of *Escape Me Never* was an Austrian actress, Elisabeth Bergner, who had come to England with her film producer husband, Paul Czinner, because of the growing pressures of the Nazi regime on their professional lives. She had played Shakespearean rôles, St Joan in Shaw's play, and other leading parts on the Continent, and spoke reasonably good English. Charles Cochran, the impresario, engaged her for the lead in Margaret Kennedy's play because a slight foreign accent was not amiss in the part. She was an immediate success. Slightly built, with an appealing face and an ability to suggest pathos, wide-eyed courage and innocence combined, she slipped into London stardom with her first part there.

Peter Scott, who had met Miss Bergner and was one of her admirers, had already seen the play and was sure Barrie would like it. Barrie did not often go to the theatre, but Peter Scott's enthusiasm was such that he went with the young man to the Apollo Theatre, and was quickly caught up in Miss Bergner's performance. He was stirred as he had not been for many years by an actress. His godson took him round afterwards to meet the young star, and they talked. Barrie asked her to come and see him at Adelphi Terrace. Bergner, who seldom accepted invitations from people she had just met, said she would be delighted.

They talked again—and each cast a spell over the other. Where does conscious charm leave off and unconscious charm take over?

Or the other way round? They had very much in common, these
two, in spite of the great disparity in their ages. Elisabeth Bergner
had played the part of the fourteen-year-old schoolgirl in *Escape Me
Never* to perfection, but she was looking for a part with more depth
to it. There had been a suggestion that Bernard Shaw might write a
Marie-Antoinette play for her, and now Barrie tentatively mentioned
Mary, Queen of Scots. Elisabeth Bergner smiled but said nothing.
Then Barrie asked her if there was any part she herself wanted to
play?

The answer was unexpected. The actress told him that she had
seen a painting of the Biblical David in Italy, and had often thought
of that dedicated young man. If a play could be made on such a high
theme—David and Saul—David and Goliath—she would like to
play the boy David.

Tinder struck on flint. Before she had finished speaking Barrie
knew that he was going to begin writing again. The Boy David.
The very title was an inspiration. Elisabeth Bergner had hardly gone
before he was at his writing-table, making notes, finding his Bible,
reading and making more notes. Next day he sent Cynthia out to
search the bookshops for works on Jewish history and customs.
When she came back with a pile under her arm she found that he had
filled one notebook and started on another.

He began to talk volubly about his theme, and wonderful Miss
Bergner, and Cynthia suggested diffidently that he should not say
too much about it to his friends, as he was now fond of doing with
a new idea; and he must not give anyone a chance to say that he was
writing another *Peter Pan*. She tried to make him see possible
dangers. When he chose an original subject of his own, he could
develop it as he liked; but when he took a subject from the Bible
where the end of the story was known, he must treat history with
respect. This would not be easy—fantasy was his strong line—but if
he did not remember this essential fact he would be heavily, and
rightly, criticized.

Elisabeth bergner was committed to go to America with *Escape
Me Never* when it ended its London run, so the new play would not
be able to go into production for some time. J. M. Barrie was
accustomed to having his plays go into rehearsal when they were
finished, usually before; but in this case he had to await events.
Not only was there *Escape Me Never*, but Miss Bergner had film
commitments.

He finished the outline of the first act in February, but could get no further. A correspondence later began between him and the Austrian actress, and soon Barrie was writing his usual Dulcinea letters, flattering her, calling himself a dull dog: the kind of letters he had been writing to attractive women all his adult life. Reading those letters now, one has the sad feeling that most of them came out of his pen of their own accord, whether held in the right hand or the left hand.

*   *   *

Cynthia Asquith was very ill in 1934, and when she had recovered sufficiently Barrie took her and her family on a Mediterranean cruise. He wore an anti-seasick belt and swallowed quantities of anti-seasick pills, but never had a single bout of seasickness. Cynthia records:

Socially, he passed with characteristic rapidity from a phase of considerable moroseness to one of excessive geniality. For fear of autograph hunters his name had been omitted from the passenger list, and he stubbornly refused to attend the 'get-together' dinner. He couldn't keep this up long, however, he was soon speaking to strangers, and at the Gala night at the end of the trip he wore a paper hat out of a cracker and blew a tin trumpet with the best of them. He still kept up his walking, he walked round and round the promenade deck, he played quoits and throwing rope rings and seemed quite content. He coughed less, he complained less of insomnia.

The cruise was such a success that the following year they went again. Cynthia wrote:

I had never seen Barrie so much moved by anything outside his own mind as by the beauty of Athens, to catch the first glimpse of which he rose before dawn. He didn't in the least mind the steep climb up to the Acropolis and down again, but his health was pretty poor. He was subject to sudden collapse after the descent. This would end in black depression, but afterwards he didn't remember the bad moments . . . Athens, for the rest of his life, glowed in his memory.

The fits of depression came more often. He had finished the *David* play, which Cochran was putting on, but his initial enthusiasm was being swamped by irritation. Cochran had asked Augustus John to design the sets. This may have been due to Cynthia's influence— John was an old friend—or to Cochran's desire to have a well-

known name for a designer. The well-known name also had a
flamboyant personality, and Barrie disliked him. Augustus John was
not slow in showing reciprocal feeling: there was mutual antipathy
from the beginning.

Augustus John had only worked as a theatre designer once before,
and he was exceedingly casual about delivering his sketches. The
scene-builders and painters, as well as the costumiers, could not get
on with their work without detailed sketches to work from, and
John's promises turned out to be like pie-crusts, made to be broken.
Even when he did, after much prodding, produce sketches, he only
bothered to indicate the upper half of a torso, so that the costumiers
did not know how the skirt of a tunic was to be made, or how long
a cloak was to be.

Even Cochran lost patience in the end, and called in an Austrian
painter, Ernst Stern, who had been chief designer to Max Reinhardt,
and who had already designed the sets for several of Cochran's
musical shows. It was not easy to explain to Augustus John that he
was now to have a collaborator, but Cochran was tactful, and the
two artists got on well, Stern taking over the costumes. Barrie came
down to one of the early rehearsals on the stage of His Majesty's
Theatre, and began to find fault with everything, especially Augustus
John's conception of Bethlehem, which John had imagined as 'an
austere little hill-town, decorated with olive-trees such as are found
in Provence'. Barrie produced, according to him, 'a mediocre sketch
made on the spot by a friend'. Augustus John preferred his imaginative conception to the flat reality of the friend's drawing.

Neither would give way, and, in any case, there was no time to
have new scenery painted, even if Augustus John had agreed. Ernst
Stern was later able to persuade him to agree to alterations in the set,
but there were difficulties of all kinds. Barrie and Augustus John
clashed whenever they met in the theatre.

Bergner was upsetting Barrie, too. She walked through her part;
she told Cynthia that she always did this in the early stages of
rehearsal, and she didn't want Barrie to be there until she had
warmed into the rôle. Barrie insisted on going, and there was a
thunderous atmosphere. Bergner said she was sure the part of David
should have been played by a boy. The donkey on which she rode
on to the stage refused to move out of the wings. Cochran, who
described the play as 'the most important event in my career',
remained patient and conciliatory. He himself was in constant pain

from arthritis, and wore a splint. Barrie developed a high temperature, and had to stop coming to rehearsals.

The company were waiting to go to Edinburgh, but they did not get there. Elisabeth Bergner was taken ill with appendicitis and an immediate operation was necessary. This was the final blow. Cochran had to cancel the try-out and dismiss the cast and technicians until he knew when rehearsals could be resumed.

It was October before they reassembled. Cochran had engaged Theodore Komisarjevsky as the producer, and Ernst Stern, recalled from New York, where he had gone, was now in sole charge of the design side. He went to Adelphi Terrace to consult Barrie, who was in bed, ill. Stern intended to use Augustus John's sets wherever possible, but Barrie did not like the last scene at all. He wanted cornfields and sheep, real sheep, with bells that tinkled. He was querulous, demanding and somehow pathetic. Ernst Stern remembered that he was seventy-six, and patiently explained that it was too late to make alterations: the try-out in Edinburgh was fixed for November, and they could not take any chances. The sets would have to be adapted for the smaller stage at the King's Theatre in Edinburgh, in any case, but no major alterations were possible.

Barrie's reply was one of his terrible fits of silence. He was feeling old and ill, and no one seemed to be taking any notice of him any more. His sister Maggie had died. The tenacious family feeling he had always had, composed of a sense of duty and incurable romanticism, made her going seem unendurable. He had nobody really belonging to him, except his nieces. The three remaining boys—now men—of 'the Five' ran their own lives, married and with homes of their own. Nicholas had joined his brother in the publishing firm of Peter Davies, and though they kept up an affectionate relationship with him when they met, they did not meet very often.

His health was worrying him badly: the play was worrying him. He was hardly ever well enough to go to the final rehearsals at His Majesty's. The company and scenery got up to Edinburgh three days before the opening, but the stage wasn't big enough for the enormous number of warriors, and 'Komis' demanded complicated lighting which was only possible in a very large London theatre.

Barrie managed to travel to Edinburgh, but took to his bed with lumbago, in his suite at the Caledonian Hotel, and had to remain there, missing the first night of his play. He was not, in fact, able to get to it at all. Cynthia arrived a day or two later. She had to break the news to him that Gilmour had died. Another link broken. Barrie was grey with pain, and this new shock made everything worse.

Cynthia hurried back after the first night and reported that Elisabeth had been exquisite, but she did not add that the applause had been tepid, and that many things would have to be altered before the play came to London. Barrie felt too ill to do much then, but once back in London at the flat he began to feel better, and was hopeful as the opening at His Majesty's drew nearer. The newspapers were humming with a Royal scandal, and everyone was wondering if the King would abdicate. Fleet Street remembered that Lady Cynthia Asquith had written a great deal about the Royal family, especially about the Duke and Duchess of York and their children. Cynthia noted in her diary:

The Daily Mail would commission article on Yorks whatever the circs. £100 if abdication £70 if not, so I cleared my afternoon. Morrisons and Mary H lunched. He was straight from Cabinet. In spite of reticence which we naturally respected I got impression of abdication. Rested an hour then got to work on article.

*　　　*　　　*

Edward the Eighth abdicated, and the first night of the London production of *The Boy David* came immediately after. No connection —but Simon Asquith told the present writer that he heard no one discuss the play in the intervals, as everyone was talking about the Abdication.

Barrie had been too ill to go. On January 19th, having gone away to a country house for a few days, Cynthia wrote in her diary that she had had a letter from Barrie saying that after she had left the flat the previous day he had found that his temperature was over a hundred degrees. 'Why must he always get ill when I go away? Telegraphed enquiry and had answer to say temp. normal and doctor satisfied.'

Cynthia was relieved: she had not wanted to be called back to town at this moment. She was again very worried over her money affairs. Hutchinson's had commissioned her to write a book about the Queen, and she had sent off the manuscript and was waiting for the proposed advance on royalties. Now her literary agent wrote to say that the publishers found the book much too short, and she would have to add at least another thirty thousand words. This was a shock, as she was already beginning another book about Princess

Elizabeth, for which she hoped to get a further advance. She now wrote to her agent suggesting that she should write the Princess book and have it included in the proposed original advance. She was feeling nervously ill herself, and did not know what she was going to do—she simply had not got the material for a further thirty thousand words for the Queen book.

She was also depressed on Barrie's account. The Press notices had been damning. She received a letter from him written from Adelphi Terrace on January 19th, 1937:

My precious Cynthia,
. . . The play alas will evidently be off in a fortnight or so tho' profitable now Cochran is insistent that it will soon be losing ground, i.e. after next Mdy when the libraries' deal ends. It wd all have been incomprehensible in the old days & ordinary theatres but I daresay he is right about today and His Majesty's. The worst mistake was going there, but probably it is not what the great public cares for. I am not depressed for myself and know it is one of the 'pin-pricks' but I grieve for Miss Bergner. She is coming in to see me tonight & seems to be taking it in a wise spirit which is nice of her.
Later
E B has just been in on way to theatre & has taken an oath against bitterness.

Loving

MASTER.

On January 31st Cynthia, still feeling very unwell, travelled up to London and went straight to the flat. She found Barrie in bed 'and pretty wretched. He confessed he had sat up till 4 & drunk too much whiskey the night before.' William Winter was staying with him, looking ghastly; cancer was suspected. Barrie admitted that the play coming off had been a great disappointment, and having William there was an added strain—though he himself had invited his brother-in-law to stay while he was in London consulting specialists.

Cynthia could not get Barrie out of his black mood. A few days later he insisted on her telephoning his agent, Golding Bright, to get the play away from Cochran, as he wanted to make alterations in it, but Cynthia knew that no altering would make it into a success. Granville Barker, in his Preface to the published version of the play, says of the highly critical Press notices of *The Boy David*: 'They wanted to know why an author who had become famous for his power to create characters should go to the Bible for a theme and then distort the story, and in any case, why have a woman, and a foreign woman at that?'

*   *   *

It was a bitter swan-song to a long, wonderful career, and an even more bitter disappointment was to follow. On February 8th, Cynthia went to tea with the two Royal princesses. The Queen came in and was charming, saying how sorry she was to have missed Sir James Barrie's recent play. Lady Cynthia at once took the opportunity to say: Why not a Command Performance? The Queen said Yes, and Cynthia knew how glad and proud Barrie would be.

He was 'pathetically delighted' at the idea of a Command Performance, which he talked about constantly, though he was wretched with pain. His doctor was now Lord Horder, whom Cynthia called in, as Barrie was demanding heroin to ease his sufferings. Horder diagnosed neuritis and gave him a palliative, refusing to prescribe heroin.

The Queen gave a date for the Command Performance, a great relief to Cynthia, who wanted all the details to be settled. She rang up Charles Cochran to give him the news, and Cochran immediately hedged, saying that the difficulties of an extra performance with such great stage problems would be insuperable. Cynthia insisted that the performance must take place, no matter what difficulties were involved. On March 12th came a bombshell. The Palace only wanted a charity matinée, not a Command Performance, as the latter might be considered injudicious because the star was of German origin. This decision put Cynthia in a very awkward position, and she did not know how to tell Barrie.

It had to be done, and the result was what she had feared—he was 'in an awful state'. She had never seen anyone so disappointed or upset. There was nothing she could do about it, and she left him in a very dejected frame of mind. Cynthia and Beb had been allotted seats with her parents in the forthcoming Coronation in May, and she was frantically busy, making arrangements for her gown and borrowed jewels. One evening when she came home Thurston rang up to say he feared Sir James had pleurisy, and she rushed round to the flat. Barrie appeared to be in such a dire state that she telephoned Lord Horder, who came immediately. Barrie was a tight ball of impotent fury: he demanded heroin, or else injections. Horder spoke very plainly, exhorting him to self-control, and left after giving him a sedative.

Barrie said that Cynthia must get Sir Reginald Poole round as quickly as possible. Poole, who had succeeded Sir George Lewis in the same firm, was now his solicitor. He wanted to talk to him about his Will. This was a familiar story. Of late years Barrie had taken to talking a great deal about his Will. He had hinted several times that Cynthia would be 'all right' when he finally quitted the scene, but she knew well enough that though he had made a Will several times, he had been so upset at the actual idea of death that he had not signed the most recent one. Whenever she had tried to get him to make up his mind about a Will he had retreated into silence, refusing to discuss the matter.

She said that she would ask Sir Reginald Poole to lunch, but within an hour Barrie was telling her to put Poole off. It was a nightmare day. Poole told her on the telephone that Lord Horder had rung him up to say that Barrie's was a case of pure hysteria, and he must be treated carefully but firmly. Cynthia was exhausted, as she often was at the end of such scenes with Barrie. How long was he going on like this?

Not long. On April 14th she went to the flat to find him up and in good spirits. They lunched together: 'He was very sweet, and gave me absolutely staggering cheque.' But she knew that he would plummet to the depths again, and within a week he was torpid and depressed, and again demanding to see Poole. When he became very ill the thought of his unsigned Will always worried him. Poole came, but Barrie talked of everything but the Will, and the solicitor left without having taken it out of his pocket.

The see-saw went on. Cynthia was deeply distressed when Lady Wemyss died at the end of April; they had been closer than most mothers and daughters, sharing a like temperament so that each understood the other completely. Cynthia travelled to Stanway and remained until May 5th, when she came back to London, and went to the flat. Barrie was in a worse state than she had ever known him. He seemed really crazed, unrecognizable, and he looked at her with an unseeing stare. The following day when she went again: 'Most incredible metamorphosis. Exalted. Never known him sweeter, nicer, in every way at his best. Staggering suggestion. He says he wanted if possible to buy Stanway for me!'

Three days later he announced his intention of doing 'a sort of

Lear' regarding her. At the end of the month, when Cynthia was feeling ill herself and had decided to stay in bed, Barrie rang her up and was very queer on the telephone; 'he said he had no money and might be flung into gaol.' She hurried round to him. He was perfectly normal. A few days later H. G. Wells dined with Barrie and the Asquiths at Sussex Place, and Cynthia found Wells very entertaining and Barrie as merry as a grig. But the following day he could not, or would not, remember anything about anything, and said she must arrange every minute of his life for him.

She was almost worn out; she felt she had to get away. Her son Simon had his exeat, his half-term holiday, from Westminster School, and she wrote to Barrie saying that the doctor had insisted on her having a complete rest. Barrie sent her 'an angelic reply', telling her that he himself was being taken to a nursing home in Manchester Square. Cynthia was relieved. She and Simon travelled to Bude, where Beb was to join them the following day; she left her Bude address and telephone number with Thurston at the flat, in case of an emergency.

The emergency was not long in coming. Two days later, on June 13th, Peter Davies rang up in the evening to say that Barrie's condition had deteriorated and he was seriously ill. Cynthia hired a car and started for London, thankful that Beb had come and she could leave Simon. She motored through the night, arriving at the nursing home very early the next morning. Freyberg was there; he, Peter and Nicholas had been sitting at the dying man's bedside in four-hour shifts.

Barrie looked ghastly ill, and Cynthia was torn by pity and alarm—and by a very different kind of apprehension. The Will. He had not signed his last Will. He appeared to be in a coma—he might not come out of it. She felt a little desperate.

Lord Horder had been sent for by the doctors at the nursing home, and Sir Reginald Poole was also there. Cynthia had a long talk with the solicitor: he would understand. Later, Poole talked to Lord Horder. A little later still, Horder gave Barrie an injection, and presently the dying man revived. Horder spoke to him, and put a pen into his hand. The solicitor had brought Barrie's last Will, and laid it on the bed before him. Barrie slowly wrote his name on the last page. Horder and Reginald Poole were the witnesses. The Will had been signed at last.

Barrie was able to speak a little, but he soon relapsed into unconsciousness again. Mary Cannan had heard the news and had come over from France, where she had been living. She was allowed to go up to the sick-room, and stood for a few moments by the bed, looking down on the man who had been her husband, long ago.

There seemed to be some improvement in Barrie's condition, but the end was not far off. He died on June 19th. The only people with him were Cynthia Asquith, Peter and Nicholas Davies. Barrie had remained unconscious; he slipped away, in the end, like a character who might have come from that once-remarkable mind.

James Matthew Barrie was buried at Kirriemuir, in a grave beside those of Margaret Ogilvy, his father, sisters and brother David. Sir James Irvine was one of the eight pall-bearers, and there were many well-known public faces in the procession that followed after. Reporters and newsreel men came to record the last rites amid the flower-laden graves. There was an open-air memorial service in the Old College Quadrangle of Edinburgh University, and, at the end of June, a memorial service at St Paul's Cathedral. Margaret Ogilvy's son had travelled a long way from the place of his birth, a lad with a few pounds in his pocket and much ambition in his head, before returning, world-famous, to rest in peace in the burying-ground above the sunlit Hill of Kirriemuir.

Appendix

THE WILL

❦

BARRIE left £173,000 gross. His Will was a long one, and it came as a shock to his near relations and to others. He appointed Barclay's Bank, Lady Cynthia Asquith and Peter Llewelyn Davies as executors and trustees, and directed that all matters concerning his literary and dramatic works should be dealt with and decided by Peter Llewelyn Davies and Lady Cynthia Asquith, as his literary executors.

He left thirty thousand pounds to Cynthia Asquith, six thousand pounds to Lieutenant-Commander John Llewelyn Davies, R.N. (Jack), three thousand pounds to Nicholas Llewelyn Davies, one thousand pounds each to his four nieces (Lilian Barrie and her sisters), three thousand pounds to his niece Madge Murray, two thousand pounds to Elizabeth Lucas, five hundred pounds to Mary Hodgson, two thousand pounds to Charles Turley Smith, a thousand pounds each to Frank Thurston and Mrs Stanley, two thousand pounds to 'my loved Elisabeth Czinner professionally known as Elisabeth Bergner for the best performance ever given in a play of mine', five hundred pounds to Bernard Freyberg. To 'my dear Mary Cannan with my affectionate regards' he bequeathed one thousand pounds and an annuity of six hundred pounds during her life free of income tax.

Six thousand pounds was bequeathed on trust, the annual income to go to Willie Winter, Maggie's son. Five thousand pounds was left to Edinburgh University, and five hundred pounds to the Bower Free Church, Caithness, in memory of the Reverend James Winter. After sundry other legacies came the most valuable bequest of all. He bequeathed to Lady Cynthia Asquith all rights in his plays and books, other than the play *Peter Pan*, which he had already made over to the Great Ormond Street Hospital for Sick Children, several years before. His furniture, manuscript books, letters and other papers were to be divided between Lady Cynthia Asquith and Peter

Llewelyn Davies; and they were also to share equally his real and personal estate. But the lion's share, taken all in all, went to Cynthia.

*   *   *

When Cynthia went to the flat she felt that in that uniquely strong atmosphere it seemed incredible that Barrie should not walk in at any moment. It was a grim business going through drawers and cupboards, and sorting in the dust of ages. There was also a huge accumulation of letters to be attended to.

She was in a queer, in-between state of relief and unhappiness. The Will would cause a lot of gossip. She wrote in her diary on June 27th: 'I think it barbaric that wills should be published, and that adjective "loved" was only added in pencil before Miss Bergner's name because he wanted to please her . . . She will hate the publicity, too.'

On July 2nd she wrote in her diary that she was feeling utterly miserable. 'Continue to torture myself for having left James that last week-end and thinking how different I would have been to him all the last months if the doctors had not said it was Hysteria and warned me.'

The chief bequest in the Will had been as much a surprise to her as to the others. She had understood from Sir Reginald Poole that the book rights and professional and amateur rights in the plays were to have been divided between her and Peter Davies, and she found the situation very embarrassing. She wondered how Peter would react to it, but when he called on July 6th: 'To my great relief he had already fully realized about the true version of the will. I am afraid it has been a great shock but he couldn't have been less embarrassing about it, and we laughed a lot. Renewed protestations of intention to help from me.'

The next weeks were fraught with worry. Among the stacks of letters which continued to come to the flat she found one from a niece of Barrie's saying she had always had an allowance of £350 a year and had been left only one thousand. 'Heaven help me. It's all going to be hell!' Cynthia wrote in her diary. Then the Bank said that there was £40,000 less in securities than they had estimated. And Peter told her that he had seen a draft of an earlier will, though he did not tell her what it was. She stayed on at the flat, replying to the letters, black depression settling on her. She felt like a slowly sinking ship.

On July 20th Peter came to the flat 'to have a heart to heart. Very nice but implication that I should surrender half the professional rights. It's all too perplexing and depressing.' Now came a startling development from an unexpected quarter. On July 24th she wrote: 'Rung up by the Press Association . . . about caveat against Barrie's will issued by Willie Winter. Charming! Implying he was not in testamentary condition when it was signed. Rung up Sir Reginald who was away and the solicitor's office. As far as I can gather he would be no better off under penultimate will. So afraid this may generally greatly delay my being able to leave London. Hell! . . . One of the most disagreeable days I remember.'

There was more trouble on July 30th. Mr Howe, the Bank Executor, had asked her to come and take an affidavit for the probate of the Will: 'Very unpleasant shock to hear Peter had refused to sign them! Howe seemed a little grim and warning about it. I told R.P. [Poole] who immediately rang up Lord H [Horder]. Cannot believe P.D. would collude with W. Winter, but suppose he may be hoping for him to succeed and therefore not want to stymie himself? But it's unpleasant and disturbing.'

Peter Davies asked if he might come and see Cynthia. She wrote: 'Most extraordinary interview. Thankful that Beb was there and that he is a lawyer.'

She went out to Italy to stay for a few weeks with Elisabeth Bergner and her husband, who had a villa in Cortina, thankful to get away from the atmosphere of the Will troubles. When she returned, she was asked to prepare *The Boy David* for publication, as she had the Prompt Copy and was used to Barrie's handwriting; there was much to sort out for the final manuscript.

Further meetings with Peter Davies could not be avoided. She had a meeting with him and the Bank Executor in late September, to discuss which securities were to be sold to pay estate duties, and lunched with him a month later at Romano's, when he suggested the possibility of her giving capital to a trust for his brother Jack, rather than shares, as had been proposed. They also discussed the sale of the contents of the flat. When they met again the following month at the Bank Executor's office, they were both stunned to find that the Inland Revenue had demanded £30,000 as their assessments of Barrie's copyrights, and they would have to decide what securities to sell to pay this vast sum. Then there was Scott's last letter to Barrie, which Cynthia had included in his letters and manuscripts for

Sotheby's: 'His widow takes a very uncompromising line about it. Decided to take it out of the sale.' but Willie Winter had dropped the caveat, which was a relief.

On December 10th, Cynthia Asquith left the flat in Adelphi Terrace House for the last time; the remainder of the lease had been sold and the place was already empty. She walked all the way to Sussex Place without realizing it. Nineteen years! Looking back, she thought of those years. Barrie had said she would be 'all right' and he had kept his promise—but it was not of the money that Cynthia was thinking. All that would sort itself out in time: there would be more worries, more unpleasantness, more moments of desperation at the tangle in which everything was getting. She walked along, thinking of Barrie himself.

'Curious how the gathering fog of worry and weariness overhanging the last phase lifts,' she wrote in her diary that night, 'and one remembers only the best and happiest times.'

Selective Bibliography

Selective Bibliography

Collections

The Novels, Tales and Sketches of J. M. Barrie, 8 vols. New York, 1896
The Plays of J. M. Barrie, 12 vols. London 1918–38
The Works of J. M. Barrie (Uniform Edition), 4 vols. London 1925–32
Letters of J. M. Barrie, Edited by Viola Meynell. London, 1942

Biographies, Memoirs, etc.

ANSELL, MARY: *The Happy Garden*, London, 1912. *Happy Houses*, London, 1912
ASQUITH, CYNTHIA: *Haply I May Remember*, London, 1950. *Portrait of Barrie*, London, 1954
BLAKE, GEORGE: *Barrie and the Kailyard School*, London, 1951
DARLINGTON, W. A.: *J. M. Barrie*, London and Glasgow, 1938
HAMMERTON, J. A.: *Barrie: the Story of a Genius*, London, 1929
KENNET, LADY (LADY SCOTT): *Self Portrait of an Artist*, London, 1949
MACKAIL, DENIS: *The Story of J.M.B.*, London, 1941
MARCOSSON, I. F. (and D. FROHMAN): *Charles Frohman: Manager and Man*, New York, 1916
MAUDE, CYRIL: *Behind the Scenes with Cyril Maude*, London, 1927
MAUDE, PAMELA: *Worlds Away*, London, 1964
ROY, J. A.: *James Matthew Barrie*, London, 1937
SCOTT, PETER: *The Eye of the Wind*, London, 1961

Articles, etc.

Barrie wrote hundreds of articles in his early days. Many of these can be consulted in the British Museum Newspaper Library at Colindale.

There are countless articles about him and his works in the

theatrical collections at Lincoln Center in New York, and in various university and other libraries in America. The small archive in the National Library of Scotland, in Edinburgh, contains his university notebooks. The Haldane archive there is particularly useful, in that it throws more light on Barrie's obsession with the archetypal mother-figure.

Index

Index